Acclaim ,   *NWAY'S*

TRUE NORTH

"A compelling character. . . . A fascinating life."
—*The Toronto Star*

"Lyrical . . . compelling and poignant. [Conway's] analyses of women's position in academe and in society are important and intriguing. . . . I was fascinated by this book."
—*The Calgary Herald*

"While Conway unflinchingly discusses . . . her private and professional joy and pain, she also fills her book with lessons: about women's history, feminist theory, geographic adaptation, professional ambition and personal courage. . . . [Her] honesty and intelligence crystallize in her words. . . . A powerful story by a woman who's learned to balance heart, mind and work."   —*Cleveland Plain Dealer*

"Nothing is missing . . . Conway is a remarkable woman—spunky, intelligent, immensely capable."
—*The Globe and Mail*

"In lucid, tactful prose, Conway details how she became a groundbreaking feminist scholar and—almost by accident—a pivotal voice for gender equality . . . a riveting assessment of the propulsive middle years in the life of a remarkable woman."   —*Bazaar*

"[Conway is] the best sort of storyteller—wise, fearless and enormously engaging and blessed with what appears to be seamless recall. . . . Conway's passion for learning and teaching, her regard for the friendships that have leavened her life and, most of all, her honest joy in the delicately balanced intimacy and independence of her marriage will buoy even the crankiest, most skeptical reader."   —*Miami Herald*

Also by JILL KER CONWAY

The Politics of Women's Education
(with Susan C. Bourque)

Written by Herself:
Autobiographies of American Women (editor)

The Road from Coorain

Learning About Women
(editor with Susan C. Bourque and Joan W. Scott)

Women Reformers and American Culture

The Female Experience in 18th-
and 19th-Century America

Merchants and Merinos

JILL KER CONWAY
TRUE NORTH

Jill Ker Conway was born in Hillston, New South Wales, Australia, graduated from the University of Sydney in 1958, and received her Ph.D. from Harvard University in 1969. From 1964 to 1975 she taught at the University of Toronto and was Vice President there before serving for ten years as President of Smith College. Since 1985 she has been a visiting scholar and professor in M.I.T.'s Program in Science, Technology and Society, and she now lives with her husband in Boston, Massachusetts.

TRUE NORTH

TRUE NORTH

A Memoir

JILL KER CONWAY

Vintage Canada

A Division of Random House of Canada

VINTAGE CANADA EDITION, 1995

Copyright © 1994 by Jill Ker Conway

All rights reserved under International
and Pan-American Copyright Conventions.
Published in Canada by Vintage Canada,
a division of Random House of Canada Limited,
Toronto and simultaneously in the United States
by Vintage Books, a division of Random House, Inc.,
New York. Originally published in hardcover
by Alfred A. Knopf Canada, Toronto.
Distributed by Random House
of Canada Limited, Toronto.

Canadian Cataloguing in Publication Data
Conway, Jill K., 1934–
True North: a memoir
ISBN: 0-394-28120-9
1. Conway, Jill K., 1934– 2. Canada—Civilization.
3. University of Toronto—Faculty—Biography.
4. Women college teachers—Ontario—
Toronto—Biography.
5. Australians—Canada—Biography. I. Title.
LE3.T518C65 1995 378.1'2'092 C95-931231-5

Printed and bound in the United States
10 9 8 7 6 5 4 3 2 1

For John

Contents

Foreword

In September 1960, I set out for Harvard and Cambridge, Massachusetts, in the complex state of euphoria and anxiety that accompanies major life transitions. I was en route for graduate study, although the choice didn't represent the fulfillment of a life shaped by the dream of a scholarly career. I'd arrived at the choice by exhausting all the possibilities of interesting careers in Australia, discovering, one by one, that they were not open to women. This process of elimination left me with my love of studying history, and my passion to understand the deterministic forces which constrained human freedom of the will. I'd seen those deterministic forces overwhelm my rural family, and needed to understand for myself to what extent human action is free.

So my setting out was not exactly the departure of a conquering hero, but more the ambiguous result of deciding that I had to get away from Australia to view life from a different perspective. The future of a woman alone in the world in the 1950s was a blank page, because no one I knew had lived that way, and the rules of the culture were clear that they shouldn't. So I experienced my leave-taking as a farewell to the known, a jump off the edge of the world into an unknowable future. As I went through the motions of departure I was emotionally drained by all the endings, both public and unacknowleged, of the previous months of leave-taking—farewells to my childhood Australian backcountry, to the seductive beauty of Sydney in its early September surge of spring's perfumes, to my neurotically dependent mother, herself alternating between the positive urge to encourage flight and the stronger need to exact promises of return, and to the friends of school and university years, a cohort slowly setting forth toward private destinies. My imagination kept flitting, like a badly managed camera, between the fully delineated world being left behind and the dim outlines of an unknowable future.

Since mine wasn't the usual flight of the nestling eagerly flexing newly developing muscles, but a somewhat delayed break for freedom from a suffocating family, from a culture actively hostile to aspiring women, and from the constraints of a still-colonial society, my mood as the Boeing 707 took off and climbed away from Sydney mingled triumph at the long-awaited moment, guilt for the betrayal of leaving, grief at the lost world of youth, and the overwhelming anxiety induced by the social attitudes of the 1950s, at being a young woman traveling about the world bent on her own individual purposes. Every verbal and visual message of the world I'd grown up in telegraphed that a young female belonged with somebody else, preferably a male partner, but failing that, family, friends, anything that would signal to the world that she was going about the business of being a helpful and charming female bent on caring for the needs of others. Without the talisman of such a comforting relationship, life presented an endless set of challenges requiring the constant justification of a solitary existence. I knew I wanted such a life, yet nonetheless insecurity nibbled at the edge of every moment.

My free-floating anxiety was temporarily relieved by the discovery that the captain of the flight was someone I knew, an old friend of my brother's. The anxieties of the moment vanished when I settled in the cockpit and began observing the fascinating process of piloting and navigating the aircraft that then represented the most advanced wonders of the Boeing company's contributions to modern jet aviation. Far too strung out for sleep, I spent the long flight gazing out at the stars, watching the moon come around the curve of the earth—a new sensation when seen for the first time from such an altitude—learning about the wonders of modern navigational aids, watching first the outlines of the Fiji Islands come up ahead and then, many hours later, the glorious white-rimmed, velvety green chain of the Hawaiian Islands, the romance of their presence way out in the vast Pacific so powerful that they subdued the modernity of large airliners and screaming jet engines the moment one stepped out the door and drew a moist breath filled with the scent of pineapple and frangipani.

Alone in one of the forests of steel and glass hotels that line Waikiki, I fell into the kind of depression that can only be induced by jet lag, awake because of the sunlight and scenery yet almost catatonic with fatigue. Truly a liminal creature, suspended between one state of being and another, I felt close to disembodied as I wandered around the ugly tourist shops and hamburger joints surrounding Waikiki, too tense to lie on the beach and soak up the sun, too lonely for sleep. Toward evening, I looked down from my fourteenth-floor room to what I would come to love on future journeys, the lyrical enclosed space of the Halekulani terrace, sheltered by an arching cypress and tall palms leaning into the wind, where a Hawaiian band plays and exquisite Hawaiian women perform the islands' dances as the setting sun lights the horizon and sends the shimmering ocean golden. Seen from above, the pygmy figures, dwarfed by the scale of the cement jungle enclosing them, seemed as surreal as I felt. But even from fourteen stories up, the movements of the dancers were novel and captivating, though I was too shy and tentative in my new state of being to muster the energy to descend, find the terrace, and enjoy the new aesthetic experience in human scale.

In San Francisco my mind came out of its deep freeze and began to register immediate sensation again. I could savor the beauty of the city, enjoy watching the sunset dim and the lights of the skyline emerge. I was still tense, expecting to find myself at any moment in the midst of some Hollywood crime film. I was just as uncertain about being entitled to occupy space in the world by myself, but the drama of the new continent was beginning to make itself felt. The next day, when I saw the confluence of the Mississippi and the Missouri, the great inland waterways that made the settlement of the United States so different from the experience of my native Australia, America began to seem real. The physical geography of this continent, which I knew in imagination from its maps and charts, its landscape painting, and its literature of the West, was immensely reassuring. A few lines began to form on the blank page of the future.

Halfway across the country the familiar outlines of mountains, lakes, and rivers disappeared beneath thick clouds, and I learned that there was to be a stormy welcome on the East Coast. We might not land in the exciting New York I was tensing my nerves for after all. Because of the force of the winds battering the Northeast, our destination could be Pittsburgh or Washington, or some point even farther south. An hour or so later the captain pointed out the eye of a hurricane swirling several miles below us, and told us the storm was of record-breaking dimensions. I was half-irritable at what I took to be typically American sensation mongering, half-panicked at the thought of arriving in some city not part of my travel plans.

Nonetheless, the sight of the storm prompted the first of many mental adjustments required when we move beyond the local and the familiar. I'd grown up with the chauvinistic belief that everything—nature, landscape, people, distances—was larger than life in Australia. Perhaps there were some forces of nature on this continent more powerful than the heat and drought I knew at home. I couldn't imagine what was happening down there below the cloud vortex, but it was strong, dynamic, visual proof that I was entering a new climate zone, one in which I'd arrive at my destination in a fog as thick as the fog that veiled the outlines of my future; but now, three days into my travels, I was beginning to be philosophical about that. I settled back in my seat and wondered what Pittsburgh would look like, or, if it was to be Washington, whether I could take in the sights before continuing on.

I didn't quite believe it when the pilot said we were over New York's international airport, and there were ninety planes ahead of us, all stacked in neat layers, waiting to land. "We'll hang around as long as our fuel lasts," he said laconically, "and only divert at the last minute if we can't make it in." The contingency of this approach to life struck me as disarming. It was far less stuffy than Australian approaches to air traffic control. Then I thought about the ninety planes circling around out there in the dark, many times the number of Australia's entire commercial airline fleet. The number made it seem real that the stormswept city below contained more people than the entire Australian continent. If we didn't run out of fuel I was clearly arriving somewhere much larger than I'd ever known. I settled down to wait, feeling diverted by the idea of so many people hurtling around in the bumpy night sky, checking their watches and wondering what to do about their disrupted schedules. I was one of too vast a crowd to fuss about my individual plans.

Jill Ker Conway

TRUE NORTH

I.

NORTHERN
LIGHT

WITHIN HOURS OF MY arrival in September 1960, New York astonished and delighted me. The astonishment was instant. I stepped from the plane at what is now called John F. Kennedy Airport but was then called Idlewild into a wall of water, my first encounter with an East Coast hurricane. The scene inside the airport resembled a Brueghel run wild. Sodden people lurched in all directions, colliding in their frantic search for lost luggage and nonexistent taxis. Some laughed and told war stories of other major storms. Others interrogated all comers, anxious for news.

Accustomed to a prim British stiffness when with strangers, and doubly wary because of repeated warnings delivered by well-traveled Australian friends about the dangers of life in New York, I was monosyllabic at first in response to friendly and cheery questions about where I was from and where I was going. I could scarcely believe the hive of activity at the airport at 2:00 a.m., or the philosophic figures draped over every chair and bench seeking sleep amid the hubbub.

The reasons for the chaos emerged slowly. The hurricane, named, for reasons I couldn't understand, Donna, had flooded all the roads leading to the airport, preventing ground crews, taxis, indeed all forms of transportation from reaching Idlewild. The crowd seemed to accept this situation with easy familiarity. I, accustomed to Australian good weather, thought it highly disruptive of well-laid plans. These people seemed much more flexible than I was used to, and much more friendly. I broke down and began to exchange stories with my neighbors about how long my flight from San Francisco had circled the airport (an hour and a half). I wondered out loud how I could make it to the International House at Columbia, where I was staying for a few days to explore the city. "Oh, there'll be a night watchman to let you in, no matter what hour we get into Manhattan. The buses will make it first. Just take a Carey bus to the East Side Terminal. There will be taxis there. It's only a short ride to Columbia." The speaker was a lanky young man with a crew cut and thick-lensed, horn-rimmed spectacles, who turned out to be a graduate student headed for Yale. He eventually helped me extract my heavy suitcases from the mountains of luggage suddenly produced by a few drenched and harassed baggage men, and showed me where to load them on the bus headed for the East Side Terminal.

The night watchman at International House was a friendly and dignified black man. "I thought you'd show up soon. I've been listening to the radio, wondering how you were doing in this storm after coming all the way from Australia." As he spoke over his shoulder, leading me to my room, the image of Manhattan as a vast impersonal city, an image created by countless movies, antiurban novels, and crime stories, faded farther into the background. I fell asleep relishing the comforts of a room far less spartan than the Australian dormitories I'd grown up with.

The next day was sunny and steamy. Not in the least like the fall weather Australian travelers to New England had told me to expect. At breakfast I met a diminutive blond girl from Oklahoma, bound for graduate work in history at Columbia. Over fruit and coffee she quickly corrected my political attitudes. Eisenhower, to me still a hero from the 1939–45 war, was a villain to her. Her eyes flashed as she told me how Ike had catered shamelessly to the red-baiting Senator Joseph

McCarthy, and how he had presided over the buildup of the defense industry. Despite my initial puzzlement at these views we took an instant liking to each other and agreed that we would meet the next morning to explore the city. Reassured by having found a companion for sightseeing, I set out on my own to find Fifth Avenue and the city's fabled emporia of fashion.

The cab I hailed on Amsterdam Avenue was of a type I came to love as a New York fixture. Rattletrap, dirty, driven by an overweight man in a windbreaker, it slowed to my wave. Where did I want to go? I gave the address of an American Express branch on Fifth Avenue at midtown, intending to replenish a dwindling supply of dollars.

"Where're ya from?" the driver asked, eying me in the rearview mirror. Still a little tense about talking to strangers in a city I'd been told was a dangerous place, I said I was from Australia. His face broke into a happy smile. "This your first day in the city?" When I admitted it was he leaned across and turned off the meter. "Well, honey," he said, "I'm gonna show you Manhattan. I was in Sydney a few times during the war. People were very nice to me there, so I want to pay a bit of it back."

We worked our way down to Battery Park, looked at the Statue of Liberty, stopped at the Fulton Street Fish Market, had coffee in a place in the Village where he told me the jazz was good at night, strolled around Washington Square, stopped to examine the Chrysler Building (Frank, my guide, said the Empire State Building was crummy), took in Sutton Place ("where Marilyn Monroe lives"), rode through Central Park, all to Frank's ironic and witty monologue about the city and its inhabitants. At the end of three hours we were fast friends. I knew all about Frank's experiences at Bataan and Corregidor, the names and ages of his wife and children, what he'd done in the fifteen years since the war, still clearly his most vivid experience. He had oriented me to the city and made it seem safe. He had also corrected permanently my thirdhand view of America as a cold and competitive place.

Instead of fearing I would be ripped off by every New Yorker I met, I knew I was going to love the city's electric mood, its pace, its contrasts, and its dazzling beauty.

The next morning I rode the Circle Line Ferry around Manhattan with my Oklahoma friend. Both of us were intoxicated by the sparkling, crisp morning. We each fell into a companionable reverie listening to the usual tourist blurb over the loudspeaker. I began to fit the colonial history I knew to the skyscrapers and the grand houses of the West Side, and to imagine the seventeenth-century port alive with sailing ships and buccaneers. As with all new sights in Australia, I could never resist trying to imagine what each new vista of the land looked like to the first Europeans. I tried stripping away the buildings to arrive at this low-lying island bounded by rivers with the great land mass beyond. I could see why F. Scott Fitzgerald had found it so romantic, this little wisp of land at the edge of a great continent. It was not that I had come like a Fitzgerald hero to conquer this new territory. I had come looking for knowledge, the discipline of study, and the challenge for someone of my overindulged life implicit in the simple circumstances of a scholarship student. Yet these resolves began to pale because I could barely contain my excitement leaning there on the rail, gazing at Manhattan. The light seemed dazzlingly bright, the buildings more visually challenging than one could tell from the most spectacular photographs, and the aspirations that had found expression in the city seemed to vibrate palpably in the air. My somber sense of exile from Australia dissolved like a fog in sunlight. I was going to enjoy myself here.

On the train to Boston the next afternoon my excitement subsided. The coastline which was revealed as the train rattled along was unexceptional, the grey pebble–ringed Atlantic a disappointment to a denizen of the lyric blue Pacific. The neat towns with their white churches, their meaning as yet concealed from me, flashed by like so many postcards. The most startling sights and sounds were inside the Pullman car, where I heard my first Boston Irish accent, and where, unwary about seeking a nonsmoking car, I found myself seated in a fog of cigar smoke, listening to loud talk about horseraces and football.

I couldn't fit the places to the images their names evoked. New Haven. Was such a nondescript platform really the place where one descended for such a seat of learning? Providence, visible from the train, was a run-down place, not the grand eighteenth-century city I expected. And Boston. When the kindly conductor assembled my bags and helped me down at South Station I seemed to have come to a depressed industrial city, not the center of learning and high culture I'd read about.

The cabdriver spoke the same nearly incomprehensible dialect. "Mass Ave. or Storrow Drive?" he asked impassively, sounding as though some strange spell had stretched out his vowels. We settled on Massachusetts Avenue, a mistake in the evening rush hour, and a worse one because it carried me to Cambridge past scenes of urban blight worse than any I'd ever encountered. "Where's that?" I asked, gesturing toward a quadrilateral of teetering buildings festooned with decaying neon signs, crisscrossed with trolley wires. "Scollay Square," the driver remarked, apparently untouched by the ugliness outside his window.

I began to reflect on the folly that had taken me from the beauty and comfort of Sydney to this decaying city. Every unfolding scene confirmed my gloomy prognosis. Harvard Square, when reached, was no grand square, but an ellipse of shops converging on the low buildings of Harvard Yard, shadows in the dusk. Mercifully the Radcliffe Graduate Center, at 6 Ash Street, was a modern, pink-brick neocolonial building on a quiet side street. After piling my bags in the hall and tipping the driver far too much, I went to find the Head Resident. To my surprise she was a fellow graduate student who was administering this residence for three hundred graduate women as a part-time job while she finished her doctorate in English Literature. Barbara Charlesworth was a beautiful, willowy woman, just my age, whose soft voice had a faint Scottish burr, something I learned was part of her Canadian heritage. Abundant light brown hair framed her heart-shaped face, remarkable for its delicately chiseled features and large luminous grey eyes. It was plain to see that she looked on life with humorous detachment, her passions all directed to the world of ideas. I liked her at once.

My premonitions of discomfort about the new world were confirmed by her laughing explanation that dinner, which had begun at 5:30 p.m. (the time for nursery tea in my calendar), would conclude in a few minutes, at 7:00 p.m. The knots in my stomach at the thought of the graceless girls boarding school I'd entered subsided at Barbara's cheerful offer of help in getting my bags to my room, where I could begin settling in while she prepared a snack for me in her apartment.

So began a friendship which became, within a very few weeks, a shaping influence on my life. Barbara was a student of Victorian literature whose love of language fit easily with my own. She had attended the Canadian variant of my Australian/British girls boarding school. She had come to hers from the wildly exotic setting of a Colombian mining camp, where her father's career as an accountant had carried the family. At her Toronto convent, she had, like me, been a stranger, struggling to translate between dissonant cultures. I had found someone, on the other side of the planet, who shared my experience almost exactly. Moreover, though our cultural journeys had set out from different points on the compass, they had produced the same result: a driving passion for knowledge—mine, historical; hers, literary—and a shared need to push below the surface of things to look for deeper meanings.

I began to relax when Barbara offered me a stiff Scotch, chatting easily while she opened a can of soup, produced a hearty sandwich, and found the components of a fine salad in the recesses of her refrigerator. As I took stock of her quietly elegant rooms, other lively and interesting people began to appear. I forgot about how ugly Boston had seemed, as it dawned on me that I had come to live in one of the world's greatest concentrations of intellectual women. It was a sign of my low level of awareness of such things that I'd given great thought to the Harvard faculty I would meet but none at all to my fellow women graduate students. Although the odds against such happenings are astronomically high, I met, within the next hour, sitting in Barbara's comfortable rooms, three other women who were to be lifelong friends. The first to erupt into the room were Mina Farhad, a woman one would have thought to have stepped straight out of a Persian miniature, until the sound of her wicked belly laugh made her seem utterly contemporary, and her improbable suite mate, Jana Moravkova, a Czech woman, daughter of implacable resistance fighters against the Nazis. Jana's accent was French because of her undergraduate education at the Sorbonne, but her Gallic joie de vivre was matched by a spirit and intellect clearly from pre-Enlightenment Europe. Her manners were formal and aristocratic, while in appearance she looked like the wood carvings of youthful Madonnas one saw in baroque churches. Both women were working in the molecular biology program which had recently contributed to the discovery of DNA, and both conveyed some of the excitement that went with the awareness that one was working on the edge of great discovery. Their easy curiosity about who I was, and comfortable acceptance that any woman in her right mind who wanted to achieve something as a scholar would come to Radcliffe, eased the memories of hundreds of careful explanations to uncomprehending Australian friends and acquaintances about why I wasn't satisfied to settle at home, or study at Oxford or Cambridge.

Promptly at 10:30 p.m. Carla Levine arrived, invited by Barbara to meet me, because Carla's room was across the corridor from mine in our distant wing of the building. Just home from the library, Carla was petite, dark haired, and strikingly beautiful. Everyone laughed at the promptness of her arrival, because, they told me, one could set one's watch by Carla's hours of departure for the library, and her equally predictable return. Several years younger than I, she was already a year into her doctoral program in Middle Eastern Studies, intent on understanding Arab-Israeli conflicts at a scholarly rather than ideological level. One could see that this woman from Kansas City, Missouri, was no typical Midwesterner. I'd had few Jewish friends, and was unprepared for her wildly extravagant sense of humor, or for the laughing way in which she told me I looked like the walking Jewish stereotype of a goy. After we returned to our rooms Carla and I talked until the small hours of the morning about our dreams as scholars, where we had come from, and why we were in Cambridge.

The conversations all evening were so easy I took to them like an addict to a drug. I'd never lived in a place where I didn't have to censor my words and edit my emotions. In Australia, one mustn't offend by being too abstract. Puns based on too much learning would certainly fall flat. Double entendres based on several languages would miss the mark. Admitting that one wanted to be a great scholar, perhaps the best in one's field, just wasn't done. It was a shameful secret to hide behind a well-polished exterior carefully contrived from the pages of *Vogue* and *Harper's Bazaar*. Suddenly I could say whatever came into my mind, not just to a lover, but to a group of people like myself. I wasn't quite sure what would happen if I began to express my innermost thoughts, but I could feel the surge of adrenaline that the very idea of actually being myself set going.

The next morning I set out to find the Harvard History Department, making my way along Brattle Street, and turning right along the shabby storefronts along Massachusetts Avenue to find Holyoke House, an address firmly lettered across all my correspondence with the admissions committee. I looked for an imposing building at the stated address on Massachusetts Avenue just across from one of the entrances to Harvard Yard. What I found after several dry runs and queries to passersby was what seemed like a run-down apartment building with a creaky and uncertain elevator. The corridor leading to the departmental office was shadowy and the floor tilted at odd angles. The general impression was of brown—brown walls, brown linoleum floors, brown muddy light from an inadequate light bulb. Inside, a woman with a dazzling smile and a charming southern accent introduced herself to me as the Department secretary. Her manner radiated genuine hospitality. Of course I could see the Chairman, no longer Professor Gilmore, but now Professor Wolfe. What did I want to talk about? I explained that since I'd been teaching history at the university level for eighteen months, had published several monographs, and produced a prize honors dissertation based on independent research, I wanted to be excused from one of the two mandatory years of courses for graduate students in History at Harvard.

She looked up with the friendliest of laughs. "Our problem is usually to get people to move out of here. Most of them aren't in such a hurry. But I'm sure you can do it if you want to." Used to Australian bureaucratic ways, in which such a request would have required written statements in triplicate for scrutiny by academic committees, registrars, and an academic senate, I asked whether my request would need any documentation. "Oh, no. He's off the phone now. Why don't you go in and tell him what's on your mind. If he says yes it's settled."

The Chairman was memorable. When first seen, seated, he seemed almost completely round, not in a flabby sort of way, just firmly round. He was rosy-cheeked, bright-eyed, slightly choleric, and when he stood, quite tall. He had the determined high humor one sees in people subject to depression, very precise tailoring, and manners of exquisite courtesy. He remonstrated with me, in a voice which managed to be both throaty and a little plummy, for being in Cambridge less than twenty-four hours, and seeming already hell-bent on shortening my stay. But if I felt I needed only a year to prepare for the much dreaded General Examination, then I could have my wish. Did I need anything in writing? I inquired nervously. "Goodness no. The Department secretary and I aren't likely to forget." I wandered back down the hall to the wheezing elevator reflecting on the American talent for getting things done. I later learned that there were several apocryphal stories about the Department Chairman being trapped in the Holyoke House elevator while making a Sunday visit to catch up on departmental matters. The elevator was of the uncertain kind that cried out for such stories. It was a puzzle, such speed of decision and such eccentric shabbiness.

The bright sunlight of a brilliant early fall morning shone on the Harvard Yard as I took my first stroll around it, stopping to find Harvard Hall, Sever, and the large modern building named for Emerson, where most history classes were conducted. Strolling around the Yard I pondered the dates of the buildings, which ranged from the early eighteenth century to the mid-twentieth. I stopped to examine the statue of John Harvard, whose 1636 bequest had established the university. This wasn't the United States of my imagination, filled with Hollywood images of crass modernity. It was old, by any standard, and sparer, in a fashion I could not quite comprehend, than any urban landscape I'd yet seen. The vast shading elms overhead, the busy squirrels, the building where Washington had slept while his Revolutionary troops camped in the Yard, all seemed to revolve around two larger structures: Memorial Church, with its serene white steeple and soaring golden weathervane, and the massive bulk of the Widener Library, its heavy columns and veritable piazza of steps daring anyone to approach its fabled contents lightheartedly.

I went up the commanding sweep of steps, bent on securing my own stall in the Widener stacks, a place where I could read and, luxury like a banquet to a glutton, charge out to my desk as many volumes as I liked. My stall, when I found it, was on the Yard side of Widener, looking through an ivy-draped window across to Memorial Church. I wandered happily around the stacks for a while, proving to myself that it was indeed true that every book one could ever imagine was to be found in the Widener's holdings. Then, emboldened by having claimed a place of my own, I went to find the office of the Librarian of Harvard.

Paul Buck was a friend of Andrew Osborne, Librarian of Sydney University, who was one of the most enthusiastic supporters of my plans for study in the United States. My Sydney friend told me to ignore whatever was the current vogue for graduate courses in the History Department, and seek out Paul Buck's advice about my course of study.

When I found my way to his office on the landing halfway up the steps to the main reading room, I knew only that he was a distinguished historian of the American South, and now close to retirement. Had I known that he had been the autocratic Dean, and later, Provost of Harvard, ruling with an iron hand from 1942 to 1953 while President James Conant was away, first on the Manhattan Project and then as the American Commissioner responsible for administering the Allied section of postwar Germany, I might have thought my plans too insignificant to bother him with.

Once again I was startled by the easy good manners and cordiality of my welcome. He seemed to know who I was, and to have time to talk. He began reminiscing about his own graduate school days, describing the common mistakes budding young historians made in preparing for their profession. When I began to talk about his book on the Reconstruction era in the South, and to inquire about the course he would be teaching on Southern history, he brushed my interest aside. I shouldn't plan to study for credit with the famous names in the Department. I could audit their courses if I liked, but their ideas were all in books I could read, and it wasn't likely that they would have anything much new to say, himself included. One should work with the rising young stars of the Department, whose ideas were still developing. They would be shaping the profession I would be entering, and I would learn the most from their teaching. When I asked who were the coming men in American history, he answered without hesitation. I should study colonial history with Bernard Bailyn, one of the youngest scholars ever to be tenured in the Department, someone who was going to change the way we thought about the development of American culture and ideas in the seventeenth century. And, since it sounded as if I was interested in intellectual history, I should work with Donald Fleming, very recently arrived in the Department, a man who was interested in the impact of science on American culture. That conversation settled the matter. When the time came to enroll, I registered in Bernard Bailyn's and Donald Fleming's graduate seminars, and signed up for their lecture courses. It turned out to be splendid advice.

My next visit was to the Radcliffe Graduate School, an easy stroll along Brattle Street from the Graduate Center, its offices located in one of the graceful neo-Georgian buildings which formed a leafy courtyard closing out the bustle of Brattle Street. The hallways, painted in pale colors, were well lit, and the waiting rooms actually contained flowering plants. The Dean was a small, elegant woman, soft-spoken and gracious, her face transformed by a brilliant smile when she sensed my barely controlled excitement at being in Cambridge and on the verge of beginning what I'd dreamed of doing.

The Associate Dean was a pure Cambridge type; sensibly tailored, firm voiced, and ironic, she coped effortlessly with the petty details of immigration, medical requirements, where to enroll, and tuition payments. Fooled by her manner, I took her to be the quintessential bureaucrat, someone who wouldn't bat an eyelid if one of her charges were abducted by an excitable Middle Eastern sheik, or eloped with an Indian rajah. She raised her eyebrows when I told her about my plan to eliminate one year of courses. Then she laughed, becoming a different woman. "Why not?" she said companionably. "It's a good way to dodge the anxiety states most people get themselves into about the General Examination, and from what I hear they'll have made their minds up about you inside a year anyway." I liked her bright, intelligent face, and left with the sense that these two women were on my side, not in any emotional or sentimental way, just benign presences who wanted to see me succeed.

I remembered them with some vehemence that evening when the first get-together for graduate students entering the history program was held in the large sitting room in what I was coming to think of as my own Radcliffe Graduate Residence. There were slightly more than fifty new students present when Professor Wolfe, accompanied by several colleagues, walked to the podium and began what was billed as welcoming remarks. His first words of welcome were speedily contradicted by the much used chestnut: "Look to the left of you, look to the right, one of you won't be here at the end of the year." I, being a sage twenty-five, with a life and identity in another world, took these remarks to be childishly intimidating, though many of my fellow students, fresh from college, seemed to take them gloomily to heart. Soon the small administrative details and introductions to the Department were over, and the group began to mingle around a bar stocked with beer, wine, and a new cultural symbol, pretzels.

The student group was almost entirely male, and the faculty exclusively so. My eye was taken by the brilliant smile and shining eyes of a slightly older student standing by the bar, with the erect carriage of an athlete. He turned out to be Sam Wells, an ex-Marine, just home from posting in the Pacific, and about to begin a doctorate in diplomatic history. His soft Southern voice, easy humor, and obvious ambition were as attractive as his friendly greeting. It turned out that we were taking many of the same courses, and we agreed to watch out for one another at the first class meeting. By the door, on my way out, I met Neil Harris, just back from a year of study in England, bookish, with thick spectacles, and a voice which mixed Oxbridge with East Coast American intonations. Neil was already professorial, in an utterly unpompous way. It was not that he paraded his learning or that his speech was pedantic. It was just that one could not imagine this man in any setting where ideas were not the principal focus of attention. We were also enrolled in the same courses, and Neil, who'd been in town for more than a week already, knew where every building and classroom was.

GRADUATE STUDY IS supposed to be lonely, but mine was the exact opposite. On my first weekend in Cambridge, Barbara, Mina, and Jana took me with them to a party in a run-down frame house on Dana Street, a ten-minute walk from the Yard. It was a gathering of their circle of friends, all convening after the travels and adventures of the summer. Just as my new women friends were kindred spirits, the group of young men promised to be also. The party was lively and high spirited, but not rowdy as its Australian counterpart would have been. The male members of the group were unlike any I'd met in my twenty-five years. To begin with, they talked— about themselves and their feelings, about ideas, about their responses to beauty, about poetry, music, art.

Al Gelpi was from New Orleans. About my age, of medium height with shining brown eyes, and a memorably beautiful deep, slightly husky voice, he talked with real emotional urgency about religion and poetry. Joel Porte, the embodiment of Jewish learning and ambivalence about life, had struggled to find his way from his impoverished New York childhood to Harvard. His eyes, owlish behind thick spectacles, his smile gentle, he talked brilliantly about literature and despondently about the impossibility of ever mastering all he needed to know. Christopher Greene, tall, dark-haired, and handsome, was the descendant of a Revolutionary general, a lineage attested to by his extraordinarily hard New England twang. To me he seemed as stern a Puritan in manner and habits of mind as his ancestors. His love of French history and French architecture was at war with his Calvinistic spirit, something he talked about volubly and with disarming humor.

His brother, Benjamin, a mathematician and student at M.I.T., was the only inarticulate member of the party, his silence accentuating the volubility of the others. When he talked about practical things—wood carving, cooking, or skiing—his face lit up, revealing its basic sweetness of expression, but there was no escaping his underlying somber mood. He seemed an island of inarticulateness amid this sea of talkers.

Bob Kiely was always the center of a group of laughing people. Half Irish, half Italian, he had the Irishman's way with a story and the Italian's sense of making the *bella figura*. His blue-eyed zest for life and his enjoyment of the absurd made him the life of the party. Yet as the evening unfolded it was clear that these surface qualities were combined with ambition, a sunny common sense, and a deeply moral temperament. He was more interested in the divine comedy than in some sardonic debunking of others.

Bob, Joel, and Al, all friends of Barbara's, were students of literature, keenly aware of language and image, intent on understanding the complexities of human interaction. Beside them, Mina's friend David Simpson seemed to be the literal embodiment of the eccentric Scottish economist. Tall, angular, and beautifully spoken, David was a passionate Scottish nationalist. His gingery hair and eyebrows quivered with intensity as he discussed the plight of colonial peoples and the inexorable economic laws which made the chances of real independence illusory. He was a student of the great economic theorist Wassily Leontief, and quoted the master with reverence not accorded any other aspect of life.

I liked them all, and spent the entire evening in animated conversation. I had lived my entire life without really *talking* to people, except in the direst emergencies. My conversations had, of necessity, been mainly with books and the minds revealed in them. Now I was learning that the spoken language could matter as much as the printed page. They were all so curious about me, asking direct yet compassionate questions about who I was and what I was looking for in life. I was accustomed to my mask and obliged for the first time to ask myself the same questions before I could answer my new companions. Searching for the answers gave me much food for thought, as I took my morning strolls by the Charles River, or gazed out the window from my Widener stall. The question of who I was and what I was about had seemed self-evident in Sydney, now it seemed to be something I was going to have to find out.

I wasn't sure any longer that my self-definition as part English, part Australian, upper middle class would do here. Mina was always teasing me when I dressed up, saying I looked just like a proper English woman, going to take tea with the natives. Was I really so stuffy? Then there was Carla's friendly amusement about my speech patterns and vocabulary, and her astonishment that anyone could live without a knowledge of classical music. Perhaps I was more of a Philistine than I thought. Why was I an historian? People seemed to want to know. One wasn't just born curious about history. The reason was I'd grown up *having* to know why things were the way they were. The droughts and sudden swings of fortune of my childhood in the Australian outback meant that I was preoccupied by questions of free will and determinism. Coming to consciousness during the 1939–45 war made me interested in the conflict of ideas and ideologies, and curious about where they came from. Then there was *my* Australia, which I was not content to see merely as an offshoot of Britain. I was different, but that seemed to amuse, not trouble, people here.

It wasn't just my new graduate student companions who were friendly. Friends in Australia who had Boston connections had written ahead to introduce me to several Boston families. I had accepted the offer gratefully, expecting what usually happens in Europe, a polite invitation of some formal kind, followed by silence. In Cambridge I had not yet unpacked at 6 Ash Street before the phone was ringing with genuine invitations. I spent my second weekend visiting the Morss family in Manchester, a beautiful seaside town on Cape Ann, just to the north of Boston. Their house was set on the shore overlooking a forbidding rock formation around which the Atlantic tides roared. To an Australian, the Morss ménage was comfortable beyond belief, its sense of ample comfort equaled only by the warmth and good humor of its inhabitants. Nan Morss was the daughter of an old New England family, a descendant of colonial governors. Everett Morss was the conscientious manager of an inherited family business, the embodiment of Boston probity. Their lives revolved around family, friends from college days, the sea and sailing, and the doings of their Boston circle.

I knew I would like Nan from the moment she called to invite me for the weekend. She promised to pick me up after the Friday afternoon Boston Symphony performance, a fixture in her life. "I'll be there at five-thirty sharp, darling. Just look for a woman with a face like a horse driving a red Chrysler." Her laughter was infectious, as was the warmth in her deep, richly timbred voice.

She was, despite her self-mockery, a woman of great elegance and genuine interest in the young. All the Morss children, a wonderfully varied group of musicians, businessmen, editors, and adventurers, had left home, so Nan and Everett had time for youthful visitors. Their kindness to me was inexhaustible. I spent the Christmas of 1960 and Easter of 1961 at The Rocks, as the Manchester house was called. I explored Salem, and all the seaports nearby with Everett in his beloved powerboat. In these cradles of New England culture I suddenly saw the grandeur of eighteenth-century England translated into colonial scale, seeming to me more beautiful than the classic statements of aristocratic power I'd observed in England. I went to the Symphony with Nan, and in time, I came to know all the Morss children, each one as distinct and captivating an individual as the parents. I became closest to their daughter, and her soon-to-be fiancé, and learned with astonishment that, for Everett, not even his new son-in-law's Harvard Law School degree could erase the disturbance in Everett's orderly world caused by the fact that he, the son of generations of Republicans, was about to give his daughter away in marriage to a Democrat.

My introduction to Thanksgiving, the true American religious feast, came in the Chestnut Hill household of a professor of archaeology at Harvard. The son of an old Boston family, married to an Englishwoman equally learned in botany and landscape design, he was a genial and intelligent host. Their two daughters and their circle of friends made the family gathering for the Thanksgiving turkey expansive. My hostess, being British, could translate the local customs and landscape for me. With her careful explanation of plants, trees, native species, the patterns of light and dark in this northern location, I began to see the landscape on its own terms instead of contrasting it to my Australian Mediterranean climate. I'd never thought there could be beauty in a palette of grey and white, but suddenly I could see in the low slanting light, the bare branches, and the gleaming snow of an early winter afternoon images I'd seen before in a Rembrandt drawing but never properly understood.

Then there was the hospitable Milton house of an Australian woman, married to a very proper Bostonian, where the dinner parties always mixed British and Australian visitors, with just the right group of proper Bostonians. Long before the world had heard of women's groups, my Australian hostess used to have grand luncheons for twenty or so of her women friends of all ages, so that I would find myself sitting with some Bostonian lady in her eighties, educated in Italy, on my right, and a youngish British poet on my left, a kind of companionship it was inconceivable I would encounter in Australia.

This easy sociability, the excitement of discovering a great university and the society that had produced it, and an emerging new aesthetic sense, overshadowed but did not obliterate the inevitable shock of moving from one culture to another. I was obsessed with the disposability of everything—handkerchiefs, napkins, plates, wrappings, packages—and, before the era of health foods, the absence of taste and texture in foods processed almost out of existence. It was true that packaged bread did not go stale or grow mold, but it also tasted exactly like cardboard. No amount of effort to enter into a new culture could make me enjoy a greasy hamburger or an utterly indigestible hot dog. Tea made with lukewarm water and teabags, and instant coffee, simply did not bear any comparison with the real thing. Indeed, to me, many of the "conveniences"—fast foods, disposable substitutes for linen or porcelain, and the ubiquitous packages—seemed like the plastic which prevented one from really examining fruit and vegetables in the supermarket, barriers to discrimination, somehow part of a huge conspiracy to convince people that speed and uniformity were all that mattered. If material objects were so easily disposed of, and flavors so attenuated, in the name of convenience, I wondered how the principle operated in human relations, and whether the passions of the heart were also attenuated and subject to a similar code.

I found myself constantly puzzling over what it meant to live in a society devoted to the pursuit of happiness, managing somehow to hold this pleasure principle in uneasy balance with the Puritan fear of the world, and of earthly beauty. I kept scanning the grand streets of Cambridge for the beautiful gardens I associated with elegant houses. In time I learned that they were not to be found, because Puritan culture discouraged cultivating any but useful plants, and New Englanders, skilled in conquering other aspects of the northern climate, claimed that gardening was too difficult.

Then there was something very troubling about the relationship between the sexes. The rules were clear. Men and women belonged in couples, and only in couples, like so many candidates for Noah's ark. I listened in astonishment as some of the women in the Graduate Center told me they felt obliged to hide in their rooms on Saturday nights unless they had a "date." When I asked what was so shameful about being alone or with women friends on Saturday nights, they explained that it was a tribal ritual going back to puberty. If one didn't have a "date," one wasn't popular, and girls who were unpopular almost didn't exist. Moreover, not to want to be paired off in this ludicrous manner meant that one was "poorly adjusted," having trouble with one's feminine nature, and headed for deep psychological trouble.

The problem wasn't just in the women's heads either. I noticed that faculty referred to graduate women as "girls" although all were well into their twenties, women in any other culture. And, to my considerable irritation, the staff in the medical center looked first for psychological problems of adjustment in women students before considering a possible physical cause of any ailment. There was a vexing incident in which a source of salmonella contamination went undetected for weeks in the kitchens of 6 Ash Street because the medical staff thought the stomach cramps and diarrhea of the graduate women were neurotic in origin. I was annoyed at the same attitude when, a migraine sufferer since my early teens, I found myself being interrogated about my sex life when I sought a prescription for my standard migraine medication. When I said I hadn't come to discuss my sex life but to get a routine treatment for my headaches, I was given a prescription along with a knowing look which conveyed that I was riddled with neurosis, and that what ailed my head would disappear if only I found a man.

I loved the heady energy of my classes, the seriousness with which everyone took their studies, and the lively sense of competition which suffused every conversation. But being British I expected competition to take place within rules of fair play. So I was astonished to discover in my class on medieval constitutional history that a trio of Law School students leapt up minutes before the lecture ended to rush to the library to hide, for their own exclusive use, all the key books and articles mentioned by the lecturer. It took me some time to understand that my ideas about fair play came from a smallish society with tiny and fairly stable elites, for whom the prizes of success were reasonably predictable. But this world was one where the competitors were drawn from a society and population the size of Western Europe, for many of whom the only rule was to win, since there was no telling where capturing the immediate prize might carry one. Of course, where winning was the only end, there could not be much joy, or sense of play, in intellectual life. In my new circle of graduate student friends, I'd found a group whose members were exceptional in their zest for learning and for their moral concerns. But there was a darker side to this competitive world in which people's talents carried them far from roots, religion, or moral constraints. It was easy for me to criticize such conduct, but I had grown up in another world, had dropped in here to see what I could learn, and would still exist, albeit somewhat chastened, if I were to fail dismally at Harvard. On some days I remembered that, and on others I could feel the heady exhilaration of reaching out for all possible prizes. It was just as well that I'd set myself a speedy timetable for my General Examination, because if I settled too easily into the Harvard world, I might easily get sucked in permanently.

Without realizing it, I was being redefined by my new circumstances. I had arrived with all the sensitivity and prickliness of the person who hasn't ever quite belonged at home—my intellectual concerns real, but defined as an eccentricity in Australia. Within weeks I began to see myself as perfectly normal, like all the other lively people around me. These people weren't the alienated left intellectuals of Australia, or the wistful exiles from Oxbridge I knew in Sydney. They were young, lively, and ambitious, and I was like them. I'd never seen this as a positive definition before, but as it seeped into my consciousness that it was, I began imperceptibly to relax, like some sea organism which has floated into a rich and sustaining habitat.

In my mind there were two symbols for how seductive this new world was. From my carrel in Widener I could watch the sun sink on winter afternoons until all the Yard was in shadow except for the gold ball and weathervane at the top of the spire of Memorial Church. It would seem to soar there above the buildings, an almost disembodied symbol of shining aspiration. I would stand at the top of the Widener steps and gaze at it before I set out to walk back to the Graduate Center in the gathering dusk, thinking about the passion for knowledge that had inspired the Puritan vision on which the chapel was modeled. Then, when I walked back to the Radcliffe Library in the early hours of the morning, to turn in the books I'd taken out on overnight loan, every building in sight would be ablaze with light. All my life in Australia, I'd been a solitary person studying late, going to bed in a darkened world, itself a commentary on my idiosyncratic interest in learning. Here, I was part of a community where everyone was awake, as intent as I was on mastering knowledge. It wasn't until I'd seen these images of a community engaged in a quest for knowledge that I realized how lonely I had been in Sydney. Here, I might be a stranger, knowing only a few charming people, and I might not yet comprehend many aspects of the culture, but in a profound sense, I knew I belonged in this country of low slanting sunlight and blazing lights at midnight. We might worship the sun in the antipodes, but never this incandescence of the mind.

2.

HARVARD

ON MY ARRIVAL in Cambridge, I was a little exasperated that I was expected to take at least a year of lecture courses on the various fields I would present for my Ph.D. orals, as well as the graduate research seminars which I equated with graduate work. In my books I was well beyond the stage of taking in fresh information from lectures. I expected to be busy at research and with work in historiography. But as the routine of the fall semester emerged, I found myself looking forward to the week's schedule of lectures.

They were so different from the low-key presentations I was used to at the University of Sydney, lectures that conveyed information laced with a very modest infusion of theory. My Harvard classes were different. Oscar Handlin, short, rotund, and wonderfully matter-of-fact, would appear puffing, seconds before the customary lecture time of ten minutes past the hour, mount the platform, and begin a throwaway monologue about the social history of the United States, a monologue which was at once sardonic and profoundly romantic. One could tell that he was deeply moved by the romance of the Puritan migration to the New World, and that, child of immigrants himself, he entered spontaneously into the emotions of the generations of immigrants who followed the Puritans. Yet the dominant theme of his course was the tragic dimension of human experience. For, of course, there was no fulfilling the dream of success inherited by the secular offspring of the Puritans. To emigrate was to be uprooted and to experience the pains of alienation. So the children of the great Eastern European Jewish migration made up for their losses by making Hollywood the purveyor of happy endings. The convention was a comfort to successive generations of immigrants unable to face the possibility that the journey had not been worth the uprooting.

In all my years of studying Australian history, no one had ever discussed what it might have felt like to be a transported convict, or the child of men and women condemned to forced labor. It was something I'd always thought about, knitting my brows in the archives, trying to imagine what my familiar world had looked like to those lonely fair-skinned people, burned scarlet by the Australian sun. I seized upon the model offered in Oscar Handlin's lectures for interpreting this experience, and quickly began to transpose it to Australia. I could see the Australian quest for the Gallipolis of life, and the often misplaced confidence in muddling through, as part of the necessary confirmation for a world of transported misfits, that life might never meet expectations and was more than likely to produce unyielding disaster. Since I craved understanding more than any other intellectual delight, each flash of insight was a heady new fix for a boundless appetite.

Bernard Bailyn taught colonial history as though it were a totally new subject. He spent one hour explaining why it was that all the dreary administrative history I'd been forced to commit to memory about the organization of the British Colonial Office, or the administration of the Navigation Acts, offered very little useful insight into the nature of society as it developed in the American colonies. Then he began to outline the important questions, the answers to which he thought might explain why the colonies separated from Great Britain, and why the new society had such a deep preoccupation with the nature of executive power and the basis of consent— preoccupations which shaped the American Constitution. I could scarcely attend a lecture without some new insight about the history of the Australian colonies exploding in my mind like a firecracker. I found myself practically dancing out of the staid historical setting of Harvard Hall because of the excitement unleashed by the new ways of examining my own history. This was what I'd wanted from the study of history—the flash of understanding, the new insight, the notion that one was living with reality, not some dusty myth from the past.

Donald Fleming, short, dapper, mannered, and beautifully spoken, presented lectures which were set performances, carefully prepared pieces of oratory which were the setting for dazzling high jinks in the history of ideas. They left the listener entranced by the new connections made between society and ideas, and between different fields, occupations, and patterns of thought. To say we looked forward to his twice weekly lectures was an understatement. It was as though we were fascinated readers of a Dickens serial, poised on the dock waiting for the newest installment of the enthralling story of Little Nell. His performances made it seem totally natural to care about ideas, and there was a panache about their delivery that was almost athletic, a high-flying trapeze of the mind. When the entertainment was over one realized that the recent performance also illustrated some important point about the social context of ideas, about the mechanisms by which ideas were disseminated, points forever fixed in the memory because of the manner of their delivery.

It wasn't possible for me to take my Ph.D. General Examination without presenting a field in medieval history, something I'd always avoided as an undergraduate, because I'd never been able to develop an interest in systems of land tenure, chivalry, or the nature of papal kingship. Now I had to rectify my oversight by attending the lectures of one of Harvard Law School's most cherished eccentrics, Sam Thorne, whose passion for medieval constitutional history could have moved a stone to interest in the evolution of the common law. We began the year with a short, white-haired figure striding

into our lecture hall in Sever, hands thrust deep into his pockets, eyes focused on the middle distance beyond the window,
coming to a dead halt in the middle of the room, to announce
that we were to see ourselves as knights who had just paid
tribute to our lord with a red rose at midsummer.

Thereafter, Sam Thorne talked to us as he wandered absentmindedly about the small lecture room, hands deep in his
pockets, eyes gazing at some distant scene in the mind's eye
far removed from the class. He never made reference to notes
but paced up and down in front of the unused lectern, leading
his listeners in successive lectures to deeper and deeper understanding of this seemingly fanciful obligation. We learned its
origin, transformation over time, and eventual replacement
with the notion of exclusive rights to property. The journey
through time was liberally enlivened by figures who were Sam
Thorne's heroes, men who had tried to understand the nature
and morality of society's status, until his greatest intellectual
hero, the thirteenth-century jurist Bracton,* had been able
to conceptualize the idea of law and justice as distinct from
obligation.

Neil Harris, Sam Wells, and I, lone historians amid the lawyers, sat entranced with these lectures and the lecturer, half
dismayed that we were modernists, unable to pursue this
form of learning further. We often extended the hour by accepting Sam Thorne's invitation to coffee, where his mind
moved easily to make the connections between the battles of
the twelfth century about feudal obligations and modern political conflicts.

My fellow graduate students in history were as diverse a
group as any I'd ever encountered before. They were from ev-

---

*Henry de Bracton, thirteenth-century judge and legal scholar whose
treatise on the various forms of legal action and commentaries on se-
lected cases made him the preeminent authority on the law of his day.
His notions of kingship were the concepts called upon in the constitutional conflicts of the seventeenth century to dispute the idea of the divine right of kings.

ery region of the United States, from every type of university and college. There were Mormons, Orthodox Jews, Japanese Americans, Jesuits, and radical freethinkers. Only a handful of women entered the graduate program. I made friends at once with the lovely young Jewish girl from New York, who was the only other woman beginning graduate work in American history in my year, and within a few weeks I also got to know the five or six women who were further along in their graduate careers in American history.

My fellow students, male and female, were mostly not a happy lot. The Ph.D. system was a European import, grafted onto American undergraduate studies in the late nineteenth century. It rested upon the assumption that doctoral students aimed to "master" a field of study, and to contribute truly original research to it through their dissertation. Students acquired a supervisor of their doctoral studies and their dissertation, and their relationship with that individual shaped the whole mood and pattern of their graduate student life. A kindly and supportive supervisor could suffuse life with sunshine. A distant or critical one could cast the world in shadow and foster the most paranoid anxieties.

The German Ph.D. system doubtless helped convert a student population given to dueling and the joys of drink to more serious studies, but for the puritanical inheritors of New England's founding culture, who desperately needed an introduction to playfulness and spontaneity, the Ph.D. system cast a blight more powerful than phylloxera or the Irish potato wilt. Each morning as the Widener opened, white-faced young men, equipped with eyeshades and green bookbags, shambled in to their Faustian task of mastering all learning in their field. As the sun set on the Yard, many of those well along in their dissertations emerged, grey of face but determined, clutching the precious thesis notes or the priceless manuscript, some so haunted by the idea of fire or flood that they deposited the priceless fragments in the vault of the nearest bank for the night.

The first great trial of this Kafkaesque world was the General Examination, an ordeal by exhaustion mounted by the candidate's department, in which four scholars questioned the luckless candidate about everything that could be asked in the space of two hours about all forms of learning in the field. Meeting this challenge was the equivalent of crossing the River Jordan, a barrier to be vaulted before the seductive joys of working on one's own to research the fateful thesis topic, a subject which could make or sink an academic career.

Every culture and profession has its own forms of hazing, but few have them so finely honed as the American scholarly world. Indeed, the hazing elements had so overwhelmed those concerned with the love of learning by the time I came to Harvard, that any detached person could see the ritual as partly comic. These were years in which students flooded to graduate school, attracted by the opportunities of a higher educational system expanding to educate the children of the post-1945 baby boom. Senior scholars took it to be their duty to winnow the fresh grain, letting the chaff of uncertainty or frivolity fall by the wayside. Graduate student colleagues encouraged one another, tried to buoy up the perpetual postponer, and, at the same time, terrified one another with rarefied discussions of historiographical theory or factual minutiae so arcane that none but the most driven specialist could possibly know about them.

The celebrations which followed the successful doctoral oral examinations were epic, a collective shout of joy at another soul released from serfdom, free at last to carve out his, or very occasionally her, destiny in the world of ideas. But the wine and garlands were a little premature, for many who leapt by the first hurdle succumbed to the dangers of dissertation work, for one's dissertation must embody sound research, meet the most exacting standards of interpretation, and be expressed in prose that captivated one's thesis adviser and the several colleagues who must collectively testify that one had met the final requirements for the degree. If the fates smiled, this committee of final judges remained friends for the duration of one's thesis work. But if the committee members fell out, absconded with one another's wives, or merely disliked one another's bidding at the department's regular poker game, the scene was set for Greek tragedy, for there were no acts of propitiation which could appease such irrationally angry gods, and the end was failure, the more crushing for being utterly unearned.

Women negotiating this Herculean set of tests encountered another hazard by the mere fact of being female. There was no way to expiate the invitation refused, however gracefully, or the sexual innuendo deliberately misunderstood. A woman's work had to be just that much better, more theoretically daring, more brilliantly researched to shame naysayers with ulterior motives. As I watched my friends run the course, it was clear that the tenderest male egos were in the sciences, and that those of us who were humanists lived in a world where chances of giving offense were fewer than for those who worked day in and day out in tight-knit laboratory teams.

Because I was an outsider, a traveler from another culture, I could afford to ignore many of the darker aspects of graduate life. Since I did not expect any of my instructors to foster my career, I could take the risk of offending by asking too many questions. Besides it was clear to everyone how excited I was by the course of study, and how much I enjoyed every new theory or new approach to history. Having fun is infectious, and has the effect of making those with whom one works relax. Thanks to good advice, I had chosen as faculty mentors people who were evenhanded and supportive in their dealings with their students, and they were generous in the amount of time and effort expended in helping me sort out how to prepare for my General Examination, and how to plan a future dissertation project.

Doubtless some may have shrugged over the chutzpah involved in planning to take one's Generals after a year, but most understood that I was somewhat older than the average graduate student, and that, in accepting a Fulbright Fellowship, I had made a commitment to return to Australia to

teach. This was something I'd vowed, when leaving Sydney
for Harvard, never to do. But once there, and free of the emotional pressures of my troubled family, I realized that this obligation was one I must meet. Australia was a vast continent,
and should offer me the space to live my own life, if I only
had the strength of will, enlarged by the vindication of this
new scholarly world, to be myself. The decision also consti-
tuted a nonmonetary form of insurance against the slings and
arrows of the Ph.D. system. It allowed me to bypass, for most
of the time, the question which haunted every other mind:
Would I be good enough to be invited to stay on at Harvard
as an instructor after I finished my degree?

For me, the dazzling discovery was that I could do very
well here. The product of a small society tormented by colonial doubts, I had always wondered how I'd measure up.
When it was clear that I was doing as well here as I did at
home, another piece in the mosaic of my new identity fell into
place. If I could hold my own here, I could hold it anywhere.
Life could be a bigger adventure than I'd ever imagined.

The question as to whether one could make it here gave
real urgency to the deliberations of one's graduate seminars,
the courses in which the practicing historian passed on his
(never her, in these days) secrets of the craft. The subject of
the seminar was usually some aspect of the research which its
leader was currently undertaking. Some were tightly organized to illuminate a single theme or period. Others ranged
widely and reflected the interests of students as much as the
instructor.

Bernard Bailyn's seminar taught me to use the social sciences to explicate a text—to read a letter, public document,
or diary entry with reference to the social reality which
formed the unarticulated context of the words. What did a
seventeenth-century New Yorker or an eighteenth-century
Massachusetts politician mean by the word *consent*? The answer to this question, we learned, meant not only reading legislative debates and court records, but letters, diaries,
sermons, account books, and bills of lading. Moreover, we

needed to trace the meanings of language, not merely in its North American context but in the complex network of communication between political groups in Great Britain and North America.

"Yes, but what does it mean?" was the most frequent question he addressed to our industrious seminar group, each of its members bent on reporting more prodigious feats of scholarship in colonial archives than the others. Each week, as the seminar members reported on their labors, we were taught to see how the same words carried new meanings for a people who struggled to give expression to a reality far removed from the political setting in which such English words as "representation," "consent," "property," and "government" had first acquired meaning. Each two-hour session was a lively intellectual workout from which one emerged with twenty new questions for each of the statements one had thought were answers.

Donald Fleming's seminar on American intellectual history was less structured but equally exciting. I was astonished when we first met around our battered seminar table, upstairs on the third floor of Sever Hall, that Donald's list of prominent American intellectuals who warranted study contained one woman for every two men. This just didn't happen in Australia, where the very idea that what women thought was the stuff of intellectual history would have provoked laughter or a dismissive smile. As I wandered about the Widener stacks skimming through the works of nineteenth- and twentieth-century intellectuals he suggested as possible research topics for us, it dawned on me that I could study the lives of other women *and* be taken seriously. It was a shock. A wonderful shock, but a startling jolt to a mind conditioned to the male point of view.

Donald's seminar was often uproariously funny. He could not tolerate sloppy thought, and was wickedly funny at the expense of the typical graduate student display of pompous erudition. Sometimes his wit ran away with him, in ways I thought left the hapless victim permanently scarred. When I got to know him better, and remonstrated with him after one such episode, he was contrite, but it didn't soften his tongue, or his relentless pursuit of clarity of thought. Week by week he taught us to see ideas as part of overarching sets of concepts, part of the mind-set of a generation, its members responding to a common dilemma or shaping experience.

He also tried to teach us how to write. Discussions on one's research topic were always informed by encyclopedic learning, but also with questions about form and style, asked by a man who took intense aesthetic pleasure in ideas, and who wanted them talked about with formal elegance. I loved his wit, respected his intellectual passions, and decided that this man could really teach me how to think. Whenever I wrote a flabby sentence in an essay, he would write in firm colored pencil in the margin "How you do run on!" I'd bridle at the comment, and then have to laugh because it was justly earned.

He was implacable in his insistence that one be committed to one's work, not just professionally but emotionally. So, after sneezing my way through many little-read tomes in Widener, I told him I had decided to do my research on one of America's great Progressive women reformers, Jane Addams. When I said I wanted to study how she had led her generation of American women to solve the problem of gaining access to higher education at a time when society had no expectation that women would use it in any but a decorative sense, he was approving. We both knew that experience had been my own personal dilemma in Australia. "One's research should always involve some element of therapy," he said, smiling. "It only counts if it's really close to the bone." I agreed, knowing I had found someone who could help me find an intellectual vocation.

For me, as for so many other graduate students, Donald's personal interest in how my studies meshed with my life gave the Graduate School a personal face. He took an aesthetic interest in the minds of his students, and his judgments, though rigorous and demanding, were delivered with insight and compassion. It was enormously reassuring that he took me and my ideas seriously.

As the time approached for my General Examination, I began to suffer the usual jitters. I would awake sweating in the small hours of the morning wondering whether I could recall some useless piece of information or the title of some recondite book or essay. My head became so crammed with knowledge that I feared tripping over and jumbling it all together through the pull of gravity. By no means immune to the pressures of the moment, I began to eat, sleep, dream the effort to digest the major body of writing on American history.

Some weeks before the day of judgment I began to realize how ludicrous the effort to know everything was. I spent the day before the exam getting a massage and a facial at Elizabeth Arden and had dinner with friends. The next morning, a sunny early June day, on my way to the Yard, two different sets of Cambridge garbage men whistled at me as I passed by. I wasn't sure what sort of an omen the irreverent greeting was, but it reminded me happily that there were other worlds and points of view than the one I was about to enter in the now familiarly shabby Holyoke House.

My General Examination followed the accepted pattern. I gave inane answers to questions I knew a great deal about, and more intelligent ones on subjects I was unaware I knew anything about. My British Empire training stood me in good stead when tea was served, because it was second nature to take over the teapot; inquire as to people's tastes with respect to lemon, cream, or sugar; and take momentary hold of events. When it was all done I left, furious with myself for the stupid blunders I'd made, yet aware from the body language of everyone present that I was going to scrape through.

The History Department still maintained its Olympian distance from such events by refusing to tell the candidate in person how she or he had performed. Instead, in those halcyon days when the express mails still performed with effortless precision, they sent a special delivery letter to the candidate's residence, where the hapless victim went home to await sentencing. When the special delivery man rang my doorbell I ripped open the letter only to burst out laughing. The letter congratulating me on passing my examination had been dated, and presumably signed, the day before.

When it was all over and I began to take stock of the year, I could see that the American adaptation of the German Ph.D. system worked well in America's activist culture. The elective curriculum of most undergraduate programs did not provide for the kind of specialized training in a discipline I had received at the University of Sydney. Instead, it offered the undergraduate a kind of intellectual exploration not available in my British world. The lecture courses and reading programs offered at the beginning of graduate study allowed for the kind of grounding in a discipline my honors program at Sydney University had provided, although only about a European world. Now the long dreamed of years of research lay ahead of me. Mine was to be conducted under the eagle eye of Donald Fleming, whose standards were exacting but whose generosity as a thesis supervisor was legendary. Other dissertation supervisors might be slow in returning draft thesis chapters, and monosyllabic in comment, but Donald's comments were always prompt and helpful, albeit delivered with his characteristic acerbic wit.

THE NEXT PHASE of graduate study, doing the research for one's thesis, was normally a lonely experience. Everyone told bleak stories of sitting wearily at their desk in the Widener stacks, wondering what folly had possessed them to undertake this particularly unrewarding piece of research in order to enter this poorly paid and little valued profession. Shoe salesmen, bus drivers, construction workers, and drugstore clerks all seemed the embodiment of calm happiness and contentment compared with the scholars who pursued this dusty quest, among old books and manuscripts, for some fresh shards of truth about the past. Like everyone else, I had such moments, but they vanished on my return to a household which was never lonely.

By January of my first year in Cambridge the starchy food, uncivilized eating hours, and the noise of collective living led Carla and me to move to a flat where we could set our own pattern of life. Eventually, in September 1961, Mina, Jana, Barbara, Carla, and I set up house together. The five of us settled with a sixth American friend—Linda—in a battered frame house on Dana Street, where we established an intensely satisfying, often hilarious, and always sociable community.

We each contributed $30 a week to the rent, $5 a week for collective shopping, and divided the heating bill for the drafty, poorly insulated house by six at the end of the month. Jana and Linda lived downstairs. Barbara, Mina, Carla and I lived upstairs, each with a sizable room for sleep and study. Downstairs there was a graceful living room opening onto a dining room, and a large capacious kitchen.

We rented the house unfurnished, and took up the landlord's cheerful offer of $100 to buy used furniture. With this we bought beds, pots and pans, and some canvas chairs from the local equivalent of the Salvation Army used furniture store. Friends lent us desks and a few chests of drawers. The rest was improvisation. The furniture gave the general air of a set for *La Bohème*, but the books piled about everywhere gave the place a sense of serious purpose. Heated discussions over breakfast or coffee in the kitchen always ended with the kitchen table, which had one loose leg, collapsing, to be caught just in time by a habitué of the house, routinely prepared to grab the tabletop and steady the leg to avert catastrophe.

Life at Dana Street never palled, no matter how fruitless one's current research efforts. We were all intensely interested in one another's research, so dinner might begin with an extended conversation about molecular biology and the significance of the newly discovered DNA, move on to an

examination of the nature of historical proof versus laboratory science, and come, by dessert, to the recitation of English
poetry. Barbara, Mina, and I had all been to proper British
girls' boarding schools, so we knew our Keats, Tennyson,
Wordsworth, and Scottish ballads by heart, just as Jana,
when the spirit moved her, could declaim the Racine she had
memorized at her French lycée.

Day by day we instructed one another in the follies and
contradictions of women's roles in our respective native countries, each learning distance on our own cultural predicaments from the life history of the other. Mina's Islamic world,
Jana's Czech and French world, my Australian frontier, and
Barbara's Canadian Catholic convent were like different con-
stellations in the night sky, points of reference, from the con-
figuration of which we could begin to chart our experience
free of the internalized presumptions of our native world
about what was "natural" and "feminine."

Not being Americans, we also clung to the idea that life
should be fun, and that hard work should be accompanied by
pleasure. We gave parties, produced impromptu feasts,
dropped everything to go walking in the country, sat on the
tottering porch drinking gin and tonic on warm summer evenings, and exploded in gales of laughter over the idiocy of our
fellow students and the foibles of our teachers. Always, un-
derneath the gaiety, were serious ideas. We studied Freud and
Jung, Talcott Parsons and I. A. Richards, read Hopkins, Eliot,
Pound, Yeats, and Frost aloud to one another, and speculated,
tipsy and sober, about the universal subjects: God, sex, and
politics.

Discussions of religion had more reference points than
usual at 27 Dana Street. Barbara and Jana were Roman Catholics. Mina was a Shiite Muslim, educated in a high Anglican
English boarding school, Carla was Jewish, and Linda, our
one American resident, was a staunch New England Congre-
gationalist. My Anglican girls' boarding school in Sydney had
taught me many beautiful passages from the King James Bible, but supplied no intellectual basis for faith except the sim-

plest piety. We all roared with laughter when Mina described her first efforts at drawing when sent from Tehran to her English school. She drew a graphic picture of St. Paul falling off his horse on the road to Damascus, a story her Bible class had read and which she had found particularly action-filled. Barbara told chilling stories of the hatred and fear of the flesh instilled by the nuns in her Toronto convent. Jana described her conflicts with her liberal rationalist parents over her decision to be confirmed a Catholic. Her parents were modern Czech liberals, believers in rational man. Their daughter had watched the family's orderly world overwhelmed successively by the Nazis and by the Russian army, and, as a consequence, had a darker vision of the human predicament than her parents. Carla explained the Jewish idea of God and talked with wry humor about what it was like to be raised in a faith in which men gave thanks to God for not being born female.

Mina, the child of an arranged marriage, was the daughter of a woman who had been a child bride, someone more like a sister than a mother. She was a parent less than a generation older than her daughter. Nothing could be in more striking contrast to our Western bourgeois ways than Mina's extended household in Tehran, with its legions of servants and family retainers. The contrast led to many fruitful discussions of marriage, sexual codes, and the position of women. Mina adored her learned father, a generous patriarch who had insisted on a Western education for his numerous daughters, but who had kept fathering children until the cherished male heir eventually arrived.

Jana's parents were products of pre-1914 Europe, aristocrats with dreams for a liberal nation-state, and, when their time of testing came, fierce fighters against the Nazis. Jana's memories of her eighth year were overshadowed by watching her grandmother manage the family household in the country, under the watchful eyes of the SS officers quartered in it, while all the family, including the eight-year-old, knew her father was in hiding with the resistance. Her childhood had ended permanently in 1944 with the family's precipitous flight across the border to the Allied zone in Austria, to life in a displaced persons' camp, and a long desperate quest to find whether her father still lived, and to reunite the family.

Carla's family was of Russian Jewish descent. Her grandparents had been part of the great migration of Eastern European Jews to North America in the late nineteenth and early twentieth centuries. Her parents' store in Kansas City might sell groceries, but family life revolved around music, art, and literature. Her father had longed to be an artist but lacked the resources to study art. Her mother, an accomplished musician, had studied at the New England Conservatory before marriage altered her career plans. Both parents were proud of their brilliant daughter, living for the day when she would marry a nice Jewish boy and perpetuate the family but also encouraging and supporting her scholarly career. I often covered up for Carla when her mother called, swearing she was out dating the right young Jewish boy from the Law School, when in reality she was having a passionate affair with an Armenian fellow student from the Middle Eastern Studies Program.

Barbara's roots were in Toronto, a city where her maternal grandfather had been concertmaster of the Symphony Orchestra, a leader of the Toronto Conservatory of Music, and an important cultural figure. So was her paternal grandfather, a longtime editor of the journal *Saturday Night*. But those roots had been attenuated by many expatriations. Her childhood had been lived in Latin American mining camps, where she, along with her mother and younger sister, had accompanied her father on the many postings of his career as an accountant with an oil company. She had spent her college years in Miami, where her parents had settled, at the home office of the company which shaped her father's life. Her father was a model of quiet probity under the stresses of such a peripatetic existence, a man governed by a Canadian ethos of stoic endurance. Her mother, vivacious, sociable, and adaptable, gave balance to the partnership. This stoic code, and the Jansenist rigors of her convent life, were a heritage against which Barbara struggled in painful but creative rebellion. It seemed to me that her intellectual quest was a triumphant effort to overcome the fear of nature instilled both by life on the edge of the jungle and by the religious teachers of her childhood. Her choice of career was a decision to escape the lot of the conventional North American middle-class wife, but the focus of her studies came from the tension between civilization and the wilderness in her childhood.

Linda, our long-suffering American housemate, was a true Yankee, daughter of generations of New England Lorings—thrifty, practical, warmhearted, and by turns puzzled or amused by her polyglot household. It was hard for her to imagine that there were persons in the world who had grown up without learning to recite the Declaration of Independence on the Fourth of July. She was patient with roommates who did not have the embattled Minutemen as part of their earliest iconography, and who actually did not know the route of Paul Revere's ride, but we were a sore trial to her. She remedied the gaps in our education at the earliest possible occasion by inviting the entire household to her family's place in Lexington to watch the annual reenactment of Paul Revere's heroic dash into history. Her quizzical gaze was a steady background to our debates about the finer points of Catholic or Islamic theology, as novel to her as Paul Revere was to the rest of us. By the end of our first year there was something of a standoff. We began keeping American festivals, and Linda was *almost* ready to concede that the pope was not anti-Christ. She agreed to be present when a Jesuit priest blessed the house!

There was something magical about this household of highly intellectual women. It functioned in every possible dimension—economic, spiritual, intellectual, aesthetic—as a true community. Dinner was the moment for excited reporting of fresh discoveries, or new and potentially troublesome questions. We abandoned work and went out to buy wine the night Barbara announced that she *finally* understood Oscar

Wilde and the English Decadents. The day Mina's name was given to the new enzyme she had discovered, to be known thenceforth as Farhad's enzyme, we discarded the household budget and produced a celebratory dinner. The coming and going of male friends was the object of humorous, but always charitable, scrutiny. There was the time in Mina's long succession of adoring suitors when her handsome ski instructor friend arrived with broken English, a colossal cold, and a compulsion to leave the room before sneezing, a compulsion which left every effort at conversation fractured. Then there was Jana's conservative Catholic friend about whom the normally laissez-faire Dana Street community united in opposition. Sometimes the learned nature of the household created delightful dilemmas. Once, a heavily draped male figure rang the bell and left a note for Carla, while Mina and I were having late morning coffee. Made suspicious by the efforts at disguise, we decided she was being courted by some faculty member from the Middle East Center; yet all efforts to decipher the visitor's identity failed because his note and return address were written in Turkish, one of the half dozen Middle Eastern languages Carla was busy acquiring.

In time we became like a well-functioning family. Fluctuations of mood were treated with exquisite delicacy. People just naturally fell to lowering their voices and tiptoeing about when my migraines struck. We were always prepared to offer hours of sage advice when Mina exploded in the door early from the lab, seething about some fresh incident of sexual harassment. Jana's courtship and eventual engagement to Bob Kiely proceeded with the help of a bevy of sympathetic observers ready during the inevitable collisions and missed communications of bridging between Europe and America to translate from new world to old. After the announcement of Jana's engagement we all learned with horror of her denunciation by her thesis director. He had greeted her happy news with white-faced rage, telling her that because she entertained the thought of marriage, she was a frivolous woman who would never make a committed scientist. The attack was chilling, since it underlined all too clearly the terms on which we were participating in a male-controlled academic world. Yet it could not dim the intense pleasure we took in each other's company and the enchantment of sharing a collective life of the mind.

Little by little, by the mere fact of living in such a community, I began to surrender the guard of reserve I had built up. My roommates laughed in a kindly fashion at what they called my ingrained British Empire phlegm. In my past life my reserve had been a necessary coloration, suitable to a hostile terrain. I needed it, first to cope with a mother ready to exploit any sign of emotional vulnerability for her own purposes of control, and second to conceal from a confidently anti-intellectual Australia how deep were my passions of the mind. But my Dana Street companions were not poised to exploit a weakness, or to mock serious aspirations. They were genuinely interested in what I thought and felt. Before long I could talk about the death of my father and brother, my mother's neurosis, and my own despair without fear of revealing too much. In time I came to realize that the privacy to which I had once clung as though it were a life raft might not be necessary at all. Perhaps it was merely one more part of the bourgeois code which silenced women. Here, we each knew one another's private griefs, and understood them. I could let my feelings show, because they would be shared with genuine compassion and moral insight. Everyone had views on the vexed question of duty to family, and everyone talked through the morality of different courses of action about it.

The continuing conversation was a form of witty and humane group therapy for me. There emerged a kind of tolerant, nondirective Dana Street consensus about the pressing problems of each individual's life. The collective view which emerged about my life was immensely comforting. It was true that one had a duty to parents, but it was an obligation to honor and respect them. One owed them the best form of love one could muster, but it wasn't necessary to like them.

One owed them economic support, but not necessarily self-immolation. Besides, duty to family must be balanced by the religious obligation to develop one's talents and put them to creative use. This was a new idea to me. My evangelical church instruction had hammered away at duty, but never considered humankind as possessing some of the creativity of the divine.

The group of women at Dana Street gave me the one element that had been lacking from my sense of self. They taught me to see my talents as normal, not aberrant, and by laughingly christening me the Reverend Mother of our not so chaste female community, they conveyed the sense that I was not different out of eccentricity, but out of strength.

On the question of the creative use of undoubted talents, there were many midnight-to-dawn discussions. As a group we didn't care for the treatment of knowledge as property. We lent our notes to potential competitors, shared new insights produced by our research, and, sitting in the comfort of our shabby kitchen, and still shabbier dining room, we denounced the intellectual habits of our fellow students who saw everyone as a potential rival. What were women supposed to do in such a competitive academic arena? Did we want to be high achievers in a world of such possessive individualism? Our answer was a high-spirited "no." We reassured one another, with no supporting evidence, that we would find another way.

WHEN I ELECTED to take my General Examination at the end of my first year at Harvard, I ended my Radcliffe scholarship and had to find work as a teaching fellow to cover the cost of my graduate tuition and to provide a modest stipend to cover my living expenses. I called on Harriet Dorman, the secretary of the History Department, now an old friend, to ask whether I could be a History tutor like many of my fellow male students; she then explained flatly that women could not be resident tutors in the Harvard Houses, although she was sure that she could find me a job as a teaching fellow in the General Education Program.

All the men friends I'd come to know in our happy circle, which revolved around Barbara, Mina, and Jana, enjoyed their lives as resident tutors immensely. Their appointments gave them handsome rooms rent-free, free meals in the House dining hall, and the intellectual pleasure of organizing their own tutorial programs with students who were "concentrators" in the fields each one had chosen to enter as a professional scholar.

My appointment, when it came, was in the General Education Program, an innovation in the Harvard curriculum inspired by the experience of the 1939–45 war, and the Harvard faculty's decision that, thenceforth, Harvard undergraduates would understand the political and intellectual tradition which Western democracies had inherited from the Greeks, and from the Western European experience. The General Education Committee sponsored courses that were aimed to ensure that every graduate would be alert to the authoritarian trends which were part of the Western political inheritance, would recognize within himself (there being no herself present in the planning) the psychological sources of the modern craving for the authoritarian, would understand the intellectual implications of modern science, would recognize the aesthetic dilemmas of the modern imagination, and would be able to distinguish between genuine religious impulses and the craving to worship the authoritarian leader, the insatiable appetite to consume, or the secular mirage of success.

It was a noble educational ambition, and it stimulated some of the most inspired teaching of the Harvard undergraduate curriculum in the 1950s and 1960s. The departmental organization of university faculties means that every department faculty, dominated by the research ideal, strives to teach ever-more specialized courses in its chosen discipline, seeking to convert its students to aspire to graduate study in the field in question. This objective is in direct conflict with the undergraduate's need to sop up general knowledge like blotting paper, to try out new ideas, to test the limits of the individual imagination, and to find the moral insight desperately needed as an anchor during the intensely competitive process of being rigorously evaluated in a self-advertised meritocratic society.

The General Education Program in its heyday did not simply pay lip service to this need. It met it by recruiting the greatest rhetorical powers, the broadest humanistic concerns, and some of the faculty's most powerful scientific imaginations to counteract the specializing trend of modern institutions of learning. Doubtless, I would have benefited by being appointed a tutor in History, but by being appointed to teach in the General Education Program, I was required to overcome some of the weaknesses of my specialized undergraduate education at the University of Sydney. So, although it was hard work, because I taught fifty or sixty students while my male friends had a dozen or so tutees, I was more excited by what I was teaching than by anything I had yet undertaken in my academic life.

The first wonderful discovery was that I was obliged to move from a colonial ideal of education, in which the instructor disciplines the student so that he or she measures up to standards externally developed, to a setting in which each student was viewed as a potential Nobel Prize winner, a possible colleague whose talents might one day transform what was regarded as important knowledge. This made teaching a joy, more like an intellectual form of athletics as distinguished from some parade-ground drill.

What we read for the course in which I was a teaching fellow was a wonderful mixture of theology, passages from the New Testament, political theory, history, selections from the novels of Tolstoy and Dostoevsky, philosophy, economic history, and essays about contemporary culture. My men friends who were tutors in several different Harvard Houses told me I would enjoy working with the two faculty members from the History Department who taught Social Sciences 6. They were Harvard characters, known for the wildly enthusiastic student response to the course, and for the numbers of students who queued up from the early hours of registration day to sign up for it. Bob Kiely and Joel Porte were tutors in Leverett House, where John Conway, one of the duo who taught the course, was Master. They talked about him with admiration and respect. He was a man of unusual cultivation, they said, a person who embodied the real concerns of high culture—religion, philosophy, history, and the love of beauty. Better still, he was a wickedly witty and funny man, with a highly developed sense of the absurd.

"You haven't met Master Conway yet?" Bob Kiely asked me. "You're going to like him. He's Canadian, and a war hero as well."

3.

JOHN

WHEN I WENT to meet my new employer, John Conway, in the Master's Office at Leverett House, I already knew my way to the two modern towers which sat, linked by a graceful willow-lined courtyard, by the edge of the Charles River, at the then easternmost tip of the cluster of River Houses. Their floor-to-ceiling windows commanded a dazzling view of the Charles as it swung gently left toward the University Boathouse and of the bridge over which the Harvard Band made its high-spirited way to the Harvard Stadium, set in imperial splendor across the river next to the Harvard Business School. Leverett House's undergraduate residents boasted elegant suites of rooms, and my tutor friends who lived in the Towers luxuriated in very elegant quarters.

I'd heard enough stories about Master Conway's wit, and British ways, to know that I would like the Canadian historian for whom I was to work as a teaching fellow, but I was still unprepared for the man and the conversation which began one hot September morning, just before classes started, in my second year at Harvard.

Despite the frenzied bustle of preparation for the return of students going on in the outer office, where a harried secretary was juggling folders and making irascible sounds to her assistants, John Conway seemed totally unhurried. Instead of focusing on the course in which I was to teach, the reading, and other administrative details, he seemed genuinely curious about who I was, where I was from, and what I thought of Harvard, of the United States, of the contrasts between British and American values. I'd come prepared to be very businesslike, to demonstrate my suitability for a teaching job, but it soon became clear that this man was uninterested in anything so graceless as a credential. He seemed simply to assume that since I'd reached my current stage in my career, the mere matter of teaching undergraduates was to be taken for granted.

The conversation took off instead about our shared experience of a first encounter with the United States. His deep brown eyes shining with laughter, he propped his feet on the desk, tilted back his chair, and lit a cigarette effortlessly, despite his amputated right hand. He began to tell me about his arrival in Cambridge, fresh from his Canadian Highland regiment, to enroll in the graduate school in the summer of 1945. I had only to look at him to see the humor of the situation. I could see the kilt and the khaki jacket with its captain's insignias, the decorations, the proper low-key British approach to his war injuries (clearly visible in his empty right sleeve), and I could imagine him making the same journey in the same dusty elevator to the ramshackle History Department office. It was a delicious study in cultural confrontation.

Not to be outdone, I began to explain my biggest puzzlement at American ways. Because my childhood friends had been soldiers returned from the 1914–18 war, each one's story a personal epic of courage, endurance, injury, I had grown up admiring and valuing the warrior mentality. For me, these men, and their sons who had fought in the 1939–45 war, embodied the modern predicament in its most extreme form. I had firsthand knowledge of the passion and beauty of their individual lives, made hostage to the bureaucratic forces of modern societies—flesh and blood perilously entwined with the destructive power of modern technology. They took service as a badge of courage, even as they understood the bureaucracy and impersonality of modern war.

That was why I couldn't believe my ears when I heard my Harvard graduate student colleagues telling me with real pride that they'd been smart and found an intelligence job during the Korean War, and that my faculty instructors had served almost to a man in the OSS during the 1939–45 war. I could see, I told my silent but now very attentive listener, that it was another form of American efficiency for the state to preserve the lives of its educated elites, but it didn't square with my old British ideas about civic duty or the codes of honor I'd previously taken for granted. It made me think differently about home, I said, laughing. I had never appreciated before that the old British Empire, which I'd thought capitalist to the core, still enshrined some noncommercial values.

John's reflective face dissolved in a smile of wicked mischief. He described arriving in Cambridge in 1945, to be greeted in his first seminar not as an honored servant of the wartime cause but as "one of you men on the dole," a slighting reference to the fact that he was studying on veteran's benefits. And, to his astonishment, many fellow students equated his military service with militarism, and Britain's wartime leaders not with the fight against Nazism but instead with imperialism.

We both laughed companionably about this new way of seeing the world, and then fell to cataloging the excitements of Harvard's intellectual life, the kindness and generosity of American friends, the delights of living in a society where everything seemed possible, and where striving for one's best achievement was admired. I told him about the wonderful sense of release I felt at living in a world where ideas mattered, and the comfort I took from those lights blazing away on winter nights, their message the exact opposite of the one someone of scholarly inclination received in Sydney or, John agreed, in Vancouver.

Forgetting entirely about the business at hand I described

the self-discovery that came from living in a world where one carried no status or past identity, so that when people asked who you were, a real answer was necessary. Moreover, I said, the questions weren't idle. I'd found my graduate student friends genuinely curious, and that in order to answer them, I'd had to learn some new things about myself. John countered with a story of his own first days as a tutor in Eliot House, where he'd met similar demands that he drop his facade of formal manners and talk about what he really believed and felt.

I glanced at my watch. Although it seemed like a few minutes, we'd been talking for an hour and a half. I took pity on the secretary who had to manage this man's time, and stood up to announce my departure. As I was leaving the busy office we agreed to meet for drinks later in the week, with the three other teaching assistants in the course and with Stephen Graubard, the historian of modern Europe and close friend, who co-taught Social Sciences 6 with John.

Inspired by Master Conway's approach to life, I walked back to the apartment I was packing up to move to Dana Street not via the Square and through the bustling Yard, but along the Charles River, lingering to relish the view from the shade of the sycamores which lined the banks. On my right were the formal neo-eighteenth-century facades of the River Houses, topped by their graceful domes. Traceries of wrought iron carried the eye from solid brick walls into inner court-yards, shaded by imposing elms. From the deep, dappled shade of the sycamores one could relish the reflected light of the river, its waters already cooling with the hint of fall in the crisp nights. Like most graduate students, I knew little of the world behind these walls. Up to this point my teaching assignment had been a way of earning a living. Now I knew it was going to be fun. John had an intellectual playfulness I relished and an experience akin to mine, even if lived half a world away from my native Australia. His enthusiasm for the undergraduate life of the College was infectious, making me curious about the bright undergraduates who had seemed part of the scenery but not of my world up to this point. Moreover, there was an exquisite courtesy in John's dealings with people that I found enormously captivating. His mischievous brown eyes and rich, melodious voice stayed in the mind.

When I met Stephen Graubard, and my fellow tutors, later that week over drinks, all my expectations were confirmed. The entrance hall at 25 De Wolfe Street, the Master's Residence at Leverett House, was dominated by a perfect replica of an eighteenth-century flying staircase. The visitor's eye was immediately carried up by the sound of John's voice to the vision of his face looking cheerfully down, inviting the new arrival upstairs. My fellow teaching assistants were gathered in the paneled living room, along with Stephen Graubard. The other tutors were a lively bunch, two of them intellectual historians, one a student of British politics. Stephen Graubard was the exact opposite of John. John was Catholic, interested in theology, in questions of free will and determinism. Stephen was a man of the Enlightenment, interested in politics and in social improvement. What they shared was their zest for ideas, deep respect for the minds of the young people they taught, a love of good food and drink, and a passion for talk. After two meetings I knew they began to talk the instant they were in sight of each other, and that the conversation was one of their principal interests in life.

The course they had designed and given the name "Freedom and Authority in the Modern World" was a testament to their friendship and to years of genial argument. John believed, with Edmund Burke, that the "constraints upon men were among their greatest liberties," that human beings needed religious belief and stable social institutions to help contain the darker side of human nature; Stephen, on the other hand, was convinced, along with the great nineteenth-century liberals, that there were secular solutions to most human predicaments.

They were accomplished lecturers, splendid models for younger teachers to observe. They almost never referred to notes. They wandered about the platform as if thinking out loud. They raised and lowered their voices for dramatic effect. They told jokes, lapsed into reverie, or paused to emphasize the loaded rhetorical question. The performance was designed to lead the four-hundred-odd students, at a spirited pace, through the moral and political dilemmas of fifth-century Athens, early Christianity, the High Middle Ages, early modern political conflicts, the French and Bolshevik Revolutions, some of the great reflections of political and historical minds on the problem of free will. John was always likely to return to St. Augustine on the theme of free will. Stephen would lead the listener somehow back to Tolstoy.

Our little group of teaching assistants sat in the back of Emerson D, sometimes spellbound, sometimes critical, always impressed by the quality of the performance. Both men were apt to disappear right after the lecture for coffee and a continuation of their personal conversation, so the teaching fellows took to gathering on the steps of Emerson D, ten minutes or so before the lecture, so that we could chat about the course before going in.

John arrived a good ten minutes before the lecture hour, often looking deathly pale. A barrage of coughing always followed after he lit the inevitable cigarette. Stephen arrived precisely five minutes before the hour, briefcase in hand, *New York Times* under one arm, grey tweed chesterfield coat immaculate, grey fedora at just the right angle on his head. He could be counted on to launch into commentary on the morning's news immediately he was within hearing distance, so that our gathering usually began with a vigorous discussion of current events.

I had said airily that I knew all the texts to be taught in the course. But in fact I didn't. So my time in the Widener stacks was now divided between the first stages of research on my thesis and a frenzied rush to be just slightly better read than my students before I met the small groups, which were held for discussion, following the weekly lectures. I hadn't read about the trial and death of Socrates since my abortive philosophy course in my freshman year. Nor had I ever read St. Paul's Letter to the Romans with adult attention. The debates of political theorists about human nature hadn't been part of my government courses at the University of Sydney, which had focused on electoral politics. It was a new idea to me that political institutions were derived from a definition of the human predicament, a predicament from which the state or the ruler might offer release—spurious release in John's terms, real relief in Stephen's. I'd read the seventeenth-century British political theorists, but not the ideologues of the French and Russian Revolutions, and I'd never heard the conservative and liberal interpretations of the meaning of the state so eloquently argued.

My students were as fascinated by the two competing viewpoints and their exponents as I. They were a joy to teach, always ready to play with ideas, often full of opinions about books and essays still to be read. My teaching life in Sydney had been dedicated to stirring a response from an impassive audience. Here the argument had already started before I came in the classroom door, and it often continued as people left, pulling on coats and mufflers, slinging bookbags over their shoulders, intent on the last question of the hour. The Harvard men were walking volcanoes of talk, giving off constant puffs of conversation. The Radcliffe women were less inclined to bubble over, but more likely to have read the text.

I'd never been so happy. It seemed as though I'd found my ideal world, where people of every generation resonated to ideas, cared about them, and thought it important to talk about them, and with *me*. I began the day discussing Racine, or the French Catholic intellectuals of her undergraduate days at the Sorbonne, with Jana at breakfast, raced to Emerson D to listen to Stephen's explication of the ideas and mores of the France of Louis Quatorze, taught a group of talkative students about French absolutism, and then headed for my Widener stall, where the issues and questions about American women's education that I was studying for my thesis were so engrossing other subjects faded.

My thesis research was perfectly designed to set me answering the questions I found most deeply troubling about my own life. Donald Fleming and I had agreed that I should do a collective biography of representative types from the first generation of American women who entered graduate study, either in the United States or Europe. I wanted to see what happened to the first women to secure training as professionals. Most histories of education talked in conventional liberal terms about the opening of access to institutions for women, or blacks. I wanted to know what the experience was like, what the pioneer generation learned, and what the outcomes of the experience were. What had it been like for them to earn the prized degree, and then find that society had no acceptable work for women professionals? How had they dealt with that disappointment? What did their solutions to the problem look like now, seventy years or so after their active careers began? I was in search of a broad sample of well-documented lives which would allow me to classify my cast of characters in terms of ideal types, and draw conclusions from that classification.

The search was blessed with an embarrassment of riches. American women born in the 1860s, educated in the late 1870s and early 1880s, who undertook graduate study or professional training, had a sense of being chosen by history, called upon to demonstrate what educated women could achieve. They entered public life in the heady years of the Progressive Era, shaping some of the Progressives' most characteristic responses to urban poverty, family welfare, and the working conditions of the urban poor. They were copious writers and public speakers, memoirists and letter-writers. I was enchanted to find such a rich record of women's lives so readily available in print, and excited to know that most of them had left a collection of papers, ready to be tapped in archives around the country. It was invigorating to be studying women with active public careers, political commitments, broad social and political concerns. They were a wonderful relief from the social attitudes and values of the 1950s, and a splendid corrective to Freudian ideas about women. I was looking at myself through the lens of history, something my male colleagues had always done. It was delightful to live with this lively cast of characters, and engage in an inner conversation with them about the circumstances of my own day.

On days when I found out something intriguing about my subjects I made my way to Donald Fleming's office in Widener, just for the pleasure of hearing him talk. Donald's unmistakable voice, always heavy with irony, left one startled by the brilliant smile which suddenly appeared when something amused him. No one else I knew used the language with such precision. Certainly no one else knew the literature of his field in such an encyclopedic fashion, or shared his knowledge so easily with his students. No one else had read the printed sources about great American women's lives, and was prepared to talk about them at length with great seriousness.

Conversations with Donald were always taking sudden unexpected turns. I might arrive to ask questions about some of the nineteenth-century evolutionary thinkers who influenced my Progressive women reformers, only to have the conversation take a swift turn toward the philosophy of history. Donald was impatient with someone so parochially Western that she had not read the great Arab philosopher of history, Ibn-Khaldūn. But his mockery was companionable, and simply sent me off to correct my ignorance. My footnotes on conversations with Donald, pursued immediately in the Widener stacks, were usually so engrossing that I lost all sense of time. Sudden pangs of hunger would send me back to Dana Street, where Barbara and I, the only regular drinkers, would sip our gin or Scotch and reflect on the day before the house took up the conversation of the moment over dinner.

It was fascinating to alternate my days between Social Sciences 6 and my study of American women reformers. When John lectured on Edmund Burke and his criticisms of the French Revolution, his beautiful voice made Burke's passionate criticisms of the French Revolution real. One could understand a man grieving for a world which had permanently lost "unbought grace," and perhaps even accept the idea that inherited institutions could evolve peacefully to meet the needs of a changing social order.

When I settled in Widener with the writings of my generation of American women reformers, I identified equally passionately with their impatient struggle to bring a new social order into being in which inherited institutions did not confine women to domesticity. Yet no matter how I identified with my subjects, I could not accept the pursuit of happiness as the telos of human experience, as the best of my women reformers appeared to do. I knew I had to act as though society could be improved by human agency. But then my mind would fly back to the natural disasters of my childhood, the griefs and sorrows which had crippled and harmed my well-meaning and highly moral parents, the pictures of Hiroshima and Nagasaki which could never be erased from the mind. Then John's view of the human situation seemed the more realistic.

No matter how erratically my mind swung between these two poles, my small community of women at Dana Street gave life a golden promise. I'd never lived in such totally satisfying companionship. If my mind turned to music, there was Carla, ready to expand my limited experience. If I were inclined to seek literary parallels for the day's happenings, or to ponder the formal problems of dissertation writing, there was Barbara in her room across the hall, her powerful mind and fertile imagination primed to enlarge the question. Let some query about evolutionary thought emerge among my nineteenth-century women intellectuals, my companions at Widener in the afternoons, I had Mina or Jana, who could be relied upon to dispose of it authoritatively over dinner.

As fall 1961 gave way to deep winter, the rickety yellow frame house on Dana Street hummed with activity. Barbara's dissertation on the English Decadents grew steadily. We all watched the pile of handwritten yellow sheets mount on the desk by the window in her tiny upstairs room. Mina's seemingly endless experiments finally reached a conclusion, and were embodied in a thesis, no sooner completed than she became a student at the Medical School, forever parodying the day's lectures for our dinnertime delight. Carla's language texts, piled on her tiny desk in the airy upstairs back room, changed from Arabic to Turkish, one more language acquired in her pursuit of understanding of the Islamic world. They sat next to the radio beside small piles of notes in delicate script. She sat there night after night, ears attuned to the Boston Symphony, eyes roving over the texts she was editing for posterity.

The glow about the household made us feel impervious to the ills of graduate study. Our friendship, and our continuing interest in each other's ideas, provided a protective cocoon which sheltered us from the realities of our situation. We could be certain with one another that we belonged in this best university in the most challenging system of graduate education in our world, because we *knew* what it took to achieve real excellence. While we might have inner doubts about our own individual talents, we knew how to recognize first-rate minds, and we knew the other members of our charmed circle had them.

As winter gave way to the spring of 1962, the piles of yellow manuscript on Barbara's desk were replaced by neatly typed pages. They were physical assurance that her thesis would be turned in before April 1, the magic date which promised graduation in June. By the time the forsythia was about to bloom we couldn't avert our eyes any longer from the fact that this intellectual world which gave us such joy was not open to women in any but the most fleeting sense. Barbara's job search in the previous fall had been disconcerting for all of us. Bob, Al, and Joel were all hoping to become instructors in English. Barbara's only hope was a job elsewhere. We admired and liked our men friends, but our household at 27 Dana Street *knew* that Barbara's mind was their equal or better. We didn't begrudge them their success, but we lived through a period of intense grief that spring of 1962, ostensibly for Barbara's blighted hopes, but, at an unacknowledged level, for ourselves as well.

The injustice we were now prepared to acknowledge made a mockery of Harvard's vaunted liberalism. We had listened all fall as Barbara, who had a splendid talent for mimicry, described the nervous and self-serving conversations she had with the English Department Chairman about her future. Her thesis director, a very new arrival at Harvard, was no help. There was no getting away from it. She could be a student at Harvard, and even a poorly paid tutor, but never a colleague. They would do their level best to find her a job at some distant state university, but it would be hard. The dishonesty of such equivocation on the part of some of the country's greatest humanists helped us to stiffen our resolve. After the fall of Barbara's job search we could never again pretend to ourselves that the academic system was based on merit. When, in the spring, she won the prize for the best dissertation presented in the English Department that year, the recognition stung like a scorpion's bite. By then we knew that Bob, Al, and Joel would remain at Harvard as instructors, and Barbara would leave for a job in the University of California system. The prize was no prize at all.

As we all lived through Barbara's disillusionment, and our own, the conversation at Dana Street shifted from the usual graduate students' talk about coming out on top in a meritocratic system, to the way we understood our intellectual vocations. Why were we undergoing this rigorous training if we were not eligible for its real prizes, and could never expect a place in its elite institutions? Our answers came after many late-night talk sessions, when the two or three of us who were wakeful would watch the early dawn illuminate the parked cars, the occasional burst of spring flowers, and the errant trash on the street below us. Sometimes we took long reflective walks along the Charles River, our eyes fixed on its renewed dazzle from the spring light, our minds intent on bringing ideals and reality into some balance. Social scientists say that people faced with implacable discrimination adjust their aspirations in order to adapt. What happened to the Dana Street household, already alerted by Jana's rejection as a scientist because of her plans to marry, was something different.

We didn't adjust our standards of achievement one hair's breadth. Instead, we decided we were pursuing knowledge because it was our calling, a vocation in the Christian sense. It might bring us unhappiness, and no recognition, but knowledge was our vocation in life, to be pursued regardless of external rewards. After some of our more anguished sessions, I wandered away from my regular place in the Widener stacks among the nineteenth-century reformers. I went in search of the shelves devoted to medieval thought, needing to find a better understanding of the concept of spiritual vocation.

I was entranced by the twelfth-century idea that each human being was specifically imbued with a unique pattern of talents, gifts which could only find fulfillment in one foreordained calling. I wondered what mine was? Would I find my vocation in Australia? In being the best historian I could be? In teaching? Great religious writers like St. Augustine or St. Teresa of Avila seemed to recognize the foreordained because the answers to questions in their lives seemed inevitable. Nothing seemed inevitable to me. I had only questions about a vocation slowly emerging, and an uncertain framework within which to imagine living it.

Still, having observed the injustice of Barbara's treatment, I was prepared for John to tell me, after we'd been teaching together for a while, what a pity it was I couldn't be a tutor in Leverett House. I knew he meant it, but the pity involved was far greater for me than for him. I couldn't let the subject alone. I embarrassed Donald Fleming, my very supportive thesis adviser, by asking him what chance I stood of being invited to stay on as an instructor after my thesis was completed. I shouldn't count on it, he said. I knew the answer, but I seemed to need to hear it over and over again.

I was still pondering the question of vocations when I went, one perfect spring evening, with Barbara and Jana to the Easter Vigil. St. Paul's Roman Catholic Church in Cambridge was renowned for its choir school and the beauty of its liturgy. I settled in to listen to the flawless Gregorian chant, my mind engaged by the litany of the Saints, the careful recitation of an oral culture, literally evoking, by name, the community of men and women who embodied the Christian idea of sanctity. In my quest for understanding the idea of vocation, I'd stopped to read about the treasury of grace, a charming product of the medieval mind. People actually believed in a literal accumulation of grace, like a bank account, from which one could borrow in moments of dire need. Automatically joining the chant calling on the Virgins and Martyrs to pray for us, I suddenly understood that my small community of friends represented just such a resource for one another. There was nothing quaint about the idea. It was literally true.

A few weeks later, Barbara, Al, and I went off to Boston College to hear T. S. Eliot read to an enormous crowd crammed into the college gymnasium. It was unreal to watch Eliot's elongated, fastidious face, familiar from dozens of book jackets, bent over a lectern beneath a basketball hoop. The thin, reedy voice, precisely British in accent, made the lines of Ash Wednesday sound disembodied, floating above the vast silent assembly. To my delight, he read "The Song of Simeon," one of my favorite poems, lyric in its celebration of nature, powerfully metaphysical. I felt comforted in my anxieties about the future—more ready to accept what I could not control. I wasn't ready to say with Hegel that "freedom is the recognition of necessity," but I was intrigued by the idea that I might not have to summon up the moral resources to deal with my future all alone.

My mood of somber reflection was punctured by the bustle of preparation for the end of the academic year. At Dana Street we planned Barbara's graduation party with an attention to logistics and execution worthy of the event. There were to be about fifty guests, to be fed delectable summer salads and a variety of native cuisines. Mina planned to rush in from the Medical School to stuff grape leaves. Jana decided to make boule with white wine and sweet woodruff. A ham was to be prepared. By collective decision there must be champagne, raspberries, and an appropriately decadent cake. Carla was placed in charge of the graduation gift. We attacked the old house in a frenzy of cleaning, from its mottled floors to its grime-encrusted windows, and decided exactly where it should be decked with flowers on Commencement Day.

John kept a promise made to the teaching fellows in Social Sciences 6 by providing lobster, champagne, and strawberries for us as we met over lunch to set the course examination. The day was one of the idyllic spring days that come just before sweltering summer heat descends on the low-lying city of Cambridge, when river and air merge into one unbroken, impenetrable envelope of humidity. We were light-headed with champagne, and end of term high spirits, so our examination questions became wilder and more imaginative as the lunch progressed. When the examination was set, the talk turned to summer plans. It emerged that John was leaving right after Commencement to visit his family in Vancouver. He planned to return in early July. I was setting out on a research trip to the Midwest, followed by a stint at the manuscript division of the Library of Congress, and I, too, intended to return to Cambridge about the middle of July. Most of the Dana Street household planned to be in Europe for the summer, converging on Collanges, outside Geneva, for Jana's wedding to Bob, so I would be spending the summer alone in 27 Dana Street, until I moved to the solitary small apartment on Brattle Street I'd chosen to be my cell-like retreat, while I worked seriously on beginning the writing of my dissertation. John issued a characteristically absentminded invitation. "Call me when you get back," he said. "We must have lunch." I'd noticed that he always invited people to lunch when he couldn't quite figure how to end the conversation. Taking the cue, I glanced at my watch, exclaimed about getting to the library, and broke up the festive lunch. "I will call when I get back," I said, and meant it.

Graduation day dawned with the proverbial Harvard brilliant sunshine. I went with Jana to watch Bob receive his diploma, in the Leverett House ceremony which followed the University Graduation in the Yard. John managed a brief, witty, and affectionate citation for every graduating senior as he awarded their diplomas, and something longer and more reflective for the tutors who were receiving graduate degrees. I watched him perform, resplendent in crimson Harvard Ph.D. robes, brown eyes shining, his face alternating between mischievous teasing and serious emotion. His resonant voice lingered over each student's name, giving each his moment before an adoring family audience. I envied the Leverett House students their years under the guidance of this generous, brilliant figure. By force of character, and the passion he brought to teaching the young, he created a setting where the struggle for grades and admission to prestigious graduate schools receded behind the glow of the gifted young at their most aspiring and vulnerable moment.

4.

PARACHUTE JUMP

ALL THROUGH A sweltering June and the first weeks of July 1962, I sat, moist, dusty, and determined, reading my way through the papers of my heroines in a series of Midwestern archives. The principal cache of documents was in the archives of Rockford College in Rockford, Illinois. One of the first educational institutions for women in the Midwest, Rockford graduated a dazzling array of women achievers in its early classes, among them my main subject, Jane Addams,* and her friends, Ellen Gates Starr† and Julia Lathrop.‡ Considerable portions of their letters and papers were housed in the college archives, where there was a small

---

* Jane Addams, 1860–1935, founder of Hull-House, leading theorist and publicist of Progressive ideas, longtime leader of the Women's International League for Peace and Freedom, Nobel Laureate.
† Ellen Gates Starr, 1859–1940, classmate of Addams, co-founder of Hull-House, writer on aesthetics and industrialism, disciple of William Morris, Socialist, union organizer, Catholic convert, and intellectual.
‡ Julia Clifford Lathrop, 1858–1932, classmate of Addams and Starr, mental hygiene worker, child welfare advocate, and first head of the Federal Children's Bureau.

space set aside for reading in the attic level of the library, just beneath the baking tiles of the roof.

Even though suffering the proverbial historian's occupational disease, hay fever, I was wildly excited as I opened each dusty box, or turned the pages of yellowing files of press clippings. Each day carried me closer into the experiences of three remarkable women. After several weeks I'd read their early college papers, their letters and diaries, correspondence with friends and teachers, press clippings about their careers. By the third week I was reading the letters and papers of friends and associates, searching for mention of them, and the newspaper reports about their old age and death. Whether at Rockford College, or the county historical museum, or the archives of the University of Chicago, or the collections of the Newberry Library, I was treading in their footsteps in a way that made me more familiar with them than their closest friends had been.

An historian who is a diligent biographer sees a life in the round, from many perspectives—associates, friends, enemies, family; from intimate records of inner life to public pronouncements. Soon the handwriting is as familiar as one's own, the characteristic habit of speech leaps from many different texts to proclaim the author, the faded photographs evoke the rich, full context of a life in all its contradictions, and the memories of friends seem like the researcher's own—memories of an intimate acquaintance.

I rented a car and drove around Stephenson County, Illinois, to find the places where my subjects were born, check out where they went to school, see if I could locate the spot on the banks of the Rock River so vividly evoked in Addams's memoirs. I liked the gentle rolling countryside, with its climbing fields of corn and contented grain-fed cattle. On occasions when I lost my way searching for some little remembered landmark, I met astonishingly hospitable farm families, who gave me coffee, recalled local legends, and talked, as all farmers do, about the price of beef, the market for grain, and the inequities of distant banks. Such meetings were a window on a comfortably familiar world, a link to the present, while I spent my days almost disembodied, living vicariously in the past.

My research travels ended in Washington, in the Manuscript Division of the Library of Congress, an air-conditioned island of cool in a sweltering July city. It was a princely place to work. One could request many boxes from a collection at once, and have the unfinished ones saved overnight on a trolley which was wheeled back beside one's desk the minute one reappeared in the morning. There I read the letters and papers of Florence Kelley,* the remarkable Mainline Philadelphia woman, who became the leading campaigner for labor legislation regulating hours and conditions of work for women and children during the Progressive Era.

After the Library closed I went on the usual tourist expeditions to see the White House, to stroll around Mount Vernon, to tour Monticello. It was instructive to see how modest the state residences and private dwellings of the greatest of the Founding Fathers were. When contrasted with the palaces of Europe they seemed positively domestic in scale, appealing in their simple elegance, embodying the aspirations of the early Republic in their studious avoidance of luxury. One could see in the scale of gardens, and the carefully reconstructed plantings, evidences of the style of life encouraged by slavery, just as one could understand that the simplicity of the early presidency was belied by the underground warren of offices and communications networks which linked the simple neo-Georgian White House to the modern maze of executive branch offices. But, on the whole, the early architecture made the wish to turn away from aristocratic Europe and the display of court society a physical reality, a three-dimensional

---

* Florence Kelley, 1859–1932, graduate of Sage College, Cornell, economist, lawyer, factory inspector, Socialist, translator of Marx and Engels, resident of Hull-House, and later Executive Director of the National Consumers' League.

context for the carefully studied principles of documents like the *Federalist Papers.*

I was travel-stained, rumpled, and weary of reading difficult-to-decipher handwriting when I arrived back in Cambridge, in soggy July weather. I thought I had done enough research to begin organizing my ideas about my dissertation, by refining the analytical approach, and laying out the narrative structure my collection of lives dictated. There were still three more lives to research, and many more visits to the Jane Addams Collection at Swarthmore College to be made, but I knew enough about all my characters now to see where they fit in the general social pattern I wanted to understand. I had decided that my women could be categorized as either Victorian sages, transatlantic versions of British contemporaries like the novelist George Eliot, or modern professional experts, distinctly American types who embodied secular rather than religious values, and were precursors of new professions for women.

The house on Dana Street was echoingly empty as I sat at my desk, sorting the mountains of notes I'd taken. In the accumulated mail awaiting me was a letter that made me wish for a long conversation with Barbara, for Mina's witty, probing questions, or Jana's religious sensibility. It was from John Ward, the head of the Department of History at the University of Sydney, my alma mater, telling me that I'd be recommended to the University Senate for the new position there in American history, for which he'd urged me to apply earlier in the spring. I had applied almost automatically, wanting to keep my options open. Now the brief, single-page letter sitting on top of my papers put the whole question of my future squarely in front of me. And I didn't know how I was going to answer it.

There was something else on my agenda calling for action. I knew John Conway would be back from his summer visit to British Columbia. I knew he probably would be too absent-minded to get around to phoning me, but I had decided, during my six solitary weeks, that getting to know this man was too important for me to follow the female rule of waiting to be asked. Predictably, when I phoned him, John asked me to lunch, a week later, in the dining room at the Ritz-Carlton Hotel, his favorite Boston restaurant, looking out over the Public Garden. It was just across Newbury Street from my one haven of luxury, in a not-too-stylish Boston, Elizabeth Arden. I planned a cheerful morning of pampering there, before the lunch date, and then set out on a long reflective walk, up one side of the Charles past Mt. Auburn Hospital, and down the other to the Weeks Bridge. I liked looking back across the river at the Houses, and the parties of picnicking summer school students, dotting the broad green banks, some idly tossing Frisbees, others unmoving, soaking up the sun. From a distance the scene looked like a Dufy painting, all splashes of color and motion.

Should I try to stay in this place that had turned, in the short space of two years, into a home more beloved than I'd previously been able to imagine? What on earth did it all mean—my love of ideas, my passion to understand why things happened the way they did? Wryly I told myself that in fifty years it wouldn't matter in the least what course I chose. I was a good historian, but I couldn't pretend I was going to be Marx or Hegel, someone whose interpretation of history changed the way the world thought.

My moral obligation was clearly to return to Australia, though not if that involved self-immolation. And there were ways in which I feared that going back might be an intellectual form of suttee. My Catholic friends had taught me not to have the reductive view of oneself which is the emotional hazard of the modern consciousness, so I knew self-preservation was a moral obligation, too.

Yet choosing to remain, overwhelmingly seductive on the surface, involved other major hazards. I hadn't gone through the year with Barbara for nothing. If I stayed, I thought with typical Harvard arrogance, I'd probably end up, not at Harvard but on some remote branch campus of a state university teaching flaxen-haired, blank-eyed girls and gum-chewing fraternity boys. Not the worst predicament in the world, but not life-enhancing either.

If I began full-time teaching now, it would be years before I finished my thesis, and if I went back to Australia I'd have to write it without access to a single major library collection on American history. Moreover, I'd have no peace of mind, because, even if I refused to live with my mother, she had all the skills of the dependent neurotic finely honed, and the burden of guilt that physical proximity would impose would get between me and my best work. I'd be so inwardly tensed to guard against the phone call, the familiar voice, and the creatively contrived predicament that I'd lose all joie de vivre, and what modest amounts of creativity I had would vanish.

But if I chose to live far away from my roots in Australia, the land, the light, the scents and sounds, the overwhelming physical beauty that still nourished my imagination, whatever creative spark I had might soon fade also. I'd be an émigré, without political roots or affiliations. I stopped on the Weeks Bridge, a quiet footbridge, with no traffic, and gazed down at the swift-moving Charles, as murky in its summer crop of algae as my state of mind.

On a whim, I turned back up the Charles to the Cowley Fathers Church, a beautiful neo-Gothic building beside the walled monastery of an Anglican religious order. I went inside the exquisite small church to listen to the chanting of the Office. As my eyes adjusted to the dim light from the stained-glass window and the candles at the sanctuary, I saw that in front of my pew was a young man, no more than twenty, flung despairingly upon his knees, shoulders shaking with the sobs of some overwhelming grief. The antiphonal chant, seemingly inevitable in its simplicity, brought to mind millennia of human cries to God for guidance in perplexity. Gradually my nameless companion's emotional storm subsided and my brief meditation cleared my mind.

I should go back to Australia, but not until July 1963, rather than the January date which was set for the appointment. I would take the extra time to finish my thesis research and to get well launched on the writing. Privately, I would set a term to fulfilling the obligation, and then, if my thesis made a good book, I'd use that to find not just any job, but a good one in the United States. If I were quietly following this inner plan, I wouldn't be overwhelmed by my mother's demands, because they would spur me on to greater striving to write a book so good I could get away again. I went briskly back to Dana Street and wrote a single-page letter asking to have my appointment brought before the Senate, but on condition that I could take it up six months later than proposed.

With that piece of business disposed of, I was in high good humor when I met John in the upstairs bar of the Ritz, after a facial and the skilled attention of my friendly young German hairdresser at Elizabeth Arden. John seemed in a celebratory mood also, sipping extra-dry martinis and telling me about the beauty of his Vancouver home, and the intensity of his reaction to the grandeur and serenity of the British Columbia landscape. I explained that his reaction resonated with my own deepest feelings, and told him about some of my reflections earlier in the week.

We sat by the window looking out at the Public Garden, a riot of summer reds and blues, alive with children and with the stately voyages of the swan boats about their tiny inland sea. Two martinis, and the exchange of deep feelings, had put us in no mood to hurry, and the excellent Pouilly-Fuissé which John ordered compounded our sense of leisured intimacy. John began to tell me that he was thinking of resigning from Harvard and returning to Canada. After eighteen years at Harvard he was still torn between his native Canada—the shimmering beauty of its landscape, the vividness of his war experiences with Canadian brother-officers, the attractions of another political system, more concerned with justice and order than acquisitiveness and the Faustian drive to power—and the pleasures of the mind and the community concerned with ideas he found so sustaining across the river in Cambridge.

He was elated at being understood, and to discover that I

had been rehearsing the very same questions about Australia. By the time we were at coffee and brandy, our mutual understanding was so intense, I asked him how he came to be so severely wounded, and what it had been like to learn to cope with life with one hand. We moved from emotional intensity to high hilarity as he told about his efforts to use an artificial arm and hand, perennially being left behind in the guestrooms of astonished weekend hostesses. Eventually, a hovering headwaiter made us aware of the empty dining room, the bored waiters, and the lateness of the hour.

We were still rapt in intense conversation as we descended the stairs to the lobby, where we chanced upon Oscar and Mary Handlin on their way to a late afternoon wedding. They looked amused at John's patently lame explanation that we were just finishing a late lunch, as the cocktail hour was about to begin. On the companionable cab ride back to Cambridge we arranged to meet on Friday evening for dinner. I mentioned that Bob Kiely had left me his car for the summer, and we decided on an expedition to the country if the weather was good.

I had plenty of time to reflect on the new intensity of this friendship. My days were taken up with a summer job, filling in for the vacationing staff at the reading room of the Schlesinger Library—an airy, cool archive on the history of American women, housed on the ground floor of one of Radcliffe's quadrangle buildings. It was easy to supply the needs of the three or four visiting researchers each morning. They were the usual array of quiet bow-tied male academics in rumpled madras coats, and diligent, worried-looking graduate students. Once they were eagerly lifting files from boxes, I was free to muse as much as I liked. The day stretched out until four, when I retrieved the items checked out, locked up, and strolled home to Dana Street, and my mountain of thesis notes.

I knew that I was heading into something more than a light summer flirtation. I also knew it was something that would have to end when I returned to Australia. But there was still a year before that would happen, and I wanted to deepen the emotional bond I felt with John. He was at least a generation older than I, something the conventions of the fifties deemed inappropriate for romance. But I wasn't interested in 1950s-style romance. I had long since concluded that marriage was not for me. I was too interested in a career to fit the going style of male/female pairing. I didn't want to become the typical Cambridge-style wife—superbly educated, someone else's muse—much admired for her conversation and her excellent, crusty, homemade bread.

I seemed to do better navigating under my own steam. I wasn't afraid of being classified an old maid. I'd had deeply fulfilling relationships with lovers who had mattered a great deal to me. I just wasn't interested in settling down. I'd only very recently escaped my mother's clinging dependence, and it seemed as though my life's adventures were only just beginning. But not wanting to be married didn't preclude close relationships with men. Then, too, John was clearly settled in a bachelor style of life, so deepening our friendship didn't threaten to turn into something more binding. I knew this man had a lot to give me, and I thought I had a lot of understanding and capacity for emotional response to give him.

Friday unfolded as the perfect Cambridge summer day, with miraculously clear air, warm sun, and the hint of a cool breeze. John wanted me to see Groton, so I would understand, by seeing its actual embodiment in architecture and grounds, the kind of prep school many of my students came from. I picked him up around five in Bob's yellow Volkswagen, and we headed out Route 2, emerging quickly into the tranquil summer landscape, dotted with ample barns, white houses, and green fields decorated with solemn ruminant black and white cows.

Within minutes of setting out our conversation grew intense. John began to tell me about his sudden, devastatingly unnerving swings of mood. I began to describe the crippling death of spirit I'd experienced in the years before I met Alec Merton, the American friend and former lover who'd convinced me I should leave Australia for a larger society. Through that relationship I had gained the courage to break away from my family and its burdens. Enveloped in the comfortable anonymity of a moving automobile, our eyes on the landscape, we talked about the subjects that were mostly taboo, except as subjects for psychotherapy, in our rational meritocratic world. His description of the sudden panics that would leave him terrified and sweating, only capable of staring blankly at the wall, made me understand what personal courage went into every day of apparently normal life for him. There was now a context for the white face and shaky coughing fits of our morning meetings before lectures. I wasn't afraid of psychological complexity, only of too compulsive a pretense of normality.

When we arrived in Groton we strolled in companionable silence about the grounds, John stopping me now and then to examine a perspective, or to reflect on the English or British Empire counterparts of some aspect of the school. In the Chapel we paused before the memorial to the Groton men who had died in the 1914–18 and 1939–45 wars, a reminder of a tradition shared in common with our British Empire world. Then, as we strolled around the quadrangle, the conversation turned to the former chaplain, a Harvard friend of John's whose demeanor and zest for life had left his friends, and John in particular, astonished and troubled when he committed suicide.

The bright lights and cheerful bar of the Groton Inn quickly dispelled our elegiac mood. We were soon laughing about the cultural dilemmas of being a very young Canadian officer in the military world of England in 1940, stories I could match with English eccentricities I'd encountered during my journeys of discovery. John was an Anglophile of a mild sort, while I was a passionate Anglophobe. The tension gave an edge to our talk, allowed for suitable exchanges of bon mots, and gave just the right pungency to the conversation. Our excellent, but simple, meal was punctuated with anecdotes about Groton students John had known, and his speculations on the school's role in the development of American elites. In Donald Fleming's seminar I'd heard a lively discussion of Endicott Peabody and his influence on Franklin Delano Roosevelt, so I had questions to raise that John found new and stimulating.

When the meal was over we settled into the yellow Volkswagen as though it had always been ours. Suddenly my mood was somber, my mind carried back to my dread of sliding once again under the emotional thrall of my mother. As we were descending the incline down Route 2, which offered the first sight of the lights of Boston's few tall buildings, I asked John if his moods had ever driven him to contemplate suicide. Many times, he replied. I told him about the times I had come very close to ending my life. It seemed an odd state of mind now, but a few years back, when I had realized that my mother was a destructive person, dependent on drugs and alcohol, ruthless in her determination to sabotage any emotional bonds her children formed, I had felt trapped by the obligation to care for her. At nighttime, when her long monologues of anger and spite against my brother and his wife, and their beautiful first child, finally ended in drugged sleep, I would feel overwhelmed by sadness at all the losses in my life—my father, my brother, and, finally, the woman I'd once revered, now transformed into something so perverse.

These black nights were so oppressive, I'd stopped by the library of the Medical School at the University of Sydney and looked up the dose of Nembutal which would kill someone of my weight. Each night, before settling into a sleepless bed, I'd count out the number of capsules, prescribed in generous amounts for my migraines, and leave them in the drawer of my bedside table, just to have them at hand if the going got too rough. I had also become compulsive about doing dangerous things, like driving far too fast, waiting for the frisson of fear when I was uncertain whether I could pull the screaming wheels of the car out of the slide around a sharp corner, or wading mindlessly into a surf too heavy for me to handle, the quick stab of fear reassuring when it came, because it meant I still wanted to live.

I had never told anyone about this secret side of my apparently calm self, and I wondered what John would make of it. "I was always going to blow my brains out," he said companionably. He'd kept his army revolver for a long time in his bureau drawer, just in case he needed it. So he wasn't even surprised at my black moods, and took their extremes as a matter of course. It was the religious duty to live and hope for salvation that had kept him from pulling the trigger. I wasn't sure what had stayed my hand, when I realized along with Dr. Faustus, "Why this is hell, nor am I out of it." It was probably grace, John said. Then we were back in Cambridge, saying a subdued, but deeply companionable, good night.

As July turned into August, people began to notice our continuing conversation, carried out in favorite bars and restaurants—a conversation so intent we scarcely noticed our surroundings. We were caught up in understanding each other's ideas of religion, in sharing our sense of the comic and the wonderful absurdity of life, in thinking about critical decisions for the future. John met me one day looking as if he'd shed a staggering burden. Although the decision would not be announced for some time, he'd written to President Pusey, resigning at the end of the upcoming academic year. He was going to return to Canada, and I was sure he'd made the right decision. He was a British Tory at heart, in some important ways fundamentally unable to enter into an academic world where liberal rationalism was the received dogma. His interest in teaching, and in shaping the most creative environment for releasing the talents of the young, was far greater than his interest in being the typical research scholar. He'd left Canada at twenty-three, and scarcely knew his native country as an adult. I was sure he would feel an emptiness of the heart if he didn't return for some part of his active professional life.

On September 1, while John was taking a brief vacation in Paris, I finished working at the Radcliffe Archives and moved into a tiny apartment on Brattle Street, almost on the edge of the cluster of Radcliffe buildings. Its smallness was relieved by the airy view from its top-floor windows and its bright southern light. Although it was a wrench to leave Dana Street, its magical set of associations was already shifting, as though someone had spun them in a kaleidoscope. I was busy getting things ready for Bob and Jana's return to their apartment in Leverett House, carting boxes across the green McKinlock Courtyard, to the second-floor apartment which overlooked the river. Barbara was headed for the opposite side of the continent. Carla was close to finishing her thesis. It was just as well to settle down alone for concentrated work on synthesizing the results of my several years of research. I needed to get the bulk of my thesis drafted and the last-minute questions answered before I left for Australia.

With my borrowed desk, a new red canvas chair, a comfortable bed, and a minuscule rug bequeathed by Jana as she departed Dana Street, a few colorful posters, and a card table produced from the attic of kind friends, I settled comfortably in my new home. The sight of a few turning leaves on a hot September day sent me guiltily to my desk, wondering, as students always do, where the summer had gone. I had time to settle down to work for the few remaining weeks before the start of the semester. The quiet late summer days were surely conducive to work. I would type late into the night, until the last sounds of automobiles faded from the street, and I could hear the katydids chirping in the garden of the Radcliffe President's house just across Brattle Street. When John Ward's letter arrived saying I had been granted the extension of time before taking up my appointment, I knew I could get everything done by next July.

The late nights typing weren't lonely, because every hour or so I would stop to allow the summer to replay itself in my mind. In later years I would tell John that, although I cannot sing in tune, the yellow Volkswagen was in fact carrying a woman around Cambridge that late summer, who was inwardly singing the equivalent of *"Mi chiamano Mimì."* In fact, it was a wonder that traffic wasn't halted on Massachusetts Avenue by the triumphant sounds. I knew I was in love, and that John was also. I expected the inevitable parting, but I didn't expect our lives to follow the romantic operatic story of love and death. I expected us both to be more alive and stronger because of the power of our response to each other. I knew my deeply devout friend Jana had been lighting candles in every church she visited in Europe that summer, to reinforce her prayer that John and I should marry. But I thought that out of the question, and quite unimportant alongside the more profound experience of knowing and being known by another person whose mind and spirit complemented mine.

When John returned a few days before the beginning of classes, our evenings together could no longer take place more or less offstage. We used to dine at my apartment or at a charming local French restaurant called Henri Quatre, where John was a regular. In the past, he'd often gone there depressed, and asked the proprietor to put a screen around his table so he could be alone. Now that he had a woman companion in whom he was obviously interested, the French proprietor's response was predictably warm and welcoming. Our meals came miraculously quickly and were cooked to perfection. There were often flowers on our table, discreetly placed in a side room.

John never seemed to sleep, something I would later learn was a sign of trouble. We might part at midnight or 1:00 a.m., but an hour or two later the phone would ring and an elated voice would carry on the just concluded conversation for hours. Fortunately, I functioned pretty well on three or four hours' sleep, having learned that less sleep was better for someone with my tendency to frequent migraines. Sometimes we'd become so engrossed in our dinnertime conversation that we'd absentmindedly notice the dawn, and our empty stomachs, and stroll out from 83 Brattle Street to wander through the Yard, before ending up at the twenty-four-hour eatery, Hayes Bickfords, for scrambled eggs and bacon. One morning of preternatural beauty we watched a family of squirrels play on the steps of the Widener, skittering around like kittens, while the early-morning bird sounds made the Yard seem almost rural.

We both drank too much. We had come honestly by this excess as part of our British inheritance. England, the font from which both Canada and Australia drew their inspiration, was a culture of drink, rather than food and sex. Transposed to the colonies, this cultural theme conspired with the deprivations of pioneering to produce a world more reliant on booze than music, art, or dance to foster the Dionysian side of life. John's six years of army life, the nervous energy consumed by ignoring the difficulties of life without a right hand, the bizarre but persistent experience faced by all amputees of a "phantom limb" meant that the day was punctuated by substantial slugs of gin or Scotch. I used alcohol to dissipate my extreme shyness on social occasions, and to mute the anxieties and sorrows always lurking at the edge of my consciousness. Now, our courtship was so liberally assisted by drink that our euphoria was accentuated by lack of sleep and by monumental hangovers.

One Sunday in early October I'd invited Carla and her flatmate to inspect my new apartment. I wasn't expecting to see John that day because he was attending a wedding, and I was to dine with friends in Boston. It was hurricane weather, the air heavy and humid, the rain torrential, the dampness curling manuscript pages, the wind sudden and fierce. I could see the umbrellas of people on the street below being swept away or collapsing under the sudden gusts of wind. I was surprised when John phoned, unexpectedly, to say he wanted to call later that afternoon. He sounded unusually somber, as though something serious was on his mind.

When Carla and her friend Harriet arrived, we chatted happily for an hour or two, catching up on summer doings, giving the inevitable reports of the state of our theses, exchanging academic gossip, but as the hour approached four I began to will them to leave. They, observing the increasing downpour outside, wanted, sensibly, to wait for a slight break in the weather. Nonetheless, I hustled them out the door just minutes before John appeared, looking very formal in his navy pin-striped suit. He had just sat down, and uttered the astonishing sentence "Will you marry me?" when the doorbell rang insistently. It was Carla and Harriet in search of the umbrella they'd left behind when I hurried them so unceremoniously from the apartment. They arrived back, and, seeing John, seemed overcome by the need to chatter on every inconsequential subject that came to mind. Again I ushered them relentlessly to the door. Again, John, now laughing, uttered his proposal. Again the doorbell rang, as though some wicked genie wanted to prevent me from answering. Carla and Harriet were back in search of Harriet's boots, a sensible enough need, given the overflowing gutters in the streets, but once again accompanied by nervous chatter. When they left, the tension of the moment was replaced by relief at being alone. "Yes. I will," I said, astonished at my sudden certainty that this was the right thing to do.

I called my dinner hostess, gave the news of our engagement, and begged off dinner. John called Stephen, always his deepest confidant, and we arranged to meet for a drink at the Ritz where Stephen was to dine with a friend. It was preposterous that I should be so sure, and so calm about a decision which was fraught with uncertainty. John was, after all, about to leave Harvard. I was agreeing to make my life with him in Canada, a country I didn't know, under circumstances yet to be determined. I would be reneging on my commitment to return to Australia. I didn't think I was suited to marriage. Yet it felt *right* to be planning life with this man eighteen years my senior. I'd never had such complete certainty before. The certainty came, not from romantic love, but from the deeper bond between two adults who are old enough to know that they share spiritual and moral commitments, political goals, and professional dreams.

There was some quality in John's personality that made me sure he did not want to dominate another person. It was safe to become close to him because he was so lacking in self-interest, he literally did not know how, much less want, to manipulate others.

When we parted after an excited dinner planning our future, John said we must dine the next evening with Jack Bate, another of his close friends, a literary critic of distinction, and a much beloved Harvard figure. I agreed happily, went home and exhaustedly to bed. The next morning I woke early, and frantic. What had I done? What madness made me accept John's proposal? What would happen to my scholarly career? Why was I, the most practical of women, planning to marry someone who was abruptly changing course in midlife, and planning to move to a country I didn't know?

It was a heavy teaching day for me, followed by office hours in the now familiar Holyoke House. I was late getting back to 83 Brattle Street, where I was to meet John at 6:00 p.m. I met him standing in the doorway to the building, his whole body radiating nervous anxiety, his face such a mask of worry I could tell that his euphoria of the previous evening had vanished as quickly as mine. I laughed and explained my abrupt change of mood. As soon as John knew his worries were shared he relaxed, and began to be amused by the panic that had struck us both. I said that ambivalence was part of the human condition, and that marriage was such a gamble that we'd probably have many such days. We'd have to take it like a parachute jump, something no onset of fear could reverse.

The evening's dinner proved delightful. Barbara had taken me to several of Jack's lectures, which I had found exciting and moving because of the power of Jack's mind, the depth of his emotional investment in literature, and the freshness of his insights into the psychology of English romanticism. Now I listened as he and John, two gifted talkers, carried on a habitual conversation, now expanded to include a third voice.

After that one quiet evening it seemed as if the whole town of Cambridge was intent on feasting and celebrating John's engagement. I was touched to discover that a community which seemed superficially hardheaded was actually as soft-hearted about a fine romance as any reader of dime-store novels. John had been a popular bachelor in Cambridge for eighteen years, and now everyone was curious about his fiancée.

In the course of a few hours I'd changed status from being a lowly graduate student, defined by my Widener stall and the progress of my thesis, to someone who addressed all Harvard's luminaries by their first names. It took some effort to call President Pusey Nate, or the great Shakespeare scholar Harry Levin by his first name. For John, who was unquenchably gregarious, the celebrations were occasions for sharing his joy with a circle of friends established over his many years in Cambridge. I was a profoundly shy person, able to deal easily with people in working relationships, but for me it was an ordeal to walk into a roomful of strangers on a social occasion. It was an ordeal with extraordinary rewards, because John's Cambridge and Boston circle was filled with interesting and civilized people, and some wonderful eccentrics. After reading Edmund Wilson with wonder at his language, astonishment at the power of his imagination and mastery of style, it was a little unreal to sit next to him at dinner, and begin talking in the flesh to a man who wrote like *that*.

John's total lack of comprehension that anyone could be shy was compensated for by his unshakable conviction that his beloved was beautiful, a brilliant conversationalist, and consequently a success with his wide circle of friends. Once I'd found my course in life I had never felt the need for the reassurance of male admiration, but now I found him a constant reinforcement to a tough, but often fragile, psyche. Acquiring, so unexpectedly, a partner in life, someone who wanted to hear what I thought about everyone I met, who commented with interest and pleasure on what I wore and how I looked, was a new and wonderful experience. Nonetheless, I found meeting all these strangers utterly exhausting.

I would want to hide in a corner, look on, do anything but join in the talk, which usually left me, always opinionated, with nothing to say.

Years later, I was relieved to learn that human biologists thought shyness genetic. Mine was never dispelled by any form of public recognition. I could give speeches to audiences of thousands, present seminars challenging assembled scholarly pundits, play the gracious hostess—all roles involving forms of work I understood. But just talking to strangers was harder work than anything else I ever did. I wrote letters in preference to calling strangers on the telephone, hid behind a secretary, when I acquired one, and used every artifice within my command to escape having to talk to strangers.

Some of the new encounters were just plain entrancing. When we became engaged, John dutifully telephoned his parents, who initially thought their excited forty-five-year-old son had been drinking when he announced his news, but who were courteous and welcoming as it dawned on them that I was real. His four sisters were as warm and outgoing as their brother, interested, concerned, and welcoming. My tiny family of three suddenly expanded to encompass a band of sisters. The mere fact of so many positive and reinforcing female kin made me feel stronger.

But, although John loved his Vancouver family, it was clear to me that he had a surrogate set of parents whose approval mattered enormously. Just four weeks after our engagement, we set out to meet Archibald and Ada MacLeish, driving out to their country house, Uphill Farm, in the delectable western Massachusetts town of Conway. I succumbed instantly to their powerful collective presence, a mixture of emotional intensity, aesthetic response to life, mastery of language, and dedication to making their life together a work of art.

Uphill Farm was an eighteenth-century farmhouse, perched on a hill in some of the most beautiful countryside I had ever seen. It had been lovingly restored, and the household functioned with exquisite attention to the comfort of guests. There was a fire in my bedroom on a chilly late fall day. The flowers on every table had been arranged by a masterly hand. The newest books were on the bedside table. The bell to ring for breakfast was close at hand. But these details were merely the background for a couple I was to love as deeply as my own parents.

Ada was dressed for dinner when I first met her, a woman whose plumpness and signs of age disappeared totally beneath her talent for gorgeous clothes and jewelry. Her eyes blazing with energy; her voice musical; her powers of observation shrewd; her conversation tireless, pungent, and filled with wild humor—she was a presence to be reckoned with. Archie was a fitting partner for such a being. Tall, handsome, gifted with a flair for casual elegance in dress, his sensitivity to people as acute as Ada's, his voice overrode all other sense of his presence. It was golden, and when he spoke the intonation made one know a poet was speaking. I was entranced.

Ada set me at ease at once by telling the assembled company about all the excited phone calls they'd received from friends in Cambridge about John's new lady friend. As we were parting for the evening she told me that for Archie and herself, John was like one of their own sons, and that they had been rejoicing at observing his happiness. From that moment on they took me into the family, and began teaching a willing pupil the art of living.

When the morning came I saw Ada's garden, a perfect rectangle carved out of a fold in the hillside, formal in design, romantic in coloring, as gorgeous in its late fall color as its designer. Beyond it a view had been cut through the woods to distant Mount Monadnock, etched sharply against a frosty, grey, New England autumn sky. This was a closeness to nature I'd missed since leaving Australia. I was seeing a landscape that would become familiar and beloved.

It was reassuring to feel close to this earth, because my plans for my wedding were proceeding against a background of storms from Australia. There were none from the Fulbright Committee or the University of Sydney, which both accepted my plans to settle in another Commonwealth country, but my mother's voice had sounded utterly blank and expressionless when I called her with the news of my engagement. Then a flood of letters arrived begging me to return home for a visit before the wedding, finally turning bitter when it was clear that I would not. The ostensible ground for her anger was that I had decided that John and I should be married in the Catholic Church, but the real cause was her feeling of betrayal. She had expected me to come home, to be her companion for the rest of her life, and thought she was morally entitled to do so.

Her reaction was utterly predictable, but I'd persisted in hoping that she could be affirmative about my new step in life. And while she remained true to her standards for what was appropriate, by sending me a handsome check to cover the cost of my wedding, it was followed within days by a carefully prepared bill listing every expense she'd assumed to provide for my education, and insisting that it must be repaid before I was free to form other connections. There could not have been a clearer statement of her sense of property in her children, and the crazy letter left a bitter taste. I was enraged at the cold calculus of the bill, and determined to settle its cash components in full. Even so, it left an empty space around my heart, remembering the woman whose care for her children once knew no such accountings. My anger at being converted into a form of property settled in my psyche like a block of ice, and filled me with an icy resolve. I would return every cent to her. Under the circumstances, it would be a pleasure to take up my life with John without a penny to my name.

My mother took my decision to be received into the Catholic Church as a negative commentary on her decision not to share in my father's religious life—and in some sense it was. I thought spouses should share a common form of worship, and I often wondered whether my father might have been buoyed up in his last desperate years if his life with his wife and children had had a firm religious undergirding. It didn't bother me that the Church was run by a male gerontocracy, because for close to two thousand years that male dominance had not been able to extinguish the power of the cult of the Virgin and of the female saints. If I'd been born in Asia, doubtless I'd have looked for my sense of the numinous through the symbols of Buddhism or Hinduism, but since I was a product of the West, I was content to seek it through the symbolism of Christianity, but a Christianity which recognized female transcendence.

So, as my wedding day approached, I felt both utterly alone, devoid of the sustaining kin who should participate in the ritual, and at the same time, sustained by the new family of affection I had found in Cambridge. Barbara was my bridesmaid, Jana, pregnant with her first child, was my matron of honor, and Bob Kiely, one of my sponsors on entering the Catholic Church, walked down the aisle with me. Stephen was John's best man, and Davie Fulton, a brother officer and college friend from Vancouver, and two Harvard friends, Walter Kaiser and Keith Highet, were his ushers.

Barbara stayed with me in the guest apartment I'd moved to in the Leverett Towers two days before the wedding. The night before, the old Dana Street group reassembled to dine with me, and spend one last hilarious evening of affectionate reminiscence. Shortly after Barbara and I returned for the night it began to snow heavily. I found that the combination of fatigue, anxiety, and elation I felt ruled out all possibility of sleep, so the two of us sat, sipping Scotch, pondering the meaning of life, watching the snow swirl around the windows of the top floor of the Towers. The combination of events that had brought John and me together from different sides of the globe, from different generations, from different backgrounds, and provided us the courage to make the leap of faith involved in marriage seemed very wildly improbable, unless we'd had an overworked guardian angel, intent on bringing about some unknowable providential order. We looked out on the white outline of the Charles River, the grey and white of the city gradually falling silent under the accumulating snow of the blizzard, and I thought about Coorain, and the lonely house of my childhood, sitting amid its thousands of empty acres, baking under the summer sun. At about four in the morning, a splendid calm descended on me, and I went to snatch a few hours' sleep.

Our wedding in December 1962 had almost arranged itself. An Australian friend, very recently married, lent me her elegant wedding dress. It had been designed to complement a tall, wide-hipped Australian figure—elegant and uncluttered in line, of heavy natural silk, with many yards of material swept into elaborate gathers at the back of the empire waist. When the dress had been fitted to my shape she also ordered us a splendid wedding cake. John's purchase of champagne from a Boston wine merchant was rumored to rival in scale some of the livelier parties of the 1920s. St. Paul's Church was a block away from Leverett House and its Master's Residence on De Wolfe Street. I'd planned to walk to the church, but a limousine miraculously appeared to carry me, swathed in a sheet against the still falling snow, to the ceremony. The guests, being New Englanders by birth, or adoption, took the blizzard as merely a test of ingenuity, and arrived on foot, by subway, or jeep, to stamp their feet in the church foyer and await the wedding party. The staff of the Leverett House Dining Hall prepared the wedding reception, and served its food and wine with smiles of affection for the Master wreathing their faces.

John had hired a piper from a Scottish regiment in Montreal to play for the reception, and just before we cut the cake we asked him to pipe a reel for us, since all weddings require dancing. Champagne and the obvious joy of the crowd and the splendid pipe music had gone to my head, so that, normally a shy and clumsy dancer, I was released into an unselfconscious ease of movement I'd never known. When it came my turn to occupy the center of the circle, the crowd roared approval, and for the first time in my life I wasn't shy.

5.

NIGHTINGALES, GODS, AND DEMONS

BECAUSE WE BOTH taught, we could spend only a few days away in New York between our wedding and the beginning of the spring semester. But when the term ended we departed for a year in Europe, living first at Oxford, and then in Rome, enjoying a honeymoon of Victorian duration, an island of leisure reminiscent of an earlier era. My formal task during this European idyll was to write the first draft of my thesis, while John's was to take time for reflection before deciding where, and in what capacity, he would return to academic life in Canada. But our major assignment was to learn to live together, to forge the intellectual and emotional partnership that would give each of us the energy and capacity for fresh growth and new challenges. We were not seeking a merging of identities in the romantic mode, but an enhancement of each identity, through access to the other's broader experience.

John's enthusiasm for showing me the cherished aspects of his British and European world knew no bounds, and I was mostly a willing pupil, although occasionally my energy was sapped by the closing stages of a psychological battle with my mother, which I knew I would win, but which I found unusually exhausting. Because the leisure of a year free for study and writing left me no room for the compulsive busyness which was my normal mechanism for coping with dark moods, the struggle loomed large.

Here in Oxford, I could only look at the blank paper waiting to receive my dissertation, while my mother fired off fresh salvos of rage at my desertion. On sunny days, I thought my scholarly career, and my marriage to John, a total justification. On grey days, I felt worthless and empty, preoccupied with making the legal arrangements which would transfer to my mother, and such heirs as she chose, all the family property I possessed. The bright ray in this process of self-imposed disinheritance was the wonderfully comic Oxford solicitor's office we visited to make the necessary arrangements, a stage set for Gilbert and Sullivan, or *Jarndyce v. Jarndyce*, every flat surface ready to be overwhelmed by mountains of vellum bound up in red tape. On the day I went before the local magistrate to swear that I was transferring all my property of my own free will, the gritty task became hilarious because the procedure, set for 9:00 a.m., was delayed by ten minutes while a Dickensian clerk raced to a local bar for two solid swigs of whiskey to prepare His Honor for the task at hand. John and I didn't need to speak. By an exchange of delighted glances we knew we had stumbled into a time warp.

But the process of cutting all my ties with my past roots in Australia exacted its price. I worried needlessly about our future. Would I like Canada? Whereabouts in so vast a country might we settle? Would my thesis be any good? What if I couldn't find a job? I was usually happy to look at life as an adventure, with the ills of the future to be coped with when they arrived. But my moods swung erratically between happiness and depression. One grey, rainy day I left John at home while I set out, perfectly composed, to do some prosaic errands—a visit to the hairdresser, a stop by the fishmonger, a call at the wine merchants. Sitting with my hair dripping amid the bustle of a hairdressing salon, I felt overwhelmed with despair. I was no good, an incompetent, and ugly to boot. There was the image in the mirror to prove it. There was so much sadness in my life, I could never throw it off and live like a normal person. The thought of my father making his way into the muddy water where he was to drown, his agony at that moment, the waste of my brother's death, the tragic, empty silence in which my mother lived with her furies, seemed to overwhelm all hope. I choked back my tears, sitting with watery eyes while the hairdresser did her brisk work, went doggedly to purchase the scallops for the Coquille St. Jacques I planned for dinner, and stopped by the wine merchants, for sherry and a large supply of gin. That was what I needed. Mother's ruin to drown my sorrows in.

When I burst, rainsoaked, into our apartment carrying my damp, newspaper-wrapped parcel of scallops, my sherry and gin, I astonished John by dissolving into a torrent of weeping, unable to explain rationally why such a wave of sorrow had swept over me in the busy Oxford streets. Although it was barely noon, he began mixing extra-dry martinis, making companionable sounds, and then sat quietly with me in the midst of my emotional storm. His own sudden mood swings made him understand my predicament. He made no effort to jolly me out of it, but plied me with gin and sympathetic questions about what had been going through my mind.

By mid-afternoon he had lit the fire to help dispel my gloom, and had me talking about my moods. When had they been as bad in the past? What on earth had made a woman as competent as I feel as though anything was beyond my reach? By teatime I was ready to nibble on a sweet biscuit, and listen as John turned the conversation toward a larger context for my woes. What did I really think about free will and determinism? Why did I think there was so much pain at the center of human experience? Would it be better to lack the power of empathy and not experience the suffering of others? What did I think about the possibility of vicarious sacrifice? About the Christian virtue of hope? Soon I was answering him, beginning to put some intellectual distance between myself and my crisis.

By dinnertime I was ready to cook the delicious scallops, found lying abandoned on the kitchen table, performing with the flawless culinary skill that comes with enough to drink to abandon hesitation, but not so much as to become clumsy. After the excellent meal, John began reading T. S. Eliot's "Little Gidding" to me, and followed it with some of the "terrible" sonnets of Gerard Manley Hopkins. By chance we turned on the radio just as a glorious performance of Beethoven's 12th Quartet in E-flat Major began. This was the music that had inspired Eliot's "Four Quartets," John told me. Here was all the dissonance and tragedy of life, being reviewed by the inner ear of a deaf genius, and resolved through his art into glorious harmony. And so the day which began with catastrophe ended in strength. John's instincts all involved high-culture music, theology, and art. They were not a cultural adornment. He lived them, and that was what drew me to him most powerfully.

Because I was living with such a companion, and in such delectable places, my experience of the final ordeal of graduate life, the writing of a thesis, was different from that of the usual harried graduate student desperate for money and the security of a first real job. I still had to test every scholarly dream by the mocking emptiness of the page on which each sentence I wrote must be weighed against the work of great and seasoned scholars, but we lived in great comfort, in a series of settings so rich in history that every walk was a visual instruction about the past.

Our first home was established in the comfortable apartment of Jean and Simone Seznec, old friends of John's who had spent their honeymoon in John's ample Harvard rooms, and who were now delighted to reciprocate the favor for us. Jean was Marechal Foch Professor of French Poetry at Oxford, and a Fellow of All Souls, where John had been invited to join the Common Room for the year. Because Jean and Simone had lived in the United States, they had become accustomed to central heating, and to American notions of plumbing. This meant that their elegant apartment on the third floor of a solid brick building on Wellington Square was unusually comfortable for an English residence. Moreover, Simone's kitchen was the kitchen of a formidable French cook, its array of gadgets and copper bowls encouraging the most unadventurous chef.

Each morning as I settled down to my typewriter perched on Simone's tidy desk, her kitchen would beckon to me, urging the preparation of mousses, the concoction of elaborate pâtés, anything to defer the moment of writing. For, when I sat at my desk, I was not only anxious about whether I could write anything of substance, I also had to grapple with the inner need to perform as a super housewife to justify my career. I had grown up being constantly reminded that "brainy" women were good for nothing in the "normal" domestic arena of feminine life. Graduate school had enabled me to ignore the question of my domestic prowess. Now each perfect mousse and flawless ragout was reassuring, but, also, time consuming. I found I hadn't realized how much I needed the faces of eager students to reassure me that the knowledge I had to convey was important. Their absence left me wondering whether I knew anything at all.

While John enjoyed the fine food and better conversation of the All Souls Common Room, a pleasure I most definitely did not want to share, I would emerge from the kitchen to sit surrounded by my notes and index cards, beginning the formidable narrative task of weaving a coherent story from the collective biography of my seven subjects. The task seemed to me to call for the literary talents of Henry James, and the analytical capability of a Max Weber. I thought I could manage the analysis, but I was strangely hesitant about composing the narrative. Nonetheless, I slogged away, wondering what had happened to my love of writing. It was not until much later that I realized I had internalized the critical voice of the Harvard graduate student, and such a concern for theoretical rigor, that theory got in the way of letting my imagination engage with my story. Sometimes I would become so exasperated that I would leap up, snatch my coat, and hurry to the Oxford Market, as if driven by demons. There, surrounded by a profusion of perfectly hung game and elegantly arrayed shellfish, so fresh the barnacles still wriggled on their shells, I would buy up the most delectable delicacies, requiring complicated recipes and hours of cooking, so that John would be startled by the elaborate dinner in preparation when he came in from the library, or by the baroque structures which kept my weighty Shorter Oxford English Dictionary compressing a freshly concocted pâté, the culinary rage of the moment.

He arrived home each day as the sun's rays lengthened, so that we could while away the golden autumn afternoons, walking in the countryside, or exploring the gardens and architecture of Oxford. Pembroke was my favorite college, because of its scale and its exquisite small walled gardens. No matter how often I gazed at Magdalen or Christchurch, their cold aristocratic excellence seemed two-dimensional to me. They were so perfect it seemed hard to separate them from their postcard existence. The Codrington Library was my ideal of a library, its wonderful carved ceiling the perfect focus for meditation. It was a space in which one could expect to entertain great ideas, and so were the Chapel and Cloisters of New College, places which made me more aware of pre-Reformation England than any other place I'd visited.

And there were wonderful English scenes and visions, etched in the memory like the traditional eighteenth-century hunting scene—pollarded willows turning gold along the banks of the Isis, College feasts so cheerfully bibulous that even hardened drinkers like John and me would make our way home with heads whirling, seven-year-olds from the Dragon School with scarlet football jerseys and cheeks to match, rushing to kick a football so big in relation to their size that they immediately fell over when their eager foot met the target. When the light began to fade we would hurry home to start a fire in the Seznecs' comfortable sitting room, enjoy the English ritual of tea, and talk about the day's events. I loved the countryside, with its gentle Cotswold hills, grey stone villages, and quiet rivers, and relished the gardens and the glorious buildings; but, despite the hospitable welcome given us, I couldn't settle down easily.

I was irrationally irked by the inefficiency of English life, the slowness with which things got done, and the easy confidence of all concerned that they lived at the center of the greatest intellectual community in the world. John kept urging me to view the British as though they were an African tribe, complete with nose rings and elaborate tattoos, delightful to observe, just as one would any other strange culture. But I could not enjoy any but our private life together. The slow-moving grocery clerk, or the hapless man who announced with apparent satisfaction that the local wine and spirits shop was out of sherry, were the startled recipients of my displaced anger at my family and Australian colonial attitudes, puzzled targets of the cold fury with which I greeted each instance of English inefficiency. My inner rage at my mother's conduct seethed below the surface, while at another level of consciousness, I was happier than I had ever been.

As John introduced me to his closest English friends, I encountered a world of civilized living, where time seemed to stand still, and life revolved around enjoying the beauties of the English countryside. From the Ziegler family in Hampshire, whose houses and gardens on the edge of the New Forest were our happiest resting place, I received a welcome that simply added me to their large circle of friends and relatives. Their casually elegant country houses, their amiable dogs, ample teas, and wonderful conversation introduced me to people who read and thought for pleasure, not as work. They also lived for the out-of-doors, not as sport, but as a place to be—an attitude I knew from childhood. Colin Ziegler, the senior member of the clan, lived a life of stylish simplicity, devoted to reading, the preservation of the New Forest, his garden, the *Times* crossword, family, and friends. When we first met, he explained his age, well over eighty, and asked which volumes of *The Golden Bough* were the most important, since he feared running out of time if he continued reading them seriatim, as had been his practice. I gave my best advice, and loved him immediately—a man shaped by the old Indian Army, by 1914–1918, and by a British world I distrusted. We became instant friends, because he was genuinely curious about other worlds and unknown ways of life, and as excited by comprehending a new idea as any academic I knew. Colin's son Oliver, and daughter-in-law, Margaret, were close to us in age, indefatigably kind hosts, and amusing instructors about the finer details of English life, and the vagaries of the large cast of English eccentrics who made up their extended families.

Vera Von der Heydt, John's Jungian analyst friend, whose London apartment became the setting for many exquisite meals and illuminating conversations, was my first encounter with a cultivated European woman professional whose learning came, not from formal study, but from a life lived in Vienna and Weimar Germany, at the height of its intellectual brilliance. She had weathered abandonment by her aristocratic German husband, because she was Jewish, had arrived in London as a refugee, where, by sheer force of will and talent, she had created another life of compelling beauty and spirituality. She had no trace of self-pity, an unquenchable zest for life, and a worldly sense of the comedy of life I hadn't met in my solid bourgeois upbringing. She became a point of reference for me in thinking about the emotional bonds between men and women, and in understanding the emotional dynamics of my family. One day, after a lunch of smoked trout and fresh strawberries, she startled me by pointing out that if my mother was a formidable woman, she had brought another powerful woman into being, with whom she would always be locked in battle for the upper hand. I'd better become resigned to it, Vera suggested, with quiet amusement. What mattered was how I put to use the emotional energy and will I'd inherited. I had always dreaded being like my mother, living with every nerve and sinew tensed against sliding into her way of exercising power over others. Vera was the first person to make me think that being like her could be put to good use.

Toward the end of October there was a sudden interruption in our routine: John flew to Toronto to discuss joining the faculty of York University, a new institution, whose main campus was yet to be built on the northern edges of the city. The University's planners wanted to reform the overspecialization of Canadian undergraduate education, and wanted to recruit John to become a senior faculty member in the Division of Humanities, and a master of one of the colleges which were to provide an intellectual and social focus for a predominantly commuting population of students. A Westerner to the core, John knew little about the city of Toronto, and less about the cultural politics of Ontario's exclusively publicly funded universities. One element of the situation was clear, however. Ontario's birthrate in the postwar years, combined with a steady inflow of immigrants, now presented the province with the need to expand higher education dramatically, and York, as the first of a series of new institutions in the planning stage, would offer a fresh opportunity to design programs and patterns of education appropriate to mid-century Canada, a society hitherto slavishly reliant on models of education inherited from Oxbridge. John was intrigued by the prospect, and within a matter of days the deal was made. We would return to Toronto in September 1964.

When John asked me, in late November, where I'd like to spend our first wedding anniversary, I said, instantly, "Paris," playing the game we often played in fantasy, about where we would like to be at that instant. But he was serious, and informed me the next day that the arrangements were made. I loved his zest for experience and readiness to plan an adventure on the whim of the moment. By this time the grey damp weather had set in, bringing with it my perpetual English cold, and I had a craving to be somewhere other than England.

We began looking for new Oxford rooms, in early December, for the Seznecs were to return to claim their apartment by the end of January, after a semester in the United States. The prospect was daunting. Each place we saw was greyer and colder than the last. I would return to my desk in Wellington Square, with the prospect of chilblains and thick underwear

looming, and take up my writing labors in very low spirits.
John said, suddenly, after a week or so of looking, "Let's not
stay here. You don't enjoy England, and I've had enough of
Oxford. Let's go and live in Rome. I've met someone at All
Souls who knows exactly how to find comfortable quarters in
Rome. We should be enjoying ourselves, not worrying about
whether we'll be warm enough."

My heart began to sing at the prospect. The picture of
Rome totally changed the context of our anniversary visit to
Paris, and Christmas in England, spent with old friends from
my Sydney University days and with the Zieglers in Hampshire. Paris, which I had seen as a tourist in the summer, presented a totally different face to the world on the crisp grey
day we arrived, when a light snowfall, so theatrical it might
have been arranged for a performance of *La Bohème*, brightened the contours of the Tuileries, and etched the Seine's
bridges in white. Our hotel was on the Quai des Grands Au-
gustins, looking across to the Ile de la Cité and Notre Dame.

On the morning of our wedding anniversary the maid set
down the tray with our coffee and croissants and swept back
the heavy gold curtains to reveal the Seine and the Right Bank
sparkling in a cold winter sun, a city free of tourists, seeming
to be reserved for us alone. The cold was penetrating but dry
when we began our morning stroll, first to Notre Dame for
Mass, and then by a circuitous route admiring the anti-
quaires of the Left Bank, to Chez Lipp, on the Boulevard
St.-Germain, where we ate Jambon de Parme and perfect Brie,
our frozen limbs warmed by a delectable burgundy. In the
evening we dined at Grand Vefour in the Palais-Royale, trying, in our conversation, to evoke the cast of characters who
had strolled in its galleries in the eighteenth century. Then,
in the mood of heightened sensitivity evoked only by great
French cuisine, we walked up to Montmartre, our steps
echoing in the cold, in search of the boîte named Le Lapin
Agile which John loved from earlier trips to Paris. The guests
were served Armagnac and cherries automatically, for the real
purpose of the place was the singing, ranging from the songs

of the moment to eighteenth-century folk songs, sounds that made the city of Rousseau and Voltaire seem barely a generation away.

WE SET OUT for Rome by train in late January, stopping in Paris for a reunion with Stephen, characteristically deeply absorbed in the current battles of French intellectual circles, then preoccupied with the relationship between Europe and the United States, and the first manifestations of the West German economic miracle. We waved him farewell from the Orient Express, bound for Rome, and stepped, the next morning, into the cheerful frenzy of the Rome railroad station, on a fine late January day. It was warm enough to stroll coatless down the Spanish Steps from our hotel to claim our mail at the American Express office in the Piazza di Spagna. I was in the Mediterranean climate I knew and loved from Sydney, and my bones knew it.

Very quickly our life fell into a magical pattern. We found a commodious room, with ample space for desks, in a comfortable and efficient *pensione*, where we would both work in the mornings, and then set out walking to take a late lunch in whatever piazza took our fancy, followed by more strolling through the blessed quiet of the siesta hour, arriving at the time of opening at whatever fountain, church, ruin, or monument was to be the afternoon's object of study. In this way we gradually made the city our own—Old Rome, Trastevere, the Vatican—pausing, at whatever point took our fancy, for espresso, a glass of Verdicchio, aqua minerale, whatever seemed the right accompaniment for long reflective gazing.

On many afternoons, or evenings, we met Clotilde Marghieri, one of John's most cherished friends, a writer and intellectual of great learning and exquisite charm. Though she and John had obviously had a past attachment, she greeted me joyfully. At our first meeting, with the characteristically grand gesture of Italian high culture, she removed the pearl necklace she was wearing and clasped it around my neck as a greeting. In her early fifties, she was small, almost birdlike in movement, her profile showing the high forehead and strong aquiline nose immortalized by classical sculpture. Her sparkling eyes were such a dark brown they seemed to verge on a luminous black, and, although Neapolitan by birth, her voice, whether speaking in English or Italian, carried the Tuscan cadences of her convent education in Florence.

Clotilde's real education had come about through her long attachment to Bernard Berenson, the American art connoisseur, dealer, and shaper of taste, whose cosmopolitan circle, which revolved around the Villa I Tatti, outside Florence, where Berensen lived in baronial style, included the major figures in art and literature of his generation. Her sensibility had been formed by Berenson's notions of art and beauty, although, when I came to read her writing, I saw that she herself wrote a spare and graceful Italian, more consistent with modern aesthetics. She was spare and elegant in dress also, but extravagant in the range and intensity of her emotional life.

It was sheer unadulterated fun to sit in Clotilde's small graceful salon, and tell her about what we had seen that day. She had no interest in economics or politics, perception and the response to beauty were all that interested her. When I said the horses in the Trevi fountain were so real (although utterly fantastic in their grouping and placement) that I wanted to pat their heads and arched necks, she responded that arousing the tactile sense was the mark of great sculpture. Our conversations would range far in an afternoon. What did I think of Proust? I had read Benedetto Croce in translation? Good. Here was a volume in Italian. He was impossible to assess except in his native tongue. Which of the English novelists of the nineteenth century did I think the greatest prose artist? What accounted, say, for the stylistic difference between Dickens and Meredith? Did I read German? The German historians of classicism would surely enhance my enjoyment of Roman sculpture.

Her curiosity was aroused by my interest in American

feminism. She had the Continental European's certainty that Americans fussed too much about liberty. Clotilde was an independent woman who maintained a warm relationship with her husband but had kept a separate residence from him for more than a decade. She practiced, without ideology, the sexual freedom of such concern to English-speaking feminists, and like all good Italian liberals, she was determinedly anticlerical. "But tell me, Jeel," her musical voice would rise on a note of questioning, "what are these freedoms you need that you do not have?" I would laugh and tell her that she could not comprehend a Puritan culture, with its fear of sexuality, and its rigid rules about marriage and property. Nor could she, who had never so much as dusted a table, understand what child rearing and housekeeping involved for a society without a servant class. Surely there were issues for Italian women less educated and independent than she? "Ah, yes," she would say, decisively. "Many Italian women are priest-ridden." But it was clear that she thought the elimination of religious superstition would usher in a society of equality. It was of no use to point out to her that a rationalist world would eliminate all the myths which inspired and shaped the art she lived for. She would smile with the confidence of someone who took her high culture as a right, and ask another question about aesthetics. She entered my female pantheon along with Vera Von der Heydt, both European haute-bourgeois women, products of a culture and a class system which allowed elite women learning and cultivation, and a range of sexual freedoms reserved for males in societies shaped by the Protestant ethic.

Walking back in the late afternoon from Clotilde's apartment near the Quirinale toward our pensione provided some of the images which formed my visual sense of Rome. The declining sun would make the golden facades of the buildings luminous, the green of the pines, unvanquished by winter, would assume a deeper hue, and the low light would etch the profiles of the great statues and fountains in dark shadows and glowing surfaces. It rains in Rome in the winter, but it was the sunshine I remembered, long sunlit walks in the Borghese Gardens, small gems of courtyards glimpsed from the street, alight with flowers and reflections from water, sunlight on handsome Italian faces seated at the cafés along the Via Veneto, warmth radiating from sunny walls onto the patrons seated out of doors in the restaurants on the Piazza Navona.

Part of the warmth came from the luxury of the food. Every meal was a delight, whether it was a simple tuna and anchovy sandwich and a glass of cold Frascati, or an elaborate dinner in a grand restaurant. I loved the colors and textures of Italian meals, beautiful pink figs, or melons and prosciutto, tiny succulent beans and olives in a salad, or the many colors and flavors of pasta, all delivered with strong opinions and heartmelting smiles by waiters who became instant friends if one made so much as a second visit to their establishment.

Our pensione was a temporary arrangement. We wanted to find a small apartment, where we could spread out our books and papers and settle in for the five months that remained of our European year. Our aide in the search for an apartment was like a bit player from a 1930s American movie set in Europe. The Principessa Soldatenkov, who answered to Bebe, had been recommended to us by John's friends at All Souls. She was half Hungarian, half Italian, and in the business of introducing respectable foreigners to Roman nobility who wanted some discreet income from renting portions of their palazzi. She dressed in extravagant colors, wore strikingly eccentric clothes, and drove her customers around Rome in an open grey Ferrari sports car, in which she was accompanied by her basset hound, Basilio.

As we careened around the streets of Rome, John in the front beside the Principessa, I in the backseat with Basilio, she would ignore the traffic and turn completely around to face Basilio, shouting, "Basilio, canti, canti." Basilio would throw back his jowly head and let out bloodcurdling howls in compliance with his mistress's orders. Eventually, she found us an apartment, not in the palazzo of a Roman aristocrat, but in the very comfortable modern apartment building owned by the daughter of the engineer who had designed the Via Veneto and planned the modern buildings of the quarter. We lived on the third floor of number 45 Via Ludovisi, our windows looking out over the gardens of the Villino Ludovisi, where, when the spring came, the nightingales sang all night.

We had a bedroom, bath, and salon, furnished in exquisite taste, and the services of the dour but efficient family retainer, who prepared breakfast and took care of our rooms. There were elegant desks and tables for us to work at, and the surrounding *quartier* was all that one could desire. We could stroll across the Via Veneto to Doney's for a martini and a hamburger lunch. There was a selection of beautiful churches within a few minutes' walk for morning Mass, an elegant coiffeur on the ground floor, and a neighborhood bar which never seemed to close for supplying our liquor closet.

We settled on moving in in ten days' time following a visit to Florence and the Villa I Tatti, now bequeathed by Berenson to Harvard as a Center for Renaissance Studies. It was presided over by Kenneth and Eleanor Murdoch, old friends of John's, and old colleagues from the Harvard History Department and the General Education Program. They loved to entertain Harvard friends, and share their pleasure in exploring the delights of Florence. The Villa I Tatti was my first encounter with the elegance and style of Italian country life, and I was spellbound by its formal gardens, overlooking steep hillsides of vineyards. Much of the decor remained as Berenson had left it, complete with the early Italian Renaissance paintings of the school on which he had built his career as a connoisseur.

By day we explored the buildings and museums of Florence, and at night Kenneth and Eleanor introduced us to the English and American expatriates who made their home in Florence. One day was given to the Pitti Palace, so cold that we had to run to the cafe for brandy every hour or so to restore the circulation to my freezing feet and hands. But in February it was virtually empty, so that we could take our time, lingering wherever the spirit moved us. By the time I could absorb no more visual images, Kenneth and Eleanor's driver was waiting to spirit us back to the hills for rest and refreshment.

I had often seen reproductions of the Fra Angelico paintings on the walls of the Monastery of San Marco, but I was utterly unprepared for the impact of those representations of the saints and of early Christian life, in the context of the monastery and its simple cells. The series on the lives of Saints Cosmas and Damian, so literal in representation, so pure in spirit, and so exquisitely executed, wiped out every other image I'd seen, and became permanently imprinted in my mind along with the Duomo and the central square which commanded the city.

While the circumstances of our life on our return to Rome were now idyllic, there were dark patches caused by the return of John's bouts of deep depression. I thought of his temperament as having the qualities of a medieval stained-glass window, rich in its range of colors, complex in texture, mediating great beauty. But just as the colors of a stained-glass window vanish when the sun disappears behind a cloud, so John's beautiful personality could be suddenly, temporarily, extinguished, replaced by swift-moving moods of anger, suspicion, and despair. In time I came to see these moods as following a rigid calendar—Christmas, spring, midsummer—sometimes announced by a period of elation, always marked by a change in facial expression which was striking. John's deep brown eyes normally sparkled with laughter, and his face was mobile in its quick ebb and flow of expressions. But when darkness descended, his right eye drooped, his expression became masklike, and the sparkle left his eyes. It was as though a stranger had replaced my sensitive and loving husband, someone possessed by demons of rage, tormented by suspicion. The man I knew of heroic courage would be overwhelmed by fear and despair, silent, without energy or hope.

When these moods descended I kept remembering that they would pass, and, when I encountered outbursts of anger or exasperation, that it was the mood, not the man, speaking. With the immaturity of the young, I expected that the strength of our love for each other, and our happiness, would eventually vanquish them. Influenced by the therapeutic attitudes of the day, I expected that this suffering could be "cured" or "made better." In time, I was to come to a chastened recognition that there was nothing I could do to help avert what was to be a chronic condition. That I could be a companion but never a cure, to someone I loved so much, was to be the discovery that marked my real growing up.

MY OWN ANXIETIES about the next stage of our life were much reduced by the receipt of an invitation to join the staff of the History Department at the University of Toronto, as a temporary lecturer in American history. The prospect of teaching again, of a salary, of colleagues of my own set my juices flowing, and released a fresh burst of energy for work on the final third of the draft of my thesis. Both of us rejoiced when the offprints arrived of my first scholarly article in American history, published in what was to become a landmark issue of *Daedalus* called "The Woman in America." The elation produced by seeing my first writing on American history in print resulted in one of our most memorable Roman evenings. We set out for Doney's and some excellent martinis, talking so excitedly about my future academic career that we didn't remember to count our martinis until the attentive waiters had delivered us each four. Then, still operating on the élan of the moment, we floated down the Spanish Steps, by this time decked in their spring azaleas, to our favorite restaurant, where we consumed all the delicacies on the menu in celebration.

Warmed by some excellent cognac, we wandered back to the top of the Spanish Steps, and then sat on the balustrade watching the sun set over Rome. We began to talk about the young Keats, whose rooms overlooked our resting place, and about his early death and burial in the English cemetery in

Rome. Somehow I was weeping, explaining to John that I wanted to be buried on Coorain, and how I felt about the actual earth of my native Australia. He responded in kind. Part of his ashes must rest at Ortona, the place in Italy, where many fellow Seaforth Highlanders were buried, and part must be scattered in the Gulf of Georgia overlooked by the snow-clad mountains and pure air of his beloved British Columbia coast. It was astonishing that neither of us had a hangover the next morning. We had marked my entry into scholarly life with a celebration of epic proportions, and clearly the resident deities, Bacchus and Diana, whose images smiled at us from every wall and fountain, had decided that our revels should, for the moment, go unrebuked.

The presence of deities was a constant reminder of the Rome of antiquity. One could walk from some gleaming espresso bar straight into an encounter with Apollo or Hera, presiding deities of the square or fountain. And what one met on the surface of the earth might cover many other pasts. Without planning it, a visit to a church might prompt descending through levels of excavation that carried one back as far in the past as the imagination could reach. The Church of San Clemente, near San Giovanni in Laterano, made me most vividly aware of the layers of time enveloping every stone we stepped upon. One entered the twelfth-century San Clemente, built after the Norman sack of Rome, and descended past the mosaics, depicting the four doctors of the Church—Jerome, Ambrose, Gregory, and Augustine—and a depiction of the Triumph of the Cross, that had the four rivers of Paradise springing literally from the foot of the Cross, to a fourth-century church named for San Clemente, fourth successor to St. Peter. Here one could dimly decipher inscriptions beneath the eighth-century frescoes, thought to represent the earliest known examples of written Italian. At the third level was a first-century Roman palace, which housed a third-century temple of Mithra, complete with altar, benches, and a bas-relief of Mithrais dispatching a bull. No printed page had made me so conscious of the link between Christianity and the mystery religions, which were its contemporaries, as these three places of worship, literally resting upon one another, like successive generations in a family. Sometimes a visit to an historic site produced a startling new awareness of linkages in time. When Sheila and Myron Gilmore, Harvard friends on leave in Rome, invited us for a picnic and a visit to Subiaco, the site of St. Benedict's cave, where the founder of the Benedictine community had actually set out the rule which still guides Benedictine life some fifteen hundred years later, Myron showed me a wall painting, done by a Benedictine monk of the day, of St. Francis of Assisi, painted as a young man, on pilgrimage to Subiaco, still to find his vocation and to found his order. I thought this figure, usually represented in the familiar brown robe, with attendant circling birds, looked exactly like a contemporary student, handsome, rebellious, and clearly a problem for superiors to handle. Living daily with the many layers of culture all present in these stones and buildings made me aware of how shallow the roots of Western culture were in my native Australia. The Aboriginal people felt forty thousand years there in the dust beneath their feet, but for white immigrants and their descendants, the past was a few hundred years.

At the beginning of May John took me to see Capri, before the hordes of tourists descended. We took the train to Naples, wandered delightedly through its narrow streets and baroque architecture, and dined happily at the Transatlantico, the resturant built over the water by the docks, where urchins pestered the clientele to let them dive for coins, and the entertainment was provided by fading tenors from the Opera di San Carlo, itself a set for *Figaro*, just up the street. This was the city John had made his own as a young Canadian officer, recovering from wounds received in 1944 as the Canadian army made its way through bitterly contested territory toward the Battle of Monte Cassino. Time hadn't changed Naples much, nor the Capri we found when we climbed off the vaporetto after three days in Naples.

In a few weeks it would become a seething horde of tourists, solemn sunburnt Germans and noisy British Cockneys, intent on their version of a good time. But for the moment we shared it with only a sprinkling of fellow travelers. We could enjoy the ocean, walk alone by the cliffs over which the monstrous Emperor Tiberius had thrown those who displeased him, and watch the light play over the fabulous coastline of the Bay of Naples. In the small village of Anacapri we found our way to the local church, famous for its glorious mosaic of the Garden of Eden, perfectly preserved on the floor of the church because the peasants who had been the regular worshipers for centuries wore no shoes.

At its center was a tree of life, around which were depicted groupings of animals that mixed the humble donkeys of the local paths and streets with the wilder creatures of Africa, all with a freshness and closeness to the animal world which made it seem as though the Garden, and its paradisal creatures, might be just over on the other side of the island near the Blue Grotto. Gazing at it with fresh delight at each new scene and animal, I wondered what it would be like to grow up with such scenes as one's primal image of the Garden of Eden, glimpsed while an infant in one's mother's arms, on the regular daily or weekly pattern of visits to Mass. Eden had been so hard to imagine in my childhood in Australia. I could see Adam and Eve with some nervous kangaroos, some agitated emus, and the occasional parrot and magpie, but then Adam and Eve would be in classical draperies or fig leaves (not part of Australian history), and how was one to fit the Aboriginal people into the general iconography? It had always seemed clear that Eden was a long way away from Australia, an unthinkable predicament for a child growing to consciousness in Capri.

At the end of June, when I had set down the last word on the first draft of my thesis, and John had completed a writing assignment for the *Atlantic Monthly*, we traveled to Assisi, which John thought as holy a city as Chartres, and as important in the Christian experience. The train journey was hot, with thunderstorms rattling around the hills surrounding the train track and lightning flashes illuminating dramatic hill villages, perched high above us. Arriving about midday, we left our bags at the hotel outside the walls of the city, and continued on to the duomo, expecting that there might be a High Mass at noon. As we entered the square a trumpet fanfare sounded, and a Papal Mass began. We had arrived for the celebration of the relationship between St. Francis and the Papacy, and entered the great cathedral to an accompaniment of flawless Gregorian chant. We came to rest beside the famous series of paintings of St. Francis by Giotto. There were many pilgrims in the church, young men's groups speaking German, a cluster of French university students, a stern group of middle-aged Spanish travelers. In my mind's eye I saw the centuries of such journeys in search of the Franciscan notion of sanctity, so completely belied by the soaring cathedral, and so fully embodied in the Convent of the Poor Clares, in the valley below. Once one left the cathedral, the town of Assisi seemed timeless, its steep streets decorated with cascades of pink and red geraniums, its gates opening onto vistas of sloping vineyards, punctuated by red-roofed farmhouses. It was easy to imagine the first Franciscan community here, and to feel the presence of sanctity.

Back in Rome, in the blazing late June heat, we packed our bags, made endless trips to the Canadian embassy for my immigrant visa to Canada, and lingered nostalgically over meals in our favorite trattorias. As the plane took off on the first leg of our journey to Toronto, and my new home, I began to list the treasures traveling along with us besides the first draft of my thesis, safe beside me in my hand luggage. John and I, on our year of study, had achieved a kind of closeness no workaday routine could give. I had a new sense of time, and an enlarged aesthetic sense, a set of images which could never fade from the mind. We had savored the fun of really living in another culture, becoming familiar with its seasons and rhythms, and a little closer to its shaping myths. The Catholic

Church, with all its pagan roots, was a living reality rather than a remote history. My personal demons had been kept at bay by the enchantments of Rome, although John's had made some troubling appearances. The gods had surely come closer to us, and the singing of the nightingales would always be an omen of happiness.

6.

ENTERING
THE FORTRESS
CULTURE

THIRTY MILES OR SO to the west of Toronto the Niagara Escarpment stands out on the horizon, so straight that it looks like a firm black line drawn with a child's ruler. The Escarpment marks the shore of a great inland sea which covered much of southern Ontario, northern Ohio, and northern Michigan before the ice age. Toronto sits nestled on the bed of that primeval lake, looking across Lake Ontario to Niagara Falls. The city stretches east and west along a level terrain bordering the lake, and sprawls north, across the rectangular grid of sections and townships laid out by the colonial surveyors who mapped the area around the newly incorporated city of Toronto in the 1830s and 1840s.

As Fort York, it formed a pivotal point in the network of frontier fortifications which marked the border of old Upper Canada with its rambunctious southern neighbor. And the city which grew up around the foundations of the fort became an embattled outpost of English colonial culture, flanked on its eastern side by Lower Canada and what later became the province of Quebec; to the north by the wilderness of lakes, streams, and mineral deposits which stretched literally to the Arctic; and to the west by the vast open prairie, extending two thousand miles to the distant point where the foothills of the Rocky Mountains rise abruptly from the plain just beyond what we know as the modern city of Calgary.

The sense of being an imperiled outpost of Britishness was heightened, for nineteenth-century Toronto, by the migration of the American loyalists to the Niagara Peninsula during the Revolutionary War, and by the cannons of the War of 1812, a war in which the most decisive engagements were fought on the Great Lakes, including one in which a party of American raiders set fire to York's legislative buildings. The American Revolution and the imperial dreams of the young republic meant that history gave the cluster of colonies that, in 1867, became the nation-state of Canada a raison d'être which was cultural, so that no matter how geopolitics might pull the economic life of Canadians into a continental economy, Canada's schools, colleges, churches, and political institutions pulled in the other direction, toward enduring ties with Great Britain. And, at the center of that determined effort to keep the memory of England and Scotland and Ireland alive, and to avoid becoming like "Americans," was the country's richest province, Ontario, and its capital, Toronto.

The mineral riches of the North, the communication system of the Great Lakes and the St. Lawrence, the abundant water-power, and the merchant mentality of the Scots settlers, who came first to the Hudson's Bay Company and the fur trade and then to settle the farms of the Ottawa and Trent valleys, combined to make nineteenth-century Toronto the entrepreneurial center of Canada. It was a city of fiscally conservative banks, visionary mining and railroad engineers, and canny lumber merchants, all intent on creating wealth, first, from tapping the region's abundant natural resources and, later, from financing the development of Canada's western and maritime provinces.

The citizens of Toronto, as Fort York came to be called in 1834, had a Scottish respect for education, so that despite bitter sectarian battles between Catholics and Protestants, the Province of Ontario had a flourishing public school system by 1871, and a cluster of sectarian colleges which were joined together to form the modern University of Toronto between 1887 and 1903. The cluster of buildings which became the University were solid grey granite and red brick, Victorian in mood and style, architectural statements that learning was a serious business. They were rooted firmly beside the spot where, on a main north-south thoroughfare, ascending a gentle rise from the lake, the third and most impressive home of the Provincial Legislature was built, at Queen's Park in 1893. This, too, was an architectural statement of the relationship between culture and politics in the Upper Canadian context, for, just as the Legislature sought to embody the inheritance of a British legislative tradition, the University sought, not to release an untutored native germ of creativity, but to transmit faithfully the heritage of British learning. The tie between state-building and higher education gained more formal expression when the Provincial government assumed formal financial responsibility for much of the capital and some operating needs of the University in 1905. So, for almost the first century of the existence of higher education in English Canada, its purpose was not to plumb the Canadian experience, but to shape the Canadian identity by the rigor and energy with which British culture was explored and transmitted.

The houses of the city's lumber merchants, bankers, and railroad promoters were built of the same grey granite and red brick, located on prominent points along the series of ravines which ran south to the lake, and gave the landscape of the city its distinguishing contours. The names of the more prosperous areas signaled England—Rosedale, Lawrence Park, Scarborough—places where grand baronial houses were built, looking strangely bereft of their park, as they stood, cheek by jowl, along prosperous streets. In the less prosperous parts of the city the street names were more aggressively imperialistic—Palmerston, Mafeking, Bloomfontein. They were lined with sturdy redbrick houses, with pocket handkerchief gardens sheltering under the shade of ample green maples. The major streets of the business district recalled royalty—Richmond, York, and Sussex—or British politics—

Shelburne and Gladstone—and the scale of nineteenth- and early-twentieth-century building showed what mattered in this very British province—banks and insurance companies.

To the north of the city, cheerful garden suburbs grew reflecting British tastes in gardening, despite the short growing season, marked by late blizzards and premature frosts. But when these neighborhoods were clad in their thick mantle of spring green—trees, lawn, sidewalks all well watered by the storms that built up around the lakes which ringed the city—lilacs bending heavy-laden with purple and pink, Toronto's suburbs came close to meeting the urban pastoral dream, because the ubiquitous ravines limited the scale on which developers planned, and flawless public transport made the commuter's life the ideal rather than the nightmare produced by the automobile.

Sprawling suburbs—poorly served by transportation, creatures of expressways and traffic jams—were built quickly in the 1950s and 1960s to house the new immigrant population, which began to flow into Ontario from Southern and Eastern Europe. These typical North American urban parodies of the pastoral ideal formed a solid semicircle of tract housing and vast apartment buildings around the outskirts of the older, more genteel city with its distinct neighborhoods and neat shopping areas, where the specialty butcher and the efficient fish merchant still delivered the most modest orders. They created a modern urban desert east, west, and north of the city as its population grew from two to three million people within a few decades of the return of the Canadian forces in 1945. Nonetheless, even the new acres of asphalt and concrete were not candidates for slum status, because the metropolitan Toronto area governed itself like London. A single unitary tax base fed the coffers of the municipal government, which, using a British ideal of fair play, struggled to reallocate resources from rich to poor suburbs. The result was the development of a school system which could carry the child of Sicilian migrants from near illiteracy to university in a generation. By the late 1950s, high school graduations, once affairs for Macdonalds, Stewarts, Ryans, O'Neils, and the standard old Saxon names like Potter and Taylor, soon began to include a medley of Hungarian, Italian, Maltese, and Portuguese last names, their owners all bound for further education and jobs in Ontario's booming postwar economy.

Old Torontonians looked a little askance at the motley crew of new arrivals, although it was possible to inhabit Rosedale or Forest Hill, and make one's way a few blocks south to the business district, without seeing the polyglot world of the new immigrants. Prosperous Torontonians sent their children to private schools, modeled on English prep schools, and to the more selective of the Ontario universities—Queens, the University of Western Ontario, or the University of Toronto. There they formed a small core of elite students, whose experience differed greatly from the average commuting student or the lonely farm boy from a small-town community who inhabited the spartan dormitories of the less socially elite colleges.

The manners and mores of the old British population were predominantly Scots, overlaid with a North American interest in comfort and convenience. People's speech patterns kept Scottish vowels and a softened Scottish burr to the letter *r*. Public ceremonies were announced by pipe bands, and a school or college with no claim to its own tartan or pipe band soon found a way to invent one. Every park worth its name had a skating rink and tennis courts, where rosy-cheeked figures waged athletic contests on weekends. Children called policemen and bus drivers "sir," and a lingering remnant of a British ideal of service inspired shop assistants, cabdrivers, and government clerks.

Grafted onto this pattern were distinctive local habits and customs. Once winter came, every patch of ice, no matter how hazardously exposed to street traffic, sported its miniature portable hockey goal, where every male child old enough to stagger on skates flew after a real or substitute hockey puck. When the real snow came, red-cheeked children stuffed into bright-colored snowsuits, their heads covered with knit woolen caps, with a long tail to wrap around the neck, adopted from Quebec, careened joyously on tin trays from every incline in local parks and public spaces. Staid lawyers and corporate executives would rise in the small hours of the morning and awake their sons, just past toddlerhood, to take them, still half asleep, to the hockey rink where the best coaches offered instruction. Girls did not join in these rites of winter, except to toboggan hilariously in the snow sporting the same long caps as their brothers.

When the lilacs announced spring, the annual rite of salmon and trout fishing began, taking every man who could afford it, and some keen women anglers, north or east to a beloved spot on an untouched stream or lake where the closeness to nature was as important as the delectable fish proudly presented to friends and relatives, on the angler's return. Fishing camps, luxurious or spartan, were just one of the many forms of getting away to the wilderness which formed the core of an Ontarian's sense of place. The sparkling waters and black rocks of Georgian Bay, the mighty forests and lakes of Algonquin Park, a thousand glorious northern lakes reached by floatplane, the spotless trails maintained by volunteer hiking clubs, all of which led north across the brooding rocks and boulders of the pre-Cambrian shield, to the silence and sense of awe which awaits the human dwarfed by the power of untrammeled nature—these made up the sense of place of a northern continental people, and had no hint of Britishness about them. And this mystical sense of a permeable boundary, between the human and nonhuman, was distinctly Canadian, because a man or a woman came to the wilderness aware that the forces of the nonhuman world were too powerful for human conquest, an awareness that made conquest seem less important than for other North Americans. But if conquest was not important, courage, loyalty, and a Scottish warrior heritage made Canadians formidable fighters in Britain's conflicts. They were a people more at ease with the nondomestic than the English or Americans, and, toughened by living, in work or leisure, close to natural forces beyond human control, they had learned never to give in.

Just as the northern wilderness waited to mock the smallness and frailty of human beings, Canadian humor emerged in stories with self-deprecating, mocking endings. People might wax lyrical about the northern wilderness, and stand bemused before the tradition in Canadian painting that evoked a natural world which dwarfed the human, but story telling about public life, about the narrator's adventures, or about popular ideals and aspirations always carried a sting in the end—a touch of richly textured mockery or farce which belittled the individual or the authority figure, and made it seem inevitable that human aspiration would encounter comic deflation. One could dream big dreams in this vast continental landscape, its eastern shore looking across to Europe, and its western shore home to vessels that sailed to the Orient, but it was safest to keep them to oneself, or scale them down and introduce them to others with a deprecating remark.

WHEN WE CAME to Toronto in July 1964 I had the imagery of Rome in my eyes. I couldn't see Toronto clearly. The route from the airport to the Royal York Hotel (then the largest hotel in the British Empire and an imposing bulk on the city's skyline) came through the sprawling new developments on Toronto's western rim. The new arrival saw fast-food outlets, small factories, shopping malls, and serried ranks of housing developments, until the highway deposited the traveler at the door of the Royal York, a hotel on the grand scale, which faced across the street to the imposing Union Station, home to Canada's two great railroads, both buildings emblems of the forces which had built the Canadian union. The lake beyond the railroad station was a cool greyish green, not the blue of the Mediterranean, or of my beloved Pacific.

The city's profile in 1964 was low, with nothing shaping the skyline but the two- and three-story facades of smallish

stores, or the box shape of the country's two large department store chains, Eaton's and Simpson's. The rectangular
street patterns deviated only for the occasional interrupting
ravine, seeming, to my uninitiated eye, both predictable and
undefined. The great public buildings—the University, the
Legislature, the City Hall—looked, at first sight, heavily and
oppressively Victorian, as did the churches and cathedrals.
Since we had no automobile, I didn't encounter the great
parks of the city during our first year there, and only gradually learned about its leafy green suburbs.

We made our home in the delectable area of Rosedale,
tucked into a ravine and its slopes, set in the rectangle created
by the main thoroughfares of Bloor (running east and west)
and Yonge (running north and south). Our modern apartment sat at the end of a road overlooking a small stream,
crossed by a footbridge which led to Bloor Street and the bustle of streetcars. We lived within a brisk walk of the University of Toronto, my new scholarly home, while John traveled
north to the Glendon College campus of York University, its
initial undergraduate college, a smallish campus, to be followed by York's grand new campus on the edge of the northwest quadrant of the city, some thirteen miles from our
apartment. The new campus, still farmland when we first saw
it, was to be the educational center of the northwest segment
of the city, along with two new colleges of the University of
Toronto, which were to serve the western and eastern rims of
the expanding metropolis.

There were two main themes to our encounters with our
new society. The first was the hospitality and high spirits with
which we were greeted by the old Toronto world John knew
from his army days. We had scarcely unpacked our bags
when we were invited to the graceful Rosedale house of
Dorrie and Edward Dunlop, to a large gathering which mixed
together their broad interests in politics, journalism, and medicine. Edward, then a member of the Conservative Party in
the Provincial Legislature, was tall, as erect in bearing as a
cavalry officer, beautifully tailored, witty, and such a power-

house of energy that one only noticed gradually that his deep brown eyes had been blinded by an explosion during his service in the Canadian Army. Dorrie, the accomplished political hostess presiding over the mixture of types, professions, and interests, was a woman of great beauty, her face alight with intelligence and humor, her zest for life infectious, her laughter ringing out above the din of a successful cocktail party.

I found my old shyness returning, as John, ever gregarious, began happily to settle in, meeting old acquaintances. I, on the other hand, was swiftly introduced by Dorrie to Don Milne and his stylish blond wife, Gloria, both keen Tories. I liked Don's easy talk about his love of the woods and his home in North Bay, and Gloria's lively interest in my reactions to Toronto. Soon we were comparing notes on our Scottish ancestry, and promising to meet again.

They were as good as their word, inviting us to a similar large party at their Toronto house in the city's most affluent suburb the next week. John was to arrive late at the party after a meeting at Glendon College, so I went alone, fighting my usual fear of entering a room crowded with total strangers. The party was in high gear when I arrived, so I went purposefully to the bar and ordered a Scotch while I looked around the elegant house for some elderly person I could sit down with and observe the room.

I caught sight of just the kind of figure I was looking for across the living room. A white-haired, elderly man with sparkling blue eyes was seated on the edge of the swirling crowd, glass in hand, surveying the room. I went across, introduced myself, explained that I was a newcomer to the city, didn't know anyone, and would love to sit down. My new acquaintance said, "Just my luck to have a pretty girl come to sit down beside me," and told me his name was Bob Laidlaw.

My new acquaintance began to quiz me. Where was I from? Didn't I have a husband? What were we doing for dinner after the party? Did I like the theater? Good. Maybe we'd come to dinner soon and go on to the theater with him. He was always buying too many tickets and forgetting to ask people to join him. I began to realize that I'd sat down not beside an elderly man I'd be expected to entertain, but someone who was cheerfully and delightedly entertaining me. Soon we were in deep conversation. The Laidlaws were Scots, and had arrived in Ontario three generations ago, too poor to eat anything but potatoes and dried apples on their tiny farm the first winter. Soon they'd gone into the lumber business. I remembered seeing huge trucks on the highway marked Laidlaw Lumber Co., and realized I was chatting to the owner of the enterprise.

Just then our host and hostess were before us, John behind them, laughing. "Just like you, Bob," Gloria said, "you found the prettiest girl in the party without even being introduced." He gave her a happy smile back, looked up at John, and said, "And I'm going to take her and her husband home to dinner right after this party." Soon we were walking out of the house and climbing into Bob Laidlaw's ancient but perfectly maintained black Cadillac, driven by a chauffeur, improbably named Speedy.

Bob Laidlaw lived in a beautifully proportioned grey stone house, surrounded by a romantic and imaginative garden, occupying a full block, at the peak of the hill which overlooked the city, a mile or so above Rosedale. The neighborhood was being transformed by the new high-rise apartment buildings being built on either side of 35 Jacques Avenue, sited to command a panoramic view of the city, but our host seemed untroubled by the change. We were greeted by an extremely cross maid, whom Bob called Dora, who announced that there was only cold supper for one person. Clearly participating in a customary ritual, her employer began to wheedle reluctant agreement that perhaps Mae, the cook, had a few other scraps of food in the kitchen. We ate a cold supper in the breakfast room, sternly supervised by a disapproving Dora, whose grim face was quite unable to quench our host's good humor.

The interior of the house was redolent of the British Empire in the 1920s and 1930s, complete with photographs of a youthful Bob in 1911 in London for the Coronation, and the obligatory full-length portrait of the deceased Mrs. Laidlaw dressed in the style of the 1930s, overlooking the drawing room. The generally Edwardian decor, which matched the owner's approach to life, was interrupted only by two dazzling Canadian landscapes, which turned out to be by Tom Thomson, the great landscape artist, who had been a close friend. Though the meal was spare, the wine was superb, and before the evening was over, we were being shown the wine cellar, crammed with the vintages collected over a discerning lifetime.

I took Bob, whom I later learned all Toronto affectionately called "Mr. Bobby" to distinguish him from his deceased brother "Mr. Walter," to be a lonely elderly man, bossed around by his maids, and since he lived only a few miles from us, began inviting him for Sunday lunch. Totally ignorant of the city and its elites, I didn't know we were entertaining one of the city's richest and most generous philanthropists, the angel for the Ballet and the Symphony, the major donor to the University and the Toronto General Hospital. We had found the perfect instructor in the delights of living in Toronto and its environs, an Edwardian character of great charm, and legendary generosity. People would later talk about "John Conway's ambitious wife" who had zealously cultivated one of the city's major figures, but I had been touched by the empty house, the cross maid, and the sight of a lonely old man trying to escape a solitary supper.

I loved the stately routine of Bob Laidlaw's life. In January he left for the sun in Barbados, returning in March to prepare for the salmon fishing and the spring at the house he really loved, Moongate, on Lake Simcoe, sixty or so miles north of the city. The landscaping at Moongate taught me how to enhance nature in a northern climate. It was a perfect study in the creation of romantic vistas, whose boundaries were marked by the shades and shapes of conifers, interspersed with white birch and lilacs. Bob's love of the black ice on the lake at Christmas or New Year, and the blazing stars in the clear wintry sky, began my instruction in the joys of winter, as did his lesson in the joyous abandon of flinging oneself into the snow to sweep ones arms in a semi-circle to make angels to surround the house on Christmas Eve. In mid-June he left for London, a suite at Claridge's, and visits with English friends. His favorite son, Jeff, a crew member on an RCAF Lancaster, had been killed in a raid over Germany, and each June Bob visited the wives and families of all Jeff's fellow crew members, taking particular delight at buying toys for their children's children, quietly solving problems about health and housing, always remembering each family's needs. By August, he was back to prepare for the duck-shooting season, followed by a fall of music and theater in Toronto.

Unlike most of the North American rich, he had escaped the notion that great wealth conveyed an obligation for excessive thrift. He explained to me, cheerfully, that he had provided amply for his four living children, and arranged for benefactions to all his favorite charities in his will. That left him an ample income which he enjoyed spending to bring pleasure to others. He kept as an inspiration over his bar at Moongate an enlarged copy of a *New Yorker* cartoon, showing the reading of a will to an unhappy audience, with the caption "Being of sound mind and body, I spent it all."

This was no idle statement. It was dangerous to admire something in Bob's presence, because the largest possible version of it would arrive on one's doorstep the next morning, delivered by a cheerful and talkative Speedy. Asked what was his favorite white burgundy, John replied truthfully, Corton Charlemagne. And the best year? John gave a truthful answer, to discover a case of the year in question at the front door the next day.

Once, when Bob began to inquire whether I liked diamonds or pearls, I remonstrated firmly with him, explaining that a lady could accept only flowers and candy from a gentleman not her husband. Under pressure I extended the list to permit the odd bottle of Dom Perignon, or hundred-year-old cognac. But in due course he playfully subverted the agreement. One Christmas Eve we stopped by 35 Jacques Avenue to leave off his Christmas gift, only to find a large bin, filled with woodshavings, in the hall. "It's a lucky dip," he explained. "I do it for the grandchildren, and a few friends. Go on. Dig in. There's nothing but trinkets and candy in there." I fished around dutifully, taking the smallest package, following rules taught in childhood, while John collected something larger. When it came time to open our packages the next day, I found a large square-cut amethyst in an antique setting of seed pearls in old gold, making exactly the kind of brooch I liked to wear. When I called to thank him he was jubilant. "I knew you were well brought up, and would take the smallest package. I fooled you properly, didn't I?"

The second theme resounding through our encounter with Toronto was the distrust, often verging on rudeness, of our respective academic worlds for anyone who could be tagged "American." John's dream of returning home to apply his extensive experience of American undergraduate education was quickly shattered by a rude awakening. No one wanted to adapt or improve on the American educational system. Insofar as there was an admired model to be drawn upon, it was the University of London, or Oxbridge. The rapid expansion of Canadian universities during the late fifties and early sixties had lured many faculty from British redbrick universities to Canada. For them in particular, the United States was anathema, and any effort to foster elite education was heresy. Moreover, the new institution, which had seemed so tranquil in its planning stages, was riven by internal strife, as groups with competing goals for the future jockeyed for power. By virtue of being Master of the first College in the new university, John had no option but to join the conflict, although it was one for which he had little taste. He was a man shaped by the ideals of service and loyalty, which had governed his childhood in Vancouver and his outstanding career as an infantry officer, so that he grudged every moment he was required to spend advancing his own cause at the expense of others.

At the University of Toronto, less threatened, because of its history as the oldest university in the British world outside the United Kingdom, I encountered a more rigid adherence to Oxbridge models and, beneath the genuine courtesy of Canadian manners, a distrust of anyone who taught American history, except with the avowed motive of unmasking the evils of American capitalism. I was also back in the world I'd fled in Australia, in which history was political and constitutional history, and interest in ideas and social institutions, except in a neo-Marxist framework, was seen as frivolous.

Mine was by far the easier setting in which to function. The Department of History at the University of Toronto was large and growing. The rising generation of Canadian students were enormously curious about, though also deeply prejudiced about, American history, and it was easy to settle down to teaching large classes, filling a needed junior position, without rocking the boat. The structure of power in the Department was clear, the control of the senior full professors benevolently despotic, and the curricular battles mainly about details I hadn't learned to care about. My colleagues in the American history section were hospitable and welcoming, relieved to see a new recruit to help handle the surge of work created by a rising tide of student interest. By the year's end I was invited to remain on the faculty in a regular position in line for tenure, to take my place on the roster of people who taught the large survey courses in American history, and to begin my initation in the Department's politics by service on committees.

The group of regular faculty I then joined was in fact locked in a major generational and cultural conflict. Its old leadership had come from the British and medieval historians with Oxbridge training, who tolerated Americanists and students of Canadian history, but privately regarded these fields as trivial, offering no pathway into the understanding of a great culture, and not requiring the scholarly impedimenta of languages and paleography which marked a real scholar. These were attitudes I knew well from Australia, and they riled me just as much in the new context as in the old.

I was lucky that "Jill's interest in women," and my status as the Department's only full-time woman member, placed me somewhat outside the contending battle lines. Mine was a subject only a few thought of as having any major significance, and to which no one objected, provided I pulled my weight in the "regular" teaching schedule. Shortly after my arrival, the battle was deferred through a typically Canadian compromise, which placed a distinguished historian of British imperialism at the head of the Department, a man whose professional interests spanned both old and new worlds, Europe and its offshoots.

I was too swamped by the responsibilities of a new faculty member, teaching ten hours a week, and grading mountains of papers, to do more than observe the contending forces, forming and reforming in complicated struggles over the allocation of newly budgeted positions. Would they go to the Europeans? The Americanists? To Latin America? To Canada? To Africa? Was intellectual history an important field? History of science? What about social history? Was there a history, for instance, of Canadian society, as distinct from the battles over constitutional issues and the relationship with Britain, or the United States? Unlike John, I didn't mind the politics, because my entire young adulthood had involved a power struggle with my mother, so I was used to functioning in a world where authority was corrupt or irrational. Besides, my go-getting parents had taught me to do my best work, and expect recognition. I hadn't received it in some areas of life in Australia, had found it readily conferred within the existing gender boundaries of the United States, and was alert to see what would happen in Canada.

There was no question, in these first crowded years, of finishing my dissertation. I liked teaching, but I was serving the traditional junior faculty member's time in the salt mines, teaching as many hours as was possible, and, since I was not content to be an average teacher, I put huge amounts of psychic energy and time into preparing. I wasn't overburdened at home, because John believed passionately in my career, and himself suggested that we defer nonessentials like buying a car or owning a house, so that we could afford household help. Unlike most couples beginning married life, we didn't argue over our respective priorities about money. We worked out our household expenses, the help included, each contributing in proportion to our respective incomes, and then disposed of the remainder of our earnings as each individual chose. But I was kept happily busy supervising the renovation of the farmhouse we'd saved from the bulldozers on the York campus, a genuine piece of Ontario's history we'd chosen for a Master's residence, rather than having a new one built along with Founder's College, the first college on the new campus, of which John would be Master.

I was new to the challenges of renovating old houses, but delighted that parts of the house dated from 1812, and that there was an exquisite old garden waiting to be rescued from many decades of neglect. What I didn't find out till much later was that the plumbing was more than antiquated and the water supply quite inadequate for the kind of usage John and I would impose on it with our official entertaining schedule, once we moved there in August 1965. Meanwhile, I worked in the garden on weekends, studying gardening books to adjust my horticultural ideas to a different climate from the Mediterranean one where I'd learned my gardening skills.

I was slow to "arrive" in Toronto, because Rome was in my inner eye, and the intellectual excitement of Cambridge was in my mind. The city was harder to "see" than most, because its charms were mostly private, and its distinctive mood and culture deceptively complex and different from the other English-speaking societies I knew. The cars were large, and American in style. The same supermarkets and fast-food stores cluttered the landscape. But these visual similarities to the United States were misleading. There were the same Midwestern lumber, grain, and industrial fortunes, but there was a world of politics, art, and literature I had to understand before I could register the visual and social cues of this society correctly. It was a fortress culture, slow to reveal itself, and I, at first, was too impatient a student.

7·

LEARNING
TO WAIT

WHEN WE MOVED into what everyone called generically "The Farmhouse" in August 1965, the simply elegant white board and batten house, surrounded by lilacs, a sweep of lawn, and an ancient apple orchard, was an island of settled life on a three-hundred-acre construction site. The construction schedule for Founder's College and the library was several weeks behind the planned date of completion, and the bulldozers and backhoes were already at work behind construction walls on the second college and a large auditorium, which would eventually serve a school of fine and performing arts. The site was a flat piece of fertile farmland covering a full section running north and south between Finch and Steeles avenues. The Black Creek meandered through the back part of the campus, and created a steep-sided small ravine at the back of our farmhouse, which was set a mile and a half back from the main road approaching the campus.

I'd hired an efficient German immigrant housekeeper, who turned out to be very much a city type, and, though an excellent cook, spent much of her time climbing up on chairs and shrieking at the sight of the mice which were a part of life in a farmhouse with an 1812 unlined earth cellar. I needed a reliable backstop in the house, since I now drove twelve miles south to the University of Toronto each day, making time to stop for the long list of errands needed for a household in the country with no shops or services nearby.

The tension mounted in the white frame house as an early fall heat wave set in, the water supply ran out, and the plumbing began to display cranky country quirks. I left it all every morning to go to my sweltering office at the University of Toronto, but John had no such retreat. The ventilation system was not yet functioning in his office, and an erratic power supply deprived a man who could only write by typing with his left hand of the ability to produce drafts of memoranda and letters. The dictation which should have remedied the situation failed to be transcribed, because the secretary first hired by York's fledgling personnel department turned out to be deeply neurotic and inclined to paranoid visions.

Somehow we struggled through the ceremonies for the opening of the campus, improvising supplies of water for the farmhouse, which was the only site for entertaining guests, but shortly afterward the cook and the secretary were fired, and drastic measures were required to deal with the erratic plumbing. John's life was made miserable by the campaigns of faculty and administrators opposed to the entire college idea he had been recruited to define and shape, and the perpetual frustration of an unfinished office and a nonfunctioning residence began to fray his nerves and exacerbate his usual late autumn depression.

Into this stage-set for tragicomedy marched a personal guardian angel in the ample shape of my third effort to hire a suitable housekeeper. In the interview at the employment agency, I explained to Elizabeth Sisnaiske that we lived in an old farmhouse. She brightened considerably. When I asked if she would mind mice, squirrels, skunks, and the usual array of wildlife, and she said, with heavy German irony, that she thought she could handle that, I was ready to hug all of her three hundred pounds.

Elizabeth was a survivor of Ravensbruck, a devout Lutheran who had worked in the underground against Hitler and had been turned in to the SS by her husband, who wanted the reward of her property, a family farm in the Rhineland. She had survived, undaunted, sustained by the faith which shone out of her wonderful grey eyes. Several of her children had emigrated to Canada, and she had recently arrived to be near them. She said, with deep scorn in her voice, that she made people in Germany uncomfortable, especially when the Jews and downed Allied airmen she'd helped to escape came to find her and thank her. She'd been amused when I asked her if she minded the odd mouse in the farmhouse, remembering the things she'd had to fear in life.

As a true German with respect for learning, she loved the idea of working for Herr Professor and Frau Professor. She adored the isolation and rural character of the farmhouse, and for the next five years, her energetic and fast-moving bulk made the farmhouse shake, as she cleaned and scrubbed it, polished it lovingly and prepared delectable meals in it. We left dealings with York's physical plant department on repairs of the house to her, because she insisted on being the final arbiter of whether a job had been well done. Since I could speak a little German, and understand more, we spent hours together in the kitchen, talking about life. I borrowed the works of Thomas Mann, Goethe, and Hegel for her from the York Library, so she could assuage her need to be in touch with Germany. At the end of each day, one could see her by the window in her bedroom, reading her German Testament. She made me understand the good side of German culture as the strength of her spirit, and her inextinguishable will, permeated the house. In no time, the plumbing worked, a new water line had been laid, and the old white farmhouse began to hum with activity.

It was a real blessing to have Elizabeth taking charge, because, among her many talents, she could make John laugh, and lift him out of the terrible black mood which had come with its usual late autumn regularity, but this year, it did not lift. Slowly, before my eyes, the light within him faded, flickered frantically, and then was extinguished completely.

This blackness was different from any moods I knew—sudden moments of despair, depleted energy, lost confidence, anxiety. Though I racked my brains to try to decipher some psychodynamic origin for John's sudden swings into profound depression, they were totally unpredictable, products of a central nervous system disorder beyond anyone's control. One could, with experience, see the warning signs, sudden irascibility, flashes of suspicion, wild surges of enthusiasm, until suddenly, there was a full-blown manic episode—a rage or panic of monumental proportions—a prelude to a depression so bleak and impenetrable that no ordinary bodily cycles seemed to operate. Sleep was a longed-for but rarely available release. Instead, he would begin the familiar restless and desperate pacing of the manic-depressive, too anxious to rest, fatigued beyond my capacity to imagine, frantic for surcease. When returned to his normal, wonderful lucidity, he would tell me that the onset of these moods was like having a series of powerful firecrackers exploding in the brain, a vivid image for a profound biochemical disturbance.

Far too much later, we were to learn that he was in a deep trough in a manic-depressive cycle that could have been smoothed out by regular doses of lithium. But we didn't know that on New Year's Eve 1965, when he checked into the Toronto General Hospital, and his suffering, and my anxiety, seemed to know no bounds.

I was a product of the therapeutic culture of my generation, expecting that with the right medical intervention, and loving care, he could be "cured." So I began to bombard his doctors. What was wrong? What course of therapy would resolve the problem? Why wasn't something being done quickly to relieve this man's near suicidal depression? Nothing worked. No course of drug therapy worked (although the obvious lithium was never tested). No amount of talking brought relief. In time, I came to understand that all depressions pass. Victim and family simply need the fortitude to wait it out. Just as slowly and implacably as the mood sets in, it will eventually disperse. But as the weeks of January 1966 stretched into February, I knew nothing about chronic depression, and had only vaguely heard about manic-depressive cycles. Like everyone my age, I'd been taught to revere Freud, and not to look for physiological causes for psychic states. I wanted some medical miracle to bring back my husband of the last two years with his quicksilver moods, irrepressible wit, brilliant intellect, and zest for life.

My desire for decisive action, and John's desperate need for relief, led us inexorably to a therapy I later came to regard as bizarre, brutal, and utterly unnecessary since the drug known since classical times as a way of handling erratic moods was readily available. Electric shock therapy was recommended, something I came to see as the most extreme form of modern medicine's quest for the quick technological fix. John wanted anything that might help, and I reluctantly gave permission. So a routine set in for us. I would rise at five, and leave the farmhouse in time to sit with him when he came back from an early morning session of shock therapy, his mind temporarily a tabula rasa in which he didn't know who he was, who I was, memory returning fitfully and erratically after the electrically induced convulsion.

No matter how early I rose, and how lightly I crept about the farmhouse, Elizabeth would be downstairs, my breakfast on the table, while she stood over me to be certain that I ate. Then she would wave me away, her lips already moving in her prayers for John's recovery as I drove down the drive.

It was mid-March before John was ready to leave the hospital, still deeply depressed, but considerably calmer. Meanwhile, we composed the memoranda, and drew up the budgets needed for his administrative role, and I kept an eagle eye on communication from his hospital room, refusing blandly to identify the cause of his illness. I'd thought myself a mature adult before. Now I learned firsthand the hard lesson of the middle years of life. I was bright. I had boundless energy. I was an excellent manager of time, resources, people. But I was powerless to avert suffering from the person who was the center of my personal universe.

By midsummer it was clear that John's mood was sliding precipitously again, and he returned for another three-and-a-half-month hospital stay, accompanied by more shock treatment. Over July and August, when most academics are away on vacation, I simply dealt with the affairs of Founders College, and when the academic year resumed, and an acting master was appointed to manage the college, I dashed between the two campuses, having taught so long with John that I could step into his place and teach his classes without too much difficulty.

This stressful time took me instantly to the core of the best qualities of the new society I'd barely entered. Unobtrusively, without my being aware of it, a small group of friends coalesced alongside John's devoted but physically distant family to sustain the two of us. "Mr. Bobby," while visiting John, observed the horrors of hospital food on his tray; learning that I ate the same thing, he set off for his club to order our meals sent in. Every evening thereafter, a liveried waiter from the York Club appeared to serve in style whatever the chief steward decided looked most delectable on the menu.

Dorrie and Edward Dunlop became like a sister and brother, deciding when I looked frayed by my busy schedule, ordering me home to be cosseted, while Dorrie took over the steady routine of hospital visits. Both of them set to work calming my fears about the future. Equally quietly, my colleagues at the University of Toronto learned not to ask whether John was better, and some, unbeknownst to me, took on departmental chores that should have been mine. Henry and Janna Best, wonderful Scottish friends from the York faculty, kept a close eye on me, the farmhouse, and Elizabeth. I often came home to find the house full of flowers from Janna's farm garden, or a note from Henry checking that all was well.

Gradually, I realized that we would both survive, albeit somewhat sobered, both literally and psychologically, from the carefree couple in Rome. And by the late fall, John was home again, his mood rising at last after twelve months of

blackness. Elizabeth had every corner of the farmhouse shining, each room ablaze with the last fall flowers, a fire burning
in the study, when "Herr Professor" came home.

I had been tempered by the ordeal. My bonds with John
were so deep that I'd been forced to withdraw a little lest I,
too, was carried down by the depths of his depression. Now
I had learned all over again the lesson I'd been taught so bitterly during the five-year drought on Coorain, my outback
Australian home: Endurance is the great virtue when nature
goes awry. If one only knows how to wait, nature, of which
we are so strangely both an integral part and a distant consciousness, will renew itself.

Twelve months without my adored partner in his customary frame of mind had ended any tendency I might have had
to become a dependent wife. His moral integrity, courage,
and devotion to humanistic learning were certainly my compass point, the true north one needed to set directions on this
continent. But I now knew there were going to be times when
I'd have to navigate alone. There are such times in the life of
every couple, but I had been enough captive to the romantic
myth to expect otherwise.

Those months also taught me to accept the greatest disappointment of my life. When John and I decided to marry, I
began dreaming about the son who would have his father's
merry eyes and mischievous humor. That child, and his sister,
a less determinate figure, but real nonetheless, lived so profoundly in my imagination that it took a long time for it to
sink in that I would not give birth to them.

Since girlhood in Australia, I'd been troubled by pain, and
often by excessive bleeding, each month. Australian doctors I
saw in my twenties would give me a knowing smile, and tell
me there was nothing to worry about that getting pregnant
wouldn't cure. They would tut-tut about my age, and tell me
I'd compounded the problem by insisting on an education. I
should have been married long ago. Rebellious about most
forms of bias, I wasn't about medical authority on this score.
I accepted that the monthly ordeal was of my own doing, and

suffered in silence. It was John's astonished observation of his normally healthy and stoic wife, doubled up in agony I couldn't conceal, or pacing the floor at night, white-faced and tight-lipped, that sent me off to a gynecologist again. I was a case for a fertility specialist, I learned. I had severe endometriosis, so severe that I needed surgery to correct the pressure building up on other internal organs. My pain wasn't normal, never had been. It was caused by the wrenching around of bladder and bowel each month, as my body struggled to function appropriately. There was a chance I could manage to get pregnant and not miscarry, but it was slight.

All those in such a situation believe they will be special, part of the positive statistics, and the specialists who work to help them can't function without conveying to each case that the chances are good. I never took in how stacked the odds were against the birth of that son and daughter. My hopes still rose with each new chance, only to plummet grievously. It became cruelly hard for me to congratulate my friends at the arrival of another sunny infant. Sometimes the sales woman in the children's shop would be astonished by my brimming eyes and shaking voice as I purchased each new blue- or pink-bound gift, and wrote the card. It was a deeper grief than any I had yet had to bear, and there was no assuaging it.

I wasn't interested in adopting children. It wasn't the experience of caring for adorable infants and toddlers I wanted. It was a much more primitive desire to produce the combination of my genetic material and John's. At thirty-three, it suddenly dawned on me that the unthinkable was true. It wasn't going to happen, despite all the tests, the careful schedules that were the fertility ritual of the day. John's illness didn't diminish the grief, but his recovery sent it underground, moved the threnody to a different key. There *were* worse things that could happen. I'd have to manage somehow.

The next spring, when classes were over, I borrowed an office on the York campus, shut myself up there every morning at eight, and began the revision of my thesis, set aside while we coped with changing country, culture, and household, and with John's lengthy illness. I discovered my old pleasure in writing again, spent many happy hours in the library dredging up recondite references, found out more about the context always lacking when a beginning historian works from documentary sources. John and I would stroll home together every afternoon, to change into running clothes and follow the program of physical fitness which was a new part of our lives. Then Elizabeth would produce one of her delectable meals, and, on nights when we didn't have guests, we would listen to music, John gradually correcting the defects in my musical education. Characteristically, he loved romantic music, while I turned out to have a taste for Mozart and Pergolesi.

As the cycle of the seasons followed its course through our first years in the farmhouse, I came to accept and sometimes enjoy the Ontario winter. At first, I was haunted by images of sterility, the ice and cold a counterpart to desert and drought, and to my private grief at the life which couldn't flourish within me. But, with time, I arrived psychologically in a northern climate. There were marking points along the way which startled me. One crisp winter night we joined friends watching the important movie of the moment, *Dr. Zhivago*. I sat watching the tense scene where the heroine, Lara, is followed, her pursuer's presence suddenly borne in on her by the sound of his boots squeaking in the snow. I thought the scene a powerful one, evocative of a northern climate. Outside the theater, bidding friends good night, I heard the same sounds of boots against icy snow. "Why, I live in a northern country, too," I told myself, gaining a sense of place I'd not had before.

I came to love the icy moonlit nights when the snow reflected a gentle glow around the quiet farmhouse, the only sound the hooting of an owl, or a fox's muffled bark. I found a real pleasure in striding through a heavy snowfall on a long afternoon walk, returning to light the fire, and relish warmth and light in ways no inhabitant of a southern climate can know.

The city of Toronto, once so formless and grey, began to assume distinctive contours, no longer a shapeless unknown territory. My Italian greengrocer, Scottish butcher, and Hungarian laundress marked stopping places on every journey in and out of town. Alongside the University of Toronto I discovered a splendid patchwork of ethnic cuisines. Within a few blocks one could find Jewish, Chinese, and Portuguese restaurants and markets, a few steps into each neighborhood seeming to carry one into the immigrant world I'd always associated with the Lower East Side of Manhattan, or Chicago's great network of ethnic communities. Massey Hall was not just a Victorian building, but the place where John and I heard superb concerts. The Old City Hall was joined by a new one, a dramatic steel-and-glass frame of modern design which overlooked a skating rink, always a vivid collage of scarlet, blue, and yellow caps and parkas. And when spring came, the farmhouse sat in a sea of apple blossoms, seemingly surrounded by one single sonorous hum of bees. I learned to listen for the sound of the crows, the earliest birds to announce that the first spring thaw was at hand.

In museums and galleries I discovered evidence of a sense of the northern landscape, as powerful and mystical as any of my feelings about the Australian landscape. I began to glimpse the beauty in the woods, the black rocks and silvery streams we found when we hiked on the Niagara Escarpment. In typically Canadian fashion, we hiked across trails which were marked and maintained by volunteers, running across private property, distant from the noise and smell of traffic, utterly free of signs of human passage, each hiker assuming responsibility for leaving woods and trail as pristine as they found them. Away from all sign or sound of human habitation I could see the kind of light which fascinated Canada's great school of landscape painters, the Group of Seven, and feel the thrust of the pre-Cambrian shield beneath my feet.

As my sense of place grew, so did my understanding and affection for Canadian ways. I loved the cleanliness, order, and civility of Toronto. And as the opening stages of the Vietnam

War unfolded, I thought differently about the virtues of the fortress culture. The Canadian wish to be a peacemaker made sense. The lack of ideology, so tiresome to someone who lived for ideas, began to seem healthy, when one watched in horror, wondering how the contending forces in Vietnam could possibly know whether the tormented villagers of South Vietnam, brutalized by both sides of the conflict, were or were not Marxist, and ipso facto, if Marxist, intent on subverting capitalist governments around the world. Against my dislike of England, and rejection of things British, I had to weigh the Canadian sense of *romanitas*, the sense of the law and tradition as the basis of civilized society, not some set of rights each individual man or woman carried within. There were important strengths in a society, embodying not the imperial general will, but an inherited order from the past. It wasn't my political psyche, but I had to admire it.

8.

TOUCHING
BASE

EVERY EXPATRIATE LONGS to bring the two halves of life together, the world of birth and the world of here and now. The longing is an ache for continuity, as though our psyches were a Roman arch waiting for the last stone to join the curves into a sturdy symmetrical whole, able to frame a life completely, without disruption or discontinuity. John understood my craving to show him Australia, and to integrate him into the small, close network of friends who'd seen me into young adulthood. He, too, had left behind the great coastal range of British Columbia, with its snow-capped peaks, reflected in the pellucid waters of the northern Pacific, and a way of life utterly different from the northeast of the continent. He longed for me to know the friends of his childhood and youth, and see the familiar outlines of the old family house. But his roots were accessible, and often visited. Mine were half a world away.

Yet as deep as my craving was to touch my native earth, unlike Anteus, I couldn't be sure that I would draw strength from it. It hadn't always nourished me well, so, when I contemplated returning, I had the ambiguous feelings of a warrior entering territory that is at once both seductive and hostile. This made me determined that we would not visit Australia together until our marriage was so well established that no scene my mother could manufacture would perturb our partnership. I also wanted no unfinished business for which to be rebuked. So we did not make plans for a visit until I'd received the news in the spring of 1968 that my Ph.D. thesis was accepted, and that my degree would be awarded at Harvard's next degree ceremony.

By that time, my mother had made her peace with her son, and struck a form of truce with her daughter-in-law, and was living near them in Brisbane, the lovely subtropical capital of Queensland, Australia's northeastern quadrant of golden sunshine, rain forests, and vast unoccupied interior desert. When we made the plane reservations and settled on the hotels we'd stay in while visiting family and friends, I felt the old familiar mixture of dread and anticipation. Dread, at the prospect of navigating these stormy emotional waters. Anticipation of the lyric delight of hearing familiar bird calls, of my nose registering the idiosyncratic pungent scent of Australian vegetation, of looking down at the bony outline of the ancient continent from a plane, of the heart's ease at seeing and taking in the archetypally familiar, over which other familiarities, not organic to our birth, are only superimposed.

What I could not imagine, until the experience was upon me, was the pleasure of venturing into such dangerous territory accompanied by an impregnably loyal, urbane, and socially gifted ally. John tried to soothe me with laughter during the twenty-six hours of plane travel that separated Toronto from Sydney. "Your mother's fierce, I know, Jill. But she's a woman of the old British Empire. She won't strike a disabled veteran." Back to his gregarious and perpetually voluble self, he teased me with the possibility that Australian monosyllabic speech might be catching, and that he'd return home transmogrified into taciturnity by the encounter.

Because of the vastness of the Pacific, often misunderstood by people who study its dimensions on the Mercator's projection, there is no way to arrive in Australia from North America, except very early in the morning after a night spent on a plane. I didn't want John to have to meet my family jet-lagged and unshaven, so I told the family we were arriving two days later than we actually landed, so that John's first image of Australia would be my beloved Sydney, and so we would be rested and composed when the moment came for descending from the plane in Brisbane and meeting my mother.

Sydney on a sunny winter morning took John's breath away. "You didn't tell me it was so beautiful," he kept repeating as we wandered through the Botanic Gardens after breakfast, strolling by the sea wall to take in the harbor. Elated by his response, I led him to all my favorite points around the Gardens, the Rocks (then still a neglected old colonial corner), the grander public spaces of the city. When we ate Sydney rock oysters, and drank Australian white burgundy for lunch, he found them as delectable as I, agreeing that there was no oyster comparable. Settling down for an afternoon nap, we awoke ravenous, fifteen hours later, in time for another breakfast, another rambling walk, and the long-awaited trip to Brisbane.

There, lined up on the tarmac, were my brother and sister-in-law, three handsome nephews and a fourth in his mother's arms, and my mother, leaning on the cane she carried ever since a broken hip and imperfect knitting of a fracture had left her with one leg shorter than the other. Her hair was now all silver, but her gaze was as penetrating and resolute as ever. My brother and his family surrounding her were pale with anxiety lest the meeting not go well. Benjamin, the youngest toddler, relieved the situation by asking John, as all children always did, what had happened to his right hand. John explained cheerfully. The other children were impressed, and we all relaxed.

Over afternoon tea, with lamingtons, a favorite Australian teatime confection, at my mother's spotless and flower-decked house, the first encounter progressed, my mother formal but cordial; John equally so. Canadians were "Americans" to my mother, and Americans were disapproved of heartily because of their emotionalism, their slowness to enter wars on the side of right, and their sex-laden fiction and movies. Now faced with John in the flesh, she had to recognize the difference. John was accustomed to the English institution of tea, his accent was audibly mid-Atlantic, and he had served in Montgomery's revered Eighth Army. It became necessary for her to admit the existence of Canada as a British Dominion, which in turn required revision of her views of my apostasy in marrying a Yank. Round One went to John, and by extension to me.

For the next week, we put up at Lennons Hotel, at that time the only Brisbane hotel with standards of service and comfort that could guarantee a soothing and relaxing stay. John and I lunched each day with my mother. I spent the afternoon with her while John went sightseeing, and in the evenings, when my mother didn't want her rigidly scheduled time for eating and sleeping disturbed, we visited my brother and his family. I was amused and delighted to observe my mother's growing frustration at her inability, despite unremitting effort, to discover any aspect of John's character or manners to which she could object. A shamelessly charming conversationalist, he kept her graceful company on any topic of conversation. Did she wish to discuss the minor twentieth-century English novelists? Agatha Christie? Biographies of British statesmen—the conversation flowed smoothly and amusingly.

A keen gardener, he was knowledgeable and suitably admiring on every walk through my mother's matchless garden. Although she was now bent with rheumatism and her body weakened by osteoporosis, she still radiated physical vigor, her step, even accompanied by the cane, as quick and purposeful as ever. She had worked her usual magic with plants, and her neat garden was a delectable palette of color, achieved where most people thought it too hot and humid for flowers. Moreover, John could match her horticultural interests with accurate and detailed stories of his own. He was clearly as ready as she to spend thirty minutes discussing the right degree of fertilization for wallflowers, roses, or any other plant. There could be no objection to his impeccable tailoring, or conservative taste in shirts and ties. A much decorated war hero, he could not be made the target of criticism about his war record. It was obvious that we were very happy together, and there was not the slightest vulnerable nook or cranny of impropriety in my dress and conduct, after living for close to six years with this totally presentable man, which might provide the opening for an outburst of disapproval. It practically drove her to distraction, and her mounting exasperation pleased me enormously.

John, aware of the depth and intensity of his mother-in-law's scrutiny, was also amused by it. When I asked what he made of my mother, he responded with characteristic fairness. She was a product of the old British world he knew well in Vancouver. Her flowers, her immaculate dress reminiscent of the respectably old-shoe English, her dainty and tastefully decorated house, and her manners were all of a type he recognized. The deep lines of unhappiness etched in her face, the preoccupation of this energetic woman with her health, her psychological intensity, and lack of humor were all emblems of tragedy. Saddest of all was her inability to enter her children's world, or take pleasure in their achievements. She struck him as physically strong, but he thought that, emotionally, there was the husk of a person left. She was a woman sustained by manners and habit, her only viable emotions now the need to possess her children, and her rage at life.

I had planned for John to travel around the continent, using the around-Australia air ticket we'd purchased, but the customary Australian airline strike made air travel impossible, so we saw him off, ever imperturbable, on the train to visit Melbourne and Canberra, where we had academic friends who were eager to entertain him. I spent the week of his absence staying with my mother, who, beyond the grudging admission that John seemed a suitable husband, spent the entire week reliving the past, telling me about her current quarrels with the manager at Coorain, and reviewing the state of her health in lengthy detail.

Within twenty-four hours I was back in the same suffocating emotional climate, living with someone I loved deeply from my childhood, but whose only interest in me now was as an object to ease her own neuroses. She retained so many good qualities from the past, her canny business sense, her passion for order, her sense of beauty, her steely will. But she just wasn't interested in me and my life as a married woman. She wanted me in the old role of ever-helpful daughter, or not at all. While, on the surface, she appeared to enjoy her closeness to her son and his family, in private she boasted to me about her hope that the marriage would break up, and her intention to assist in the process wherever possible. The motivations were monstrous, but I understood them all too well. She wanted her children (without partners) permanently tied to her. Her drive to possess them was nonmoral, Greek in its intensity. For the moment there were no outbursts, although my brother and sister-in-law later told me that they had worked diligently to prevent some in the making. This formidable, but aging, psychological warrior knew when to concede, although she remained ever alert for a return to battle should she spot a vulnerable point of attack.

My brother and sister-in-law and their young family were generous and sensitive hosts. Barry and Rozlyn were clearly as tense as I, anxiously awaiting the anticipated explosions, visibly relaxing when it seemed safe to conclude they'd been averted. Rozlyn was genuinely curious about life in other parts of the world, spontaneous in her pleasure at our happiness, proud of her four handsome young sons. My brother and I renewed our quiet, unspoken affection, and to my delight, he and John genuinely liked each other. I felt less solitary in the world, a revived network of kin easing my sense of being uprooted and cut off from the past. Two of my brother's sons bore striking physical resemblances to my older brother, Bob. It was comforting to see the genetic strain carrying on in another generation. I marveled that my mother fussed only about her grandchildren's manners, and didn't seem to take joy in the promise of a rising generation.

When we climbed on the plane for the flight back to Sydney, and a week of showing John the world of my school and university years, I was utterly exhausted, weighted down, as always, by sadness at the emptiness of my mother's life, wondering, as I would the rest of my years, why it had to unfold this way. What had gone wrong with the wonderful, confident, and generous young mother I remembered? But now, when I worried over that question, I had John's insight and perspective on my family to help answer it. There was someone to laugh with and weep with about them all.

Over a relaxed dinner at the Wentworth Hotel that evening, John reported his travel impressions. Nothing I had told him about the bleakness of the Australian psyche and the cult of death had made it seem real to him, until he'd visited the Australian War Memorial in Canberra. The central monument in a planned capital city, it represented a glorification of battle in modern warfare on a scale that encompassed every engagement ever fought in by Australians. John thought it had no counterpart in Canada, England, any society he'd ever visited. Perhaps the nearest equivalent was the City of the Dead in Egypt. What was the reason? Why the cult of death? Why didn't anyone write about such an extraordinary phenomenon in a modern society?

I said I'd been conscious of it growing up, absorbing from the culture around me that life was only worth living on very circumscribed terms, and that the moment of meaning in life came with departing it. I thought the preoccupation with death came in part from the dreadful physical and psychic suffering of the convict population, prisoners of a brutal military garrison, and in part from the very high rates of participation in warfare. The loss of life in two world wars had been disproportionately high for two generations of Australians, making their small society, with a population no larger than the size of a modern city, more marked by modern warfare than others. But most of all it came from the fact that, leaving aside small pockets of deep religious sentiment, Australia was a profoundly pagan society. Despite a veneer of

Christianity, people saw the human predicament in terms of the pagan "flight of the sparrow." Australians were essentially pagan in the acceptance of life as having only transient existential meaning. The country was just too remote from Europe for people to absorb its central worldview.

Melbourne had captivated John because of the Victorian mood established by its elegant Victorian buildings, the bandstands in the parks, and its high imperial institutions. Friends from my university days had taken him to dine at the Melbourne Club, and he had relished its red plush, the dress and manners of its members, savoring a stronghold of an old British world he cherished. It was in Melbourne also that he'd sampled a hotel bar at five o'clock in the afternoon, crammed with an all-male clientele, drinking as though their lives depended on it. Then there was the discovery made the next day that working-class people stopped for a beer on the way to work, like French workmen dashing into a bar for a quick Calvados. Why was Australia such a drink culture—as opposed, say, to food or sex? I explained about the shaping influence of rum as the first colonial currency (necessary because planners at the Colonial Office neglected to provide any other), and a means of exchange quite natural to a settlement ruled over by the British navy. Then there were the sizable Irish and the Scots migrations, the patterns of pastoral settlement requiring single male workers (always prone to binge drinking), and the aggressively male patterns of sociability, found elsewhere perhaps in fraternities or barracks, but central rituals of Australian culture because its patterns had been set by the forced migration of convicts in which men outnumbered women by about six to one.

All these explanations only partially satisfied John, fascinated by my native country as society and culture. Its visual and cultural impact was formidable, he said. There were no problems of identity here of the kind he was accustomed to debate in Canada. Gradually, as I took him to meet my academic colleagues at Sydney University, and introduced him to my Sydney friends, he came to modify that sweeping assertion. People did seem to be counting rather too much on their next sabbatical in England. When he praised the glorious Sydney light, one of my mother's friends responded disparagingly, "You mean the glare." The sight of swarms of uniform-clad schoolchildren proceeding to very British schools in Sydney's suburbs helped swing the balance, as did the sight of a military parade of sorts emerging from the grounds of Government House.

We made another flying visit to Melbourne to see an old Sydney University friend and his English wife, both teaching in Melbourne universities. Her account of the refusal of her colleagues to concede her academic credit for an honors degree in economics at Columbia, because "American universities have such dreadfully low standards," drove home my points about the colonial mentality. But this was contradicted by our afternoon at the Melbourne art gallery, and a tour of local galleries, where we could see the work of contemporary painters. John was reconfirmed in his earlier opinions. This work wasn't colonial at all. Why were the visual arts so far ahead of academic culture in asserting a strong Australian selfhood? His questions set me thinking about my own visual sense, and the way it had led me to question the view of Australia I read in textbooks. Word and image were different in the colonial context. It was a question to ponder.

Some returning travelers find they can't revive the same easy association with old friends that has survived in memory from times long past. My experience was the opposite. Each time I introduced John to someone important from my past it was as if we'd been carrying on our usual intimate discussions about life a week or so ago. Some friendships in life sustain themselves only at a particular life stage, products of some mutual developmental problem to be resolved together, or of some external circumstance, like being housed in the same dormitory in boarding school. Others grow out of a deeper spiritual and philosophical affinity, which continues throughout life. Mine were mostly of this kind, so that, although we now looked at life from the perspective of a very different experience, the same inner questions continued to sustain the closeness which makes conversation immediately meaningful, and set aside the component of rivalry or competition, which often lives inside more surface friendships. The affinities which shaped my deepest friendships were the ones which also drew me to John, so that my series of introductions had no flat moments. One of our most memorable evenings was spent with Nina, the closest woman friend of my Sydney University years, and her mother, in the flat in Mosman I knew so well from Nina's lively parties of our youth. The two women began talking to John about their first experience of Europe. He responded with tales of marching through Sicily and Italy, living by the Bay of Naples. Music was Nina's passion in life, and also John's great solace. When it transpired that they both loved Wagner, the evening gained another level of intensity. Nina's deep faith had always been important to me. It gave her interest in art and music a greater intensity, beyond mere connoisseurship, and gave her face the radiance of inner grace. "Your friend has great beauty of spirit," John said, as we drove home. "I see why the two of you were so attracted to each other."

We left for the airport after a hilarious luncheon with my old friend Cam McKinney, another close and cherished university companion, now a successful Sydney advertising executive. I'd always relished his wit, his sensitive antennae for the finer gradations of contemporary taste, and his wildly creative energy. His wickedly witty responses to John's questions about Australian culture were so engrossing we nearly missed our flight home. There was no mystery about the Australian cult of death, he assured John. It came from the horrors of Australian suburbia, which John could never imagine unless he lived here, and watched the death of the spirit in those vast agglomerations of red brick, redder roof tiles, and burgundy-flowered Axminster carpets.

At the airport, there was the appropriate sting in the tail of my return to my native city. I tried to buy some magazines in a hurry, because our flight was due to depart. I must have pressed the lackadaisical newsstand attendant a little harder than she could bear. She flung my change at me, with typical Australian contempt for service. "Why don't you bloody Yanks stay home," she snarled, as I turned to depart. It was just the squeeze of lemon juice I needed to stop becoming misty-eyed as the plane banked over a sparkling Sydney Harbor, with its shoreline clad in a grey-green mantle of eucalypts, and set out on the first leg of the long journey east, toward North America, and what I now realized was home.

9.

HISTORIAN

IN THE FALL of 1968, freed from the albatross of my dissertation, I suddenly realized that I was serious about being a historian. At thirty-three, about to be thirty-four, I saw myself as a scholar. I was not just someone going through the motions of scholarship to please some distant thesis supervisor, or to win some other medal or prize, but the real thing. History was what I did, and would do for the rest of my life.

Thirty-three might seem late for such a discovery, but a woman develops her sense of her working self on a different time trajectory from that of a man. Because society defines children as a woman's prime responsibility, she needs to clarify what her reproductive life will be, and whether she is to be single or a member of a partnership. She may be working to the limit of her capacity throughout her twenties, but, when her inner discussion on these subjects arrives at a firm resolution, her working self blossoms, and she enters a highly productive stage of life.

After 1968, I knew that John and I were an unbreakable partnership. I knew I would never return to Australia for any part of my active professional life. No longer on probation, I knew I was a working historian. At thirty-four, I gave up all hope of having children, and decided that I must put that recurring grief to one side. I never saw a young mother, or a delectable baby, or a window display of maternity clothes, without an involuntary surge of feeling, but, by an act of will, I moved the sorrow to the background, rather than the foreground of consciousness, and concentrated on other things.

When I wrote the last word of my dissertation I had solved a problem which perplexed me more and more as I read my research notes, and mulled over the way my cast of characters had lived their lives. Every one of my subjects had been a rebel, either refusing marriage or insisting on a very unconventional marriage union. They had all founded institutions or professions for women, and, because of their voluntary expatriation from prosperous middle-class America to the slums of industrial, immigrant cities, they had all been powerful social critics. Some were privately conscious of a drive to power. All of them made things happen. Some, like Jane Addams, settled for the comforts of wealth and establishment status. Some, like Florence Kelley or Ellen Gates Starr, were genuine radicals, progressively casting off the trappings of property and position, arriving in old age at a deeply religious simplicity.

In real life their language was pungent, their schedules were enough to daunt a professional athlete, and, for those who worked with them, their force of character something of primal dimensions. Florence Kelley's associates used to joke about the way Kelley ticked off President Theodore Roosevelt when he threatened to renege on an election promise concerning child welfare. Jane Addams intervened forcefully with the Chicago police after President McKinley's assassination, insisting that the event did not justify an overzealous attempt to round up members of Chicago's anarchist clubs, and won her point. Julia Lathrop was an effective lobbyist in the rough and tumble world of Washington politics in the late 1920s and early 1930s. Kelley was a master political planner, choosing targets for investigation by the National Consumers' League, which could be used to advance her lifetime commitment to just labor laws. She was a master at timing leaks to

the press, feeding a story to seize and keep front-page head-
lines. Her private correspondence shows her zest for a good
fight, and her scorn for anyone afraid of battle on behalf of
a good cause. But when the time came for each of these
women to write her memoirs, each presented herself as the ultimate romantic female, all intuition and emotion, tugged by
the heartstrings to random encounters with the important
causes, which, in reality, this group of women had discovered
and led.

The puzzle to be solved in my dissertation was why had
they done this? Had they chosen deliberately to deceive? If
they had, to what purpose? Or did they really experience life
the way they described it? Was it possible that they had lived
literally unaware of the import of their actions? How could
that be? What would lead them to suppress the power and
drama of their lifetime of crusading?

The more general problem for historians of American society, writing in the 1960s, was why it was that the major social reform movements seemed to have lost momentum in the
1920s, the young being drawn not to social justice, but to
jazz and bootleg gin. Specifically, there was the issue of why
the long-fought battle for woman suffrage, concluded in
1919, produced such insignificant results in American political life. Women then voted in much lower proportions than
men, and, in most cases, just like their fathers or husbands.
My study held a potential answer to these more general questions, because, if I could figure out why my subjects hadn't
wanted, or hadn't been able, to pass on their real-life experience to the next generation, I might have a piece of the answer to the larger question of why reform efforts became so
unfashionable in the twenties.

To help solve the puzzle, I read more about the lives of
women reformers in other eras, paying special attention to
the giants of the abolition movement. I knew I was on to
something when I found out that Sarah and Angelina Grimké,
the astonishing pair who faced down critics of women who
spoke in public and addressed large audiences about the evils

of slavery as they had known it in their native South, had lived the final stages of their lives as archetypal nurturant and self-effacing females. They showed wills of steel in denying their fashionable South Carolina heritage, and a brilliant capacity for social analysis in their feminist writing. But both sisters then sank beneath the burdens of domesticity when Angelina married her Abolitionist colleague, Theodore Dwight Weld, and produced a family. Romantic love and domesticity dampened down perhaps the most radical fires to burn in a female breast in nineteenth-century America.

Shifting my focus to the 1930s, I read my way through the Depression-era media debate about whether married women should be allowed to work, and the patronizing writing of conservatives like H. L. Mencken* on women's true motivation for their increased participation in the paid work force. Mencken depicted women as playing at work, really driven by the quest for a mate. Once successful, he thought them well satisfied to retire victorious to the kitchen and nursery. The implication of his writing was that the groundswell of popular opinion against paid work for married women was justified and would harm no one if embodied in government policy.

Looking over the span of a hundred years, what was constant was the unyielding social pressure which operated to define women in romantic sexual and emotional terms. Then I saw a feasible explanation for my subjects' inability to describe themselves in nonromantic terms. For them, and indeed for every generation, the social system operated not merely to repress libido (as Freud thought), but to repress other powerful human feelings, and to prevent them from being brought to consciousness. That would mean that a woman could live her whole life seeking power and influence for the causes she favored, but not be conscious of any but the approved spectrum of emotions allocated her in the patterning of gendered

---

* H. L. Mencken, *In Defense of Women* (New York: Alfred A. Knopf, Inc., 1918).

temperaments. It could also make men unable to bring aesthetic or nurturing feelings to consciousness just as social convention had taken away men's tears in the nineteenth century. Social systems must operate to structure the psyches of both sexes to reproduce their desired ideal types, and they do so by controlling what can be thought and felt.

Several decades later, the problem I found so puzzling was to be illuminated by the deconstruction of texts, and by more subtle approaches to the analysis of narrative, most strikingly narratives by women, and by writers from ethnic minorities. Later in my career, when I had a larger public role to play, I also learned that in American society, a woman who does not fit the romantic stereotypes of the female has difficulty mustering public support. Then I understood that it was entirely possible my subjects told their story the way they did because they didn't want to damage the public response to their reforms. But in the 1960s, my explanation was new and challenging.

I thought my generation of women had been telling their lives straight, just as they had experienced them consciously. Naturally, if they were unaware of their own anger at social injustice, or of their own drive to exercise power for their own very laudable ends, they could not pass on the message to the next generation. One has to know the existence of one's rage or passion for change to transmit its energy to others.

This conclusion, in an otherwise fairly conventional collective biography (unusual only in its female subjects), seemed productive of real insight when most approaches to women's liberation were legal or institutional, and when the idea of consciousness-raising was just getting going in a few East Coast cities. When I published articles drawn from my thesis, they attracted a lot of interest, and I received a growing number of invitations to write for scholarly journals and to lecture at other universities. When I finished writing my thesis in early 1968, there was an emerging interest in more academic study of women's lives, much of the effort dependent on out-of-date, or hastily researched, writing. Within a decade there were to be several thousand formal women's studies programs in American universities, and many more in the planning stage. By following my own idiosyncratic intellectual interests I had inadvertently been working on what was to become what academics call "a hot topic."

The stimulus to develop my ideas came not from fellow American historians, whose interests were political or economic, but from the woman colleague who was to become one of the English-speaking world's leading early modernists. Natalie Davis and her mathematician husband, Chandler, were teaching in Canada, because Chandler, a committed left radical, had refused to cooperate with the McCarthy investigations into Communist sympathizers in the 1950s, had served a jail sentence for his refusal, and was then blacklisted in American universities. The political fortunes which drove them to academic appointments in Canada presented me with the ideal professional colleague.

Natalie was small and dark, her brilliant eyes and swift movements, and her love of rich, jewellike colors, evoked the beauty and intensity of a hummingbird. A woman who lived and breathed for ideas, inexhaustible in intellectual energy, daring and original in imagination, learned in more languages than I could dream of—Natalie was a shaping influence on my professional life.

Like all overcommitted professional women, we found it necessary to make appointments with each other for lunch or coffee to talk about our work. She set me reading anthropology to become more fluent in interpreting cultural symbols, introduced me to historical demography, and instructed a naive modernist on all the mechanisms by which earlier societies had controlled fertility. I, in turn, was able to introduce her to the nineteenth-century history of the social sciences, and to the intellectual forces which had shaped Western feminism.

By the time I was awarded tenure, Natalie and I were among the History Department's more popular teachers, our large enrollments prompting suspicion and sometimes outright hostility from senior colleagues. In the academic world, numbers and enrollments are the currency with which new appointments are negotiated, and on which claims for the resources that support scholarship and teaching—library funds, teaching assistants, research grants—are based. The area I studied was no longer just "Jill's work on women." Events and student interest gave it a new political flavor. I might say I was teaching urban history, or colonial history, or the first or second half of the survey course in American history, but the student response was to the way I structured the narrative, the kinds of historical problems I posed, and the texts I assigned for them to read.

Both Natalie and I cared about teaching undergraduates. We enjoyed working hard on preparing good lectures, and wanted undergraduates to be aware of new fields of study—social history, intellectual history, non-Western societies. So we quickly became embroiled in the History Department's internal battles, particularly the never-ending arena of political contention in any academic institution: the curriculum. Academic institutions may present a calm front to the outside world, and even persuade their new initiates into scholarly life that curricular discussions are based on strictly academic criteria—such as the potential interests of the fictive "student," the hours she or he can devote to study in a given week, the level of preparation she or he may bring to college-level work, new fields versus "core" subjects—but in reality, these academic concerns are merely props, a backdrop or part of the set for the stage on which individuals and groups contend for power. Sometimes the contest is polite and open, sometimes devious and ugly. It may subside for a period of uneasy truce, like some guerrilla war in an unsettled territory, but it is always smoldering, with the contenders ready to snatch up their weapons and begin a fresh assault on some battle-scarred, body-strewn curricular territory.

The curriculum at the University of Toronto became a contentious issue in 1967, when a Presidential Committee recommended that the University abandon its old pattern of

specialized honors programs and introduce an elective undergraduate curriculum, which would lead to a three-year general B.A., or a four-year honors degree. Students could elect
to specialize in particular disciplines, and departments might
impose requirements on specialists; otherwise, all subjects
were to be open to all comers. Within the History Department, this new dispensation meant that conflict simmered,
and occasionally boiled, around the issue of how students
were best introduced to the study of history. How would we
recruit our cadre of specialists, and also attract the general
student to enroll in history courses? Should it be through a
standard survey course treating medieval and early modern
Europe, with some classic readings designed to develop the
capacity to "read" and interpret historical texts? (An approach favored by the medievalists and European specialists,
who might otherwise not interest many students in their
upper-level courses.) Or should students be introduced to the
drama and debate of historical problem-solving by reading
half a dozen fine examples of historical writing, to be read in
the context of lectures which would give the student some
framework within which to understand how an historian goes
about reconstructing the past? (This kind of topical introduction might be better designed to capture the interest of young
people whose attention spans were shaped by television, and
whose high school experience of history had not been rigorous.) It was important to come up with the right answer, because few students entered historical studies by any route
other than the first year, and our well-being as a group depended on the Department's enrollments in that first year, and
our ability to retain a high proportion as interested upper-
level students.

Because no one else particularly wanted to spend time
working up a new first-year course, Natalie and I ended up in
charge of one planned around a series of readings showing
brilliant historians at work on problems which form the scaf-
folding on which historical narrative is built: class and economic interest, race, nationalism, imperialism, demography,

climate, and topography. Some dealt with the medieval and early modern world, some with Europe, some with North America, some with non-Western cultures. Because the reading was lively, the lecturers and teaching assistants involved, and the preparation solid and painstaking, students flocked to the course enthusiastically, and the major problems of the two instructors had to do with finding enough space for tutorials, and revising lectures intended for a smaller audience, so that they could hold the interest of a crowd in a large auditorium.

Although I thought of myself as politically savvy, I was too pleased with the initial success of the endeavor to be wary that the very success might be feeding the wrath of my colleagues, who had a vested interest in seeing that students plodded through a narrative history of Western Europe from Charlemagne to the French Revolution. I certainly wasn't aware of any signs of trouble when I went along to a general meeting of the Arts and Sciences Faculty, in the fall of 1968, called to discuss plans to revise the governance of the University.

The old Act establishing the University's governing bodies dated from early in the century, providing for a lay board to have fiduciary oversight of the institution, vesting academic affairs in the hands of a Faculty Senate, and delegating to student governing bodies the management of much extracurricular life, and various kinds of nonacademic discipline.

The purpose of the meeting was to hear from the President, Claude Bissell, the reasons which led him to propose establishing, in concert with the government of the province, a commission to review the University's governance and to bring forward recommendations to the Legislature for revision of the University of Toronto Act. The President was eloquent in laying out the problems he felt had made the setting of priorities and informed decision making difficult during his administration. He thought the separation of academic and fiscal decision making unwise in a social and political context, where the reality was that the Provincial government set the University's income, through its power to control grants to universities by a formula, calculated to vary according to the cost of educating a student in a given faculty. Similarly, the government of the day provided some 80 percent of the capital needs of the University. Thus, the old Board of Trustees was exercising fiduciary judgment over a smaller and smaller array of issues. Moreover, since the government set the global sum of the University's annual operating income, decisions about funding allocations within that global picture were every bit as much academic as they were financial, and needed to be deliberated upon as such.

The prospect of revising the University's governance had galvanized the student government, always a lively political force in Canadian universities. Two of its representatives spoke at the general faculty meeting about the objectives they would work for in the revision. Their concerns were nationalist and utopian, in a youthfully idealistic sense. They wanted to ensure a student voice in curricular matters, because the wholesale recruitment of American-trained academics into the humanities and social sciences in Canada's rapidly expanding university system was having the effect of downgrading the study of Canada, and substituting the American experience as normative. Their perception was correct, and I agreed with it.

Their second objective was to secure a voice in considerations of tenure and promotion. Students and their families were taxpayers, they argued, and should have their views heard when lifetime commitments of academic resources were made. There ought to be some political art which, through a genuine process of debate and deliberation, could reconcile student and faculty interests. Their utopia, to be achieved through a blending of nationalistic concerns and a new constellation of power over academic decisions, was to create a new style of academic community, in which faculty and student interests were harmonized.

As I sat listening in the meeting I thought about the extent to which the dream of a genuine community of scholars, mediating the conflict between generations, linking young and old in a mutually loving quest for knowledge, has inspired ideas about academic communities since Greek times. Then the paideia rested upon the homosexual eroticism, which mitigated generational conflict. Otherwise, as the riots of the medieval university, and its American colonial counterparts, showed, the generational tensions could at best be contained, but never removed. Still, I was sympathetic to the idea of allowing a more effective student voice in matters of promotion and tenure. I hoped Canadian universities could evolve into institutions which were not mirror images of American research universities, where I thought undergraduates were genuinely shortchanged because of the greater weight assigned to graduate teaching. One way to counteract the tendency to duplicate what existed elsewhere was to evolve some new system which assigned greater value to undergraduate teaching.

After a number of senior faculty had thrown cold water on the student proposals, I spoke briefly in favor of them. I thought the appointment and promotion process surely should be carried out by faculty peers, but it was worthwhile thinking harder about how to weigh and include student opinion. Students were not, after all, children. They had genuine academic concerns. Much later in the discussion, Natalie, who had arrived late, and was seated in a different part of the auditorium, also made a brief speech supporting the student concerns. Without giving it any thought, and without any prearranged plan, we'd managed to infuriate our senior colleagues, one of whom rushed back to the Department following the meeting and demanded an investigation of the academic standards in our first-year course. "Those women can't be trusted, and they're getting those big enrollments by lowering standards. The whole course is a scandal." Of course, wiser heads prevailed, because the course was probably more demanding than its predecessor, requiring more, and more carefully assessed, written work than most introductory courses. It was my first introduction to the realities of academic politics, in which personal rivalries and dislikes emerge clothed in self-serving academic garb.

As the year progressed, I discovered that I was beginning to enjoy lecturing, a very particular and demanding form of public speaking. One has to be part performer to hold the attention of the laggards in the class, eloquent teacher for the middle range of talent, and, by posing questions and drawing attention to unresolved problems and issues, feed the curiosity and imagination of the committed student.

If the group is large, there is the added challenge of projecting the personality to a large crowd; if smaller, the lecture hour can become more of a conversation. I found my style as a lecturer because I was subject to recurrent migraines (an affliction I shared with my brother). Since they struck without warning, I could arrive at the lecture hall with a splitting headache, and a blank white circle where my page of notes should have appeared on the lectern. Forced to rely on memory, I found that I could perform very well, speaking extemporaneously. My memory was excellent, the outline I had prepared clear in my mind, but many more striking illustrations, and points of complexity and interest, came to me when I wasn't able to refer to the printed page. Listeners become much more engaged when the person standing in front of them is thinking on her or his feet. Then the occasional hesitation in search of the right word, or the spontaneous aside, keeps the listener alert, and able to take in and retain more. I gave up clinging to the lectern, began to wander about the room a bit, stopped when students looked puzzled, elaborated, asked for questions. It became fun. Moreover, the extra surge of adrenaline required for the extemporaneous performance often relieved my migraine, so that at the end of the hour, I would be surprised to notice that my headache was diminuendo, and, although the room was waving about a little, I could see again.

Probably mistakenly, I decided not to revise my thesis and submit it for publication. Donald Fleming, my thesis director, thought it needed considerable work to make it a satisfactory book. I thought he was right. Besides, I'd grown weary of the subject and was ready to move on. I thought it required greater narrative talents than I possessed to make this complex group of characters come alive, and I didn't realize how broad and interested a readership there was for the subject. Instead, I decided to publish the best chapters quickly as articles. As it turned out it was published in 1987 in a group of the fifty most consulted theses presented in the United States in the previous twenty-five years.

A logical subject for a more compelling book might have been a biography of Jane Addams, the key figure in my group of women reformers. However, there were some important barriers to writing at length about her. She seemed to me to have been more than a little opportunistic in her emotional life, shifting from one deep emotional relationship with her contemporary woman friend Ellen Gates Starr, with whom she'd founded Hull-House, to a lifelong ménage with the much younger, much more beautiful, and much richer Chicago woman Mary Roset Smith. I wasn't sure what to make of her sex life. Was she an active lesbian? And if so, what did I think of that? Was she just sensible, in avoiding marriage ties with a man, an action which, in the 1880s, would certainly have inhibited, if not stopped, her public career? Still influenced by Freud, I was nervous about lesbianism, a subject I would come to understand better along with my generation in the feminist movement.

I was also put off by what seemed to me her hunger for fame and recognition. Reading the files that showed how she and her friends had engaged in a ten-year lobbying effort that finally succeeded in securing her the Nobel Peace Prize, shared with Nicholas Murray Butler, President of Columbia University, in 1931, it seemed to me that she had forgotten the ideals of simplicity and democratic virtue which had taken her to the Chicago slums in 1889. I wasn't sure one should plan to write the biography of someone about whom one felt so ambivalent. I was too young to understand how person and cause become blended in the identity of a public figure, and that largeness of ego usually accompanies great accomplishment. Addams hadn't become America's preeminent woman reformer through humility and self-abnegation, although as a moralistic young scholar that's what I expected her to do.

Meanwhile, I learned to love the essay as a literary form, and enjoyed tracking down some of the more recondite themes I'd uncovered while doing my thesis research. One, which taught me a lot, was a study of the way in which the social sciences had appropriated Victorian ideas about female sexuality, and assigned a biological basis to them, long before biologists actually came to understand the process by which the sex of a fetus was determined, or the actual working of the endocrine system. Until I began researching the essay I hadn't understood that the variations in endocrine levels of individuals of the same sex were greater than the difference between women and men. I'd always been taught to see the endocrine system as the unalterable biophysical base for differences in temperament between the sexes. Now that just wouldn't wash. Perhaps women and men possessed all the human traits equally, but were socialized only to express a small part of their human capability? I thought of my mother, with her strong managerial ability, her drive for power, her restless energy, sitting alone in her neat suburban house, schooled to believe she shouldn't be in business, or running an organization. What might life have been like for her if she could have recognized that side of herself and been able to act on it positively?

Eventually, I decided to broaden my interests beyond my original focus on collective biography, and to use my earlier research to enrich a more general history of the experience of women in the process of urbanization in nineteenth-century America. Having been born in a remote part of the Australian outback, I was more vividly aware than many city-born colleagues of the enormous social transformation represented by urban growth, and, in particular, of the city's potential as an environment in which women could move outside traditional rural roles. I happily signed a contract with an academic publisher, and began working delightedly on my new project. I needed longer hours in the library, and more uninterrupted time at my typewriter to fit the new project into a life in which every minute of the day was carefully allocated. I taught full-time, commuted an hour each way between the York and University of Toronto campuses, and, since there were no existing urban services in the desert of tract housing around York's once rural campus, I did all the shopping, picked up and delivered all the laundry and cleaning, stopped at the liquor store, and carried out all the errands of the household with a heavy schedule of entertaining. There was no corner store for us to run to if I forgot something, or if Elizabeth neglected to tell me to bring home some necessary ingredient for the evening's dinner party. So planning, and timely execution of the errands, made me obsessive about using time well, and usually about attempting to do two things at once. I would grade papers while dictating the day's grocery order to the store where I would race to pick it up after my three o'clock lecture. Or, dangerous but fortunately never exposed, I would find myself making up shopping lists with one part of my mind (one five-pound standing rib roast, four pounds of new potatoes, three Boston lettuce), while the other functioned apparently smoothly to deliver the lecture of the moment on the causes of the Civil War.

John, who believed passionately in my career, suggested that we each stay at the office two, or if need be, three nights a week, to allow for more library time and less rushing about. The plan worked like a charm for me, freeing me from watching the clock every day, and making possible the kind of browsing, or the periods of concentration without interruption, that I then needed to function as a writer. They also meant that on the nights we were both home for dinner, we felt freer to spend time together, each totally available to the other, not partially attending, while the mind was preoccupied with other matters. On the evenings we were home without company, we ate dinner at a leisurely pace, listened to music, or read aloud to each other. The readings were always poetry, an interest with deep roots in both our lives. John still had his battered copy of T. S. Eliot's *Poems, 1932,* which had been in his jacket pocket, and had stopped some shrapnel, the day he was wounded in Italy. I had not brought many books with me on my journey from Australia to graduate school in the United States, but I had carried with me the collected works of the English Romantics, the poetry of Donne and Yeats, my own volume of *Poems, 1932.* This ability to keep a separate life together, beyond and quite outside our professional lives, stood us in good stead, and was a practice we never abandoned, no matter how great the pressures of work and the demands of public life.

My daily academic activities kept reminding me that my field of research was of direct, immediate relevance to women's lives. As a younger tenured member of the Department, I had to take on my share of administrative tasks, some more instructive than others. Perhaps the most startling was my assignment to run the search for a junior, tenure-track appointment in American diplomatic history, in 1970–1971. The American section met, developed the job description, and, as was usual in the days before mandatory advertising, came up with a list of colleagues and heads of graduate programs from whom we should seek nominations of potential candidates. The lists of applicants for other jobs I'd seen before had always been entirely male, something that squared with my experience of graduate school. When I signed the letters which went out from me as the chair of the Search Committee, I wasn't expecting anything different. But the female name beneath the signature was a code which unleashed a flood of recommendations for talented women scholars. One eminent diplomatic historian even went so far as to write "I would not normally nominate a woman for a position at Toronto, but seeing that the Committee Chairman is a woman, and there is obviously no barrier to employing women there, I want to recommend Miss X, my best student in years. . . ." I was astonished as I read half a dozen similar comments from prominent graduate departments around the country. If one of my male colleagues had signed the letter those women would never have had a chance. As luck would have it, the two splendid women who topped our list each refused the appointment, using the invitation to extract better offers from their home institutions, so we ended up hiring another male colleague. But the concrete evidence of discrimination was bracing and unforgettable.

My delighted self-discovery as a scholar and teacher came to an abrupt halt early in 1970, when I'd been six years at the University of Toronto. In 1964, I'd been one of a large group of junior faculty entering the Department, and, although I'd been slower finishing my doctorate than the male members of my particular vintage as assistant professors, I'd begun an active publishing career, was a frequent invited speaker at scholarly meetings and at other universities, and I'd done more than my share of departmental administrative chores. But when the group was promoted to the rank of Associate Professor, all were in lockstep but me, and by some accidental remarks over lunch in the faculty club, I learned that they were all paid considerably more than I was, and had been for some time. Of course, I'd read that it was well established that women professionals encountered their first discrimination not at the entry level of their field but in six or seven years' time, when male peers were usually promoted ahead of them. Now that it was happening to me, my rage was so powerful, it startled me. An icy calm settled on my mind. I must protest this at once. I mustn't just become another statistic in the history of discrimination against women. I remembered the discrimination which had driven me to leave Australia. Then I had been too crushed and too unsure of myself to do anything about it. This time I was going to stand and fight.

I made an appointment to see the Department Chairman the next morning, and then went home seething to tell John my story. He agreed with my plan for the morning's interview, and encouraged me to challenge the judgment. White hot with rage, I was away early after a night without the faintest hint of sleepiness, coolly prepared for battle. The Chairman was actually a friend of John's and mine, genial, someone I thought something of a womanizer, and a scholar of some international repute. We had many common interests, and until this decision, which was solely in his hands, I had liked him.

After the usual pleasantries I asked why I hadn't been promoted. No one had communicated any dissatisfaction with my work, but clearly there must be some areas I was unaware of in which it had been deficient. I wanted to know what they were so they could be corrected. The response made no sense. "I was waiting for you to finish your book. Then it will be time." But, I pointed out, three of the group with which I'd entered the Department had published no book, but had been promoted. I really needed to know what the perceived difference was between my performance and theirs. The Chairman became beet red, and very agitated. "Now, Jill, don't get excited and emotional about this. You'll be promoted in good time." I said that I was not the least bit excited or emotional, although my informant looked quite flushed and agitated. I had asked a rational question, and wanted a rational answer.

I never got one. The Chairman kept repeating that "it wasn't time." Then why was it "time" for my male peers and not me? He couldn't answer.

I said that explanation wasn't acceptable, and that I'd raise the matter with the Dean. I thought he had made an error of judgment, which I'd ask the Dean to correct. I left the office and walked the length of the hall to the Dean's office and asked for an appointment, which was set up for three days away. Women often read that "man" is a political animal, but they don't universalize the idea to apply to themselves. Just to get the communication networks operating I stopped in to see two senior Department members who I knew worked regularly with the Dean, and explained my dissatisfaction. I didn't ask them to pave the way for me, but I knew the odds were good that they would.

The Dean seemed knowledgeable when I kept my appointment, listened attentively, and said he'd look into the matter. A week later I received a letter from him confirming my promotion and adjusting my salary. The Chairman stopped by my office the next day. "No hard feelings, I hope," he said. "Just a difference of opinion."

"No hard feelings," I said, meaning it to exactly the same degree as he.

10.

CLIMATES OF
THE MIND

SOME EXPATRIATES NEVER arrive spiritually in the new land. The light remains strange. The climate is perpetually measured by the standard of another geographic zone. Nature seems persistently niggardly, failing to deliver whatever was the luxurious season of a native country. New recreations retain their novelty. Sight and smell continue to be governed by the inner senses, always searching for the particular sensations of childhood and the place of birth. So, too, some émigrés can never master the pronunciation of a new tongue no matter how fluently they speak it.

My experience was different. Very slowly, almost imperceptibly, all my five senses readjusted to the Northern Hemisphere, so that its sights and sounds, progressions of seasons, flora and fauna came to play as vivid a part in my imagination and in the renewal of flesh and spirit as those of my native Australia. In part, the process was political, a gradual, but profound, transfer of allegiance to a political and social system I came to regard as fairer, more enlightened, more civilized than the Australian. But the sense of nature lies at the ground of our being because it shows us the forces of life by which we are sustained, and demonstrates, more powerfully than any other set of images, the potential for renewal and rebirth in living things.

So the process of setting down psychic roots in a new country, and drawing spiritual sustenance from the variety and wonder of creation, is a process of reordering the imagination, imprinting new images, fusing them with deep impulses and values, so that they become the inner climate of the mind.

That process began for me in the summer and autumn visits John and I made to friends who spent those delectable northern seasons in the Berkshires and in Upper New York State. Archie and Ada MacLeish's Uphill Farm, set on a hilltop in Conway, Massachusetts, the hills surrounding it gently rounded by glacial forces in pre-Cambrian times, showed me high summer ritually celebrated on the Fourth of July, a liturgical as well as political feast, and autumn, when, at long last, after an Australian childhood, I understood the imagery of Keats, in his great "Ode to Autumn." Archie and Ada were in the autumn of life when I met them, and they remain fixed in my memory in the lambent light of a New England autumn, the golden auburn glow of fall color so heavily intoxicating I always thought it far more potent than any drug-induced trance. The redness of fall color seems to seep into the air, while the clarity of light stimulates the eye the way a draught of fine champagne heightens the senses.

High summer also came to mean Northlands, the wonderful Adirondack farmhouse of the writer Walter Edmonds, who was known as Wat, and his wife, K, way off in the woods north of Syracuse, New York. There the sun never burned too hot, the lakes were always cool, the corn from the farm perfection, and the hikes in the woods a fresh instruction in the northern economy of nature. Wat, whose childhood had been shaped by summers on the farm, knew the history of New York State, and the influence of the Erie Canal, better than any academic historian. He could explain, as if teaching at a military academy, the finer points of the French and Indian Wars, and the way they turned upon the ability to mesh strategy with natural forces.

Lying in the cellar at Northlands was a cache of "medicinal bourbon," a relic of Wat's father's stratagems to escape the constraints of Prohibition. A bottle of it was produced each summer, when we hiked off into the woods, to settle down for lunch at the point where the lake which covered twenty or so acres of the property was at its most picturesque, and where one could sip one's bourbon within hearing of the nearby waterfall, while the fire was lit in preparation for broiling the best steaks of the region.

After lunch there were a profusion of trails to explore, each party armed with implements to trim back intruding branches, and to arrest the incursions of marauding brambles. The expeditions were always enlivened by the Edmondses' grandchildren, and by Bridget, Wat's Labrador dog, whose joy in this habitat, and capacity to alert the party of any bears in the neighborhood, was an emblem of the relation between dog and man. When the long day in the woods was over we would return home, often carrying a happily clinging child in our knapsacks, to change for dinner, and sit by the fire, always needed in the evening as the cold crept in from the woods.

Our Canadian farmhouse was surrounded by enough wild country to permit learning about the wildlife. There were energetic black squirrels in the big elm trees which shaded the farmhouse, so athletic that no matter how many branches we trimmed they could learn to make the wild leap that landed them in the center of the supposedly squirrel-proof bird-feeder. "They have a black heart in their black bodies," Elizabeth would say crossly, forever racing out with a broom to drive them away.

We shared the garden with a colony of woodchucks whose behavior charmed and delighted me. They liked to sunbathe on the rock garden built behind the house, lying motionless, looking like a pool of rich milk chocolate poured onto the rocks. In the spring, when their young came, they played wild games on the back lawn in the early morning, before retiring to rest in the midday sun. They seemed like followers of some cult devoted to the color pink, because they ate only the pink tulips, leaving us the red and white ones for our borders. And then there was the pleasure of watching for them in February, to see how they would predict the season for us. The garden was also supervised by a single sentinel hawk owl, which kept its motionless perch on the dead crown of a pine tree, seeming like the totem of the place. Its flight was swift and deadly, ensuring that no small rodents lived to eat our bulbs. Once, as a curtain of snow raced through the small creek valley behind the house, I saw an old grey wolf, a silent shadow moving by.

John always told me that I would be as excited by the grandeur and remoteness of nature in the Rockies as I had been by my childhood Australian wilderness. I didn't see the Rockies until I'd been in Canada five years and left Toronto on a warm mid-September day to land in Calgary in two feet of snow. I was bound for an American Studies Conference at the Banff Center for the Arts, an hour or so's drive into the mountains. All the first afternoon of the conference I sat where I could look across the conference table to the mountain range visible through the window, small snowstorms floating across its crags like delicate veils. Whether because of the altitude, or the visual excitement of the day, I spent the whole night moving from window to window in my room at the Banff Springs Hotel. The moonlight was so pure and crisp it seemed as though one could reach out to touch the mountains. The serene black and white stayed in my mind like an etching.

In the early seventies, after John had finished his term as Master of Founders College, we surrendered to convention and bought a house. For the first decade of our life together it had seemed far more important to travel, to be free to go anywhere we wanted on a research trip, not to be bound by the need to care for material things. But when we did buy a house, we found one in a section of the city three or four miles north of the center, filled with ample old houses built around 1900. We were surrounded by a chain of parks so extended that we could walk for a good three hours without encountering a hint of urban life. Because the city was so law-abiding, one could stroll there after dark, or take one's early morning jog along one of their trails, without the faintest qualm about safety. An early-rising jogger, I had the pleasure of being alone in a natural setting again, enjoying the first light as a private pleasure. Sometimes, if we had a visitor from New York, Boston, or Chicago, I would persuade them to come along, just to see how safe one could be in the middle of an urban social order which worked.

Our greatest pleasure was to set out on a fall or spring weekend to hike along the Bruce Trails, trails we began exploring on short walks, but eventually progressed to much longer excursions. The system of trails that began at the tip of the Niagara Peninsula, and made its way north all the way to Georgian Bay, offered many points of entry for spectacular day or weekend-long walks. The Niagara Escarpment provided sensational scenery for the hiker, who might, at one moment, be scrambling down a steep rough-hewn descent across enormous black granite boulders, only to emerge on some tranquil cornfield, alight with late summer poppies, or sharply outlined against scarlet maples in the fall. I often thought of these daylong walks as like scrambling across some vast stained-glass window, because we moved through so many different fields of light, always marked at the margin by the firm black lines of glacial boulders. There are countless varieties of ferns and wildflowers on the Escarpment, and one could sit still on a boulder by some noisy stream, and spend a good half hour counting all the types of vegetation supported by the moisture and the sheltering rocks.

When my schedule called for a July visit to meetings in Vancouver in the summer of 1974, we decided to rent a house at Half Moon Bay on the coast north of Vancouver, on the Sechelt Peninsula, where John had camped and explored by canoe as an adventurous youth. So I finally came to experience John's Northern Pacific paradise, in all its late summer glory.

Our house was nestled on rock, its deck, built out almost to the water's edge, shaded by a gnarled and twisted arbutus tree, its windows looking across the Malespina Straits to the snow-capped mountains of Vancouver Island. Behind us was the coastal range, its snowy peaks reflected, on still days, in the clear blue ocean. We waited to swim until the tide came in over the sun-warmed rocks, because the ocean, while warmed by the Japanese current, still reminded the swimmer that it flowed down from the Arctic. I liked to swim out a short distance and lie on my back looking back at the mountains, and their majestic covering of pine and cedar. Sometimes I would find myself observed from a high perch by a disapproving, fierce-eyed bald eagle, motionless, and so commanding that one grasped instantly the place they occupied at the top of the Coast Indians' totem poles.

The coastline around us, much of it untouched, invited long, scrambling walks over rocks and across tidal inlets. When the time came to rest, we picked the luscious wild blackberries which grew in abundance, savoring the explosion of sweetness, tasting of long sunny days and moist air. The woods combined all the colors I loved most—the delicate grey-green of lichens and the richer green of moss, the strong vibrant pink of fireweed, juxtaposed with the red stalks and strong green of salal, the luminous coral and grey of arbutus bark, and the rich velvety browns of pine and cedar trunks. I wished I were a botanical illustrator, or a designer of chintzes, so that I could carry away these colors, so pure in the crisp cool air, so vividly framed by sky and brilliant blue sea.

There was an Edenic quality to the plenitude of nature there. We often startled families of mink on our walks, all so richly clad they seemed creatures of utter luxury. The sea teemed with salmon, their silver shapes making gleaming arcs as they jumped in the water. When I swam, small schools of fish were visible in the clear water, traveling unhurriedly by. Families of seals sunbathed on the rocky beaches, and swimmers were often startled by playful baby seals, who were unable to tell a person from a fish, and would pirouette around them in the water. After a long day in the sunshine, and an evening spent watching the late northern sunset turn the ocean a glimmering silver, we would fall into bed lulled by the sound and smell of ocean. At dawn I often woke to the unique scent of the Pacific Northwest, the overpowering scent of cedar. It was a signal to step out on the deck and observe the log-boom with its attendant tug, riding quietly in the shelter of the island which shielded Half Moon Bay from the open sea. When I tried to imagine being a child here, perched on the edge of this cool ocean, a whole continent at one's back, one's eyes looking out to Japan and China, I could understand what had given John his richly romantic temperament and passionate love of natural beauty.

As time passed I also understood why after eighteen years at Harvard, John had remained a Canadian citizen. First of all, there was John's regiment, the Seaforth Highlanders of Canada, a Vancouver institution, in which, as a very young man, he had lived an epic experience from 1939 to 1945. In time of war one volunteered, indeed pled, to be accepted into the Seaforths. One wasn't drafted. The Regiment kept its ties to home, and civilian life, wherever the fortunes of war led it. So John, a very young member of the Vancouver Bar, had lived by the standards of his civilian life and calling, when, in the heat of battle, he responded to hot-headed talk about taking no German prisoners, and told his men he would personally see them tried for murder, once they got home, if they shot Germans who had surrendered. He was joined in this action by three fellow officers, with whom he'd grown up and studied law. Canadians, even in modern total warfare, had a habitation, a home, a community. The regional scale of the country removed much of the anonymity of modern life. It often threatened to undo the Canadian union, but it was a positive force in the face of much that was alienating about modernity.

One lovely summer evening on our first West Coast holiday, John's old commanding officer, himself deeply rooted in the community, gave a party for us so that John's fellow officers could meet the wife he'd married in the distant East. The general lived beside the ocean in West Vancouver, looking back to the lights of the great seaport city. After dinner, we gathered on the terrace, as the pipe-major who had piped all these now middle-aged lawyers, doctors, and businessmen into battle, and beat retreat for them at the end of an engagement, paced with the slow deliberate gait of the piper, back and forth before us, playing "Johnny Cope" and "Scotland the Brave" as the sun went down.

Then there was the order and beauty of Canadian cities. We had no sooner moved into our house in Toronto than a representative of the municipality called to point out that the great maple to the left of our front lawn was near the end of its life. What kind of a replacement would we like and when would it be convenient to have it planted? I had thought it would be a nuisance to own city property in a northern winter, remembering the snow-clogged sidewalks and icy streets of Boston and Cambridge. Snow was no problem in Toronto. For a minuscule sum added to our municipal taxes we could have the city shovel our walks within two hours of any snowfall.

When the tax bill came there was a box for a check-off to indicate whether we'd like our taxes to support Catholic or nonsectarian education. So, in Canada, the great nineteenth-century sectarian battles over public education hadn't ended in a majoritarian solution. There were in Ontario, I discovered, unions for Catholic elementary and secondary teachers, and non-Catholic elementary and secondary teachers, and a grab-bag union for teachers who didn't want to be separated by religious affiliation. All five bargained with the Province about pay and conditions of work, and all five ran their own professional development efforts. Not rational, perhaps, even quirky, but it gave variety to the school system, which students and teachers seemed to like. The one universal in the system was a high standard of public honesty, and a commitment to achieve fairness while respecting difference, something no other democratic state I knew seemed able to achieve.

I liked the fact that at the University of Toronto, belatedly to be sure, but earlier than in other English-speaking countries, there was a genuine effort to educate native people. The University ran a transitional-year program for students from the Indian bands, in which gifted tutors, some of them student volunteers, taught Indian students what they needed for high school equivalency in twelve to eighteen months, so that the University could then admit and train Indian lawyers, doctors, social workers. And then there was a wonderful polyglot mixture of old British Empire and Commonwealth peoples, all studying at the University supported by the Canadian International Development Agency, and beside them there was an equally complex mix of political refugees in flight from tribal wars, totalitarian regimes, national disasters. Their scholarships and help in resettling came mostly from public funds rather than volunteer organizations, their presence accepted as part of Canada's commitment to international development. This commitment had the support of all political parties, Canadians being determined to spend more, in relative terms, than other industrial societies, and to invest more effectively in development than the other Western democracies.

Political life was startlingly different. The vitality of local government made entry into the political arena relatively easy, while the electoral laws provided for short election campaigns. As a result, the process of recruitment into political life was different, and the national political process a system of accommodation among regional elites. This allowed for genuine ideological diversity across the political spectrum, from doctrinaire socialism to staunch old-fashioned Toryism, and one was likely to see the sons, and even some of the daughters, of the country's elite families sparring with one another in the Legislature, old friends from private school days and college even though committed to different political ideologies.

Dorrie and Edward Dunlop provided my education on Canadian political mores. They were exemplars of the Ontario Tory tradition, but their counterparts existed in every region and branch of political life. Dorrie was the granddaughter of one of the Fathers of Confederation, her Nova Scotian family strung out across Canada from the Maritimes to British Columbia. Edward, born in the Ottawa Valley, came from the staunchest center of loyalty to Crown and Commonwealth in Canada's richest province. Both of them took public service and involvement in the affairs of the Tory Party as their raison d'être. Dorrie had met and married Edward when, just twenty, she had served with the Red Cross in a wartime English rehabilitation hospital. There she had met her handsome six-foot officer husband, blinded by an explosion while training new recruits for service in the Canadian Army.

Their notion of service continued uninterrupted into civilian life, where Edward entered Provincial politics, served as a Tory member of the Legislature, and then held cabinet office in the current Tory administration in Ontario. Just as John had learned to write, to tie a tie or shoelaces with his left hand, Edward made no concessions to his blindness. Stylish in dress, erect in bearing, a fluent and witty conversationalist, Edward surprised me by the breadth of his social concerns, and his willingness to expend enormous amounts of energy to understand the details of social issues. His interest in rights for native peoples, and in the broadest possible access to education, didn't fit with my notion of the social and political conservative in Australia. When he became a member of the Governing Board of the University of Toronto, I volunteered to read the massive pile of documents which accompanied the docket for each meeting to him, a pleasant occupation which resulted in the two of us spending hours together discussing educational issues, and the niceties of University governance. Invariably the conversation broadened to political and social theory.

Edward had some of the old British Tory concern for "the people," as opposed to the special interests of commerce or industry. He valued the right to accumulate and preserve property, indeed wanted to acquire plenty for his family, but he saw this right as subordinate to broad issues of social justice. The process of political deliberation fascinated him, and he valued the parliamentary system of government as deeply as he did because he thought it the best suited to foster orderly deliberation. I could talk to him about my political interests and concerns in a way it was impossible to contemplate with his political counterparts in Australia, where social and political conservatives saw the faintest recognition of Aboriginal rights to land as a blow at all forms of property, and where class conflict and religious bigotry were endemic. Edward, an Anglican by tradition, was regularly elected by a predominantly Jewish constituency, where he was often to be seen attending religious functions in a yarmulke. I was always amused and charmed by the impassioned way Edward could speak at length on the subject of tax policy. Taxes for the Ontario Tory were not the political no-no they were for Australian or American conservatives, and the institution of the Crown corporation, a government enterprise established to operate as a freestanding entity, to perform some task that the Canadian market was too small to support otherwise, was not seen as an inefficient boondoggle, but a valued resource in building the Canadian state.

Dorrie Dunlop, always by Edward's side, but never in his shadow, had the trenchant judgment of people, and the gift for getting all kinds of people to work together, which characterizes the talented "behind-the-scenes" political person. Since she read all his Cabinet papers to Edward, she was as knowledgeable about the affairs of the Province of Ontario as any cabinet minister, and as concerned. I enjoyed watching her in every kind of setting, listening intently, registering every nuance of a situation she might need to brief Edward on later. Her delight in the extent of human folly, and her inside knowledge of Canada's major political figures, made her a wonderful storyteller, ever alert to the personal foibles which affected affairs of state. She became the friend I trusted most completely in life. Utterly discreet, always thoughtful in her responses to situations, ambitious in the best sense, with a natural habit of authority, she was a distinctly Canadian type.

As hardworking as if she held a full-time paid job, she lived for her ideal Canada. It was a country where public office-holders could be trusted, where the the best standards governed the civil service, where the machinery of the state ran smoothly, where inherited British traditions thrived, and where people gloried in the natural beauty which was Canada's great heritage.

At first I couldn't credit the response of my Canadian students when I gave them a reading assignment drawn from Alexis de Tocqueville's *Democracy in America*. When I first read this French aristocrat's classic analysis of the way a democratic society worked, based on his travels in the United States in the 1830s, I took his criticisms to apply to *all* democratic societies, mine included. My Canadian students, all of them committed to democratic institutions, read *Democracy in America* as simply one more commentary about what was wrong with the United States. I came to understand that at the core of every Canadian being is the determination to differentiate himself or herself from the supposedly crass society which presses upon Canada's southern border, and that that need operates as a set of blinkers preventing some kinds of critical scrutiny of Canadian institutions. The problem of differentiation from powerful neighbors found expression in racism in Australia, because there was no dynamic nearby Anglo-Saxon country. But at first, the Canadian attitude, just another form of the effort to differentiate, seemed sour and ungenerous, a failure of perception I couldn't explain in intelligent people. Then there were certain terms of speech which I eventually assimilated. One could not talk to Canadians about America, meaning the United States, because they would instantly point out that they lived in America, too. There was North America, and South America, within which were to be found a variety of states. They were correct to resist this linguistic example of American imperialism, but at first I was puzzled when my History Department colleagues told me that if I wanted to teach a course on "the American colonies in the eighteenth century," it must include the history of the Maritime Provinces and Hispanic America.

I was often irritated by the naysaying of Canadian journalism, a characteristic which resonated with some deep need in the Canadian psyche. Canadian humor expressed people's delight in mocking authority or deflating large ideas. This was an attitude necessary to preserve the regional and local, but there was an astringent quality to it I didn't enjoy. Canadians had to make themselves feel at home occupying the territory which separated the world's two nuclear giants, each with their missiles poised to fly over Canadian territory. This made them perpetual mockers of the heroic, insisters that no one become excited by ideas, that the only way to live was to be determinedly pragmatic. These qualities found wonderfully positive expression in Canadian peacekeeping activities, and support of the United Nations, but I thought them also a straitjacket for Canadian intellectual life, and a barrier to firing the imagination of the young women and men I taught. Those same qualities meant that great ideas, by definition, had to come from some other place, and so the gifted young left, drawn to intellectual centers which stoked the fires of the mind.

This acerbic view of life was such a constant, it became part of the flavor of Canada for me, almost as strong a sensation as the pungent smell of the Australian bush. Once, after a tense round of academic politics, in which my side lost the battle, I commented to a Canadian friend that it had been a really good fight, and I'd learned a lot from it. He refused to be comforted. "I've lived in the United States too much," he said tersely, referring to his doctoral studies at Berkeley. "I don't enjoy to lose any more."

Like every émigré, I was always keeping score, somewhere in the back of my mind, weighing and assessing what was good and bad about my new situation, testing the new society against my native one. There always seemed to be two things to which I couldn't give assent in Canada. I couldn't really like winter, couldn't make it seem natural to my southern bones. And I couldn't control my irritation with Canadian pragmatism. I lived for ideas, wanted the imagination to know no bounds, hoped my students would aspire to greatness. Each time I met the stolid refusal to think big, I fumed. One day, discussing my plans for a new American history survey course, one of my Canadian colleagues made the usual deflating remark. "Now, don't get too fancy," he said. "Give them a meat and potatoes course. That's what they really need."

My final moment of conversion came after another trip back to Australia. I'd visited my mother, now once again living in her favorite part of Sydney, having, predictably, not been able to settle down near my brother and his family. After visiting her for some days I took an early morning flight to Brisbane to see my brother and his family. In the waiting area before the flight I noticed a group of young Aboriginals. They had placards under their arms, and the air of youthful defiance that signals a demonstration somewhere in the making. There was open seating on the flight, so I followed them to the back of the plane, and began to engage them in conversation. I was behaving like my Canadian self, already keenly involved in working with the program which brought native people to the University of Toronto. Feeling something odd about the silence in the rest of the plane, I looked up to see almost the entire white population of passengers turned around in their seats staring at what to them was the outlandish prospect of a white woman apparently engaged in lively conversation with a group of Aboriginals. I'd forgotten how deep the strain of race feeling was in Australia.

When I landed in Brisbane, and walked off the plane, still chatting with the group of young Aboriginals, one of the greeting party made the archetypal Australian comment. "Those bloody Abos! Good for nothing but booze and the dole. What were you talking to them for? On their way to fake a claim to some new sacred site, I'll bet." I said they seemed like very pleasant young students to me, and then someone tactfully changed the subject.

On the plane back across the Pacific, I forgave Canadians their sour humor. Theirs was a fairer society. It had the limitations of place and history, but I would teach myself to love them. I really didn't belong in Australia now. I could spend a lifetime explaining, but I'd never be able to make my family and its circle, for whom I felt deep affection, understand how I felt about the history of white settlement in Australia and the Americas. It wasn't that I idealized traditional peoples. I didn't want to be treated by a witch doctor when I fell ill. But I wanted to live where there was some fairness and recognition of the people and cultures our ancestors had so unthinkingly despoiled. I felt the old panic of the need to get away. It was cowardly, no doubt, but I couldn't find the psychic energy here to fight every minute of every day. A kindly providence had given me the reasons of the heart that everyone could accept for living halfway around the world, and that was where I belonged. Of course, others could and later did mount the battle over the rights of native peoples in Australia and succeeded in ways I'd never dreamed possible.

Early in the winter after my return, I took the shiny high-speed train everyone called The Rapido, bound for Montreal, where I was to give some lectures at McGill. The snow had come early that year, and I was gazing reflectively out the window, watching it fall steadily on the spotless white landscape. The frozen winter landscape had always haunted me, its inability to sustain life an emblem of my own infertility. On this winter morning, the snow suddenly abated as the train slowed to negotiate icy and frozen tracks. The sun came out illuminating a line of bushes beside the tracks, turning them every color of the spectrum as it lit the icicles hanging in the winter stillness. I could see how beautiful it was and suddenly knew that I could call it home.

I'd always hated the slow and unreliable spring in Toronto. It was so dispiriting to see the crocus and early daffodils disappearing beneath a late snowfall. I had no childhood memories to make such weather a reminder of the last treasured chance for wild tobogganing, or the speedy creation of a soon-to-sag snowman on the front lawn. But in the spring following, I went again to Montreal, one April morning. It began to snow as I drove to the airport, and my seven o'clock flight was held on the ground for de-icing. It won't last, I told myself. The ground is too warm. In Montreal, my journey into the Stock Exchange Building for my nine o'clock meeting, usually twenty minutes, turned into an hour and a half of inching through heavy snow. By noon, when my committee, a group of academics and bankers, had to make our way to the St. James Club for lunch, there was a total whiteout. Not one member of the group, drawn from across Canada, was prepared for the weather. The member from Montreal stood before the glass doors opening to the street and admonished us. "It's a whiteout. Better hold hands so we don't lose one another on the way to the club. It's windy out there. I know the way. I'll lead." Looking just like a staggering group of kindergartners, we set out, slipping, sliding, falling over, all pretense at solemnity blown away by the force of the storm.

When the meeting ended at four, those of us from Toronto were too late to catch the high-speed Rapido home, and had to settle for the slow milk train. The passengers in my carriage became a cheery group knit together by the sudden frustration of human plans by the forces of nature. There was drink on the train, but no food, so the party's spirits mounted, and people grew loquacious as the hours stretched out, while our train made its deliberate way to Toronto. About ten o'clock a great cheer went up as the slow train passed the Rapido, stuck in a snowdrift on the track to our right. When we drew into a white-covered Toronto, just before midnight, I seemed to have made about twenty close friends all with war stories of spring blizzards to tell me. Instead of feeling depressed by the laggard spring, I was laughing as I climbed wearily onto Toronto's excellent subway system, still working flawlessly at midnight after four feet of snow. I fell over a few times as I plowed the short blocks home from the subway on frozen feet, but I didn't mind. The moon had come out, there were a few elated cross-country skiers moving joyfully right down the middle of the streets, and I kept laughing at the thought of the sudden childishness of holding hands with a group of near strangers, our eccentric crocodile making its seemingly drunken and erratic progress through the streets of Montreal.

II.

ACTION VERSUS CONTEMPLATION

AFTER MY CONFRONTATION with the Chairman of the History Department over my promotion, I began thinking about the situation of other women faculty. It was easy for me to stage a fight. I was tenured. I was happily married to a man whose ample salary could easily support us, should the need arise. I had no dependents. But what about women who were single mothers, or supporting aged parents? They probably couldn't risk a fight. And they needed the money which discrimination deprived them of more than I did.

There weren't that many women faculty at the University of Toronto in 1971. And they didn't have any collective voice. Always a believer in trying to make established channels do the job at hand, I went along one evening to the fall meeting of the University of Toronto Faculty Association, a meeting called to discuss the vigorously perennial subject of the faculty's impending submission to the Provincial government on faculty compensation. The submission was made annually as one component of the University's brief to the legislative committee which recommended on the higher education segment of the Province's budget. Faculty salaries were a component of the complex formula used by the Province to determine its level of subsidy for student enrollments, and, when fiscal pressure led the Province to elect to fund student access versus reasonable faculty compensation, salary levels often languished. The Faculty Association, which had an all-male executive, was planning a submission to the Province highlighting the erosion of faculty living standards and purchasing power during the recent spurt of inflation caused by the high oil prices of the early seventies. They thought the best plan was to urge the Province to make a special, onetime grant, earmarked for salaries, and designated as a catch-up effort.

Seizing the opportunity, the few women present at the meeting urged a similar request to remedy the effects of sex discrimination in rates of promotion and salary awards. We were told firmly that there was no discrimination in salaries at the University of Toronto, or (condescending concession) even if there were a *few* isolated cases, the faculty had to present a unified front. There could be no discussion of "side issues" in the faculty brief. I was still simmering the next morning when I got to my office in the Sidney Smith Building. Women faculty just weren't represented by their professional bodies. Idly, I picked up the Faculty Directory and began to count the number of women listed. There weren't many of them—just a few hundred outside the strongholds of nursing, social work, and food sciences.

Why not organize them? I called the room scheduling office, chose a date for a lunch-hour meeting two weeks away, typed out a call to a meeting of women faculty to discuss issues of common concern, stepped out to the Xerox machine, ran off 120 copies, got some friends to help stuff envelopes, and, when we dropped them in the University mail, the deed was done. On the appointed day about fifty women appeared, many carrying notes from friends who couldn't attend urging further meetings. The level of frustration with difficult to prove experiences of discrimination was near boiling point. When I told my story there were wry nods of agreement from the group. Everyone could match my experiences—and more than match them. When I said how exasperated I was with the Faculty Association's stance, there was a ripple of laughter. "I gave up going years ago," one woman said. "That's just a boy's network. We're invisible to them." The consensus was that most hard-pressed women faculty couldn't be bothered paying the annual dues to a group which refused to recognize women's professional concerns.

When the talk turned to what to do next, we quickly decided to make our own submission to the legislative committee considering University grants. The social scientists present wanted to base any comments we made on the subject of discrimination on hard data. But how to get hard data? "Let's just ask the central administration," I said. "They are probably waiting for someone to complain. They acted pretty quickly on my individual complaint." One of my new women colleagues in the History Department was a feisty British medievalist married to a good feminist husband. They had come as a team—he to be a senior administrator on one of the University's suburban campuses, and she to the History Department. She volunteered to relay the request through this impeccable line of communication.

To the astonishment of the action team designated at the meeting, the central administration cheerfully handed over the computer records of faculty salaries, and one of our statistical experts from the Psychology Department set about analyzing them. While there were no performance data to accompany them, the records showed a widening salary gap between male and female faculty over a lifetime career. At all ranks in all schools and faculties, salaries on initial hiring were routinely lower for women than for men, and slower rates of promotion contributed to the increasing differentials in pay over time. Some of my partners in the women faculty group fumed over the injustice revealed and wondered why the central administration hadn't corrected it. "Why should they make trouble for themselves with their deans and department chairs if the women themselves weren't complaining?" I asked. It made pragmatic sense for the central administration just to leave things be unless there was trouble.

Trouble was what surfaced when my colleagues made their presentation to the Legislature. On the scheduled day I was out of town, giving a lecture at another university, but my partners in crime told me they had been listened to attentively, asked a lot of questions, and promised that their brief would receive serious attention. The brief was a model of detached scholarly logic, using the data to suggest, not the fact of discrimination, but a likely presumption that bias was operative in bringing about this undeviating pattern of difference. We had labored diligently over the tone, language, and methodology of the submission, knowing that we were laying down a path for others to travel. A few days later we heard that the legislative committee had refused to vote the appropriations for the University of Toronto unless they were assured that there was a mechanism in place to correct the salary inequities revealed by the University's own salary data. Our group was met with tight-lipped hostility by our Faculty Association colleagues, but we'd made our point in a fashion calculated to grab the attention of the most sexist faculty politician.

Much of my readiness to settle down to enjoy a good faculty battle came from the splendid model John always provided me. He believed passionately that every faculty member should be a committed member of the university on whose faculty he or she served. He never complained about the dullness of faculty meetings, always alert to the broader educational issues involved in the most pettifogging faculty discussion. I'd watched in silent admiration while he led the successful faculty opposition to a presidential appointment at York which he thought would not serve the University well. He never seemed to heed the personal consequences of a good fight provided he was sure of the principles involved.

So it never crossed my mind that I was doing anything out of the ordinary when I began to pay close attention to the political process by which the University of Toronto Act was being revised in the Provincial Legislature. Because of our friendship with Stephen Graubard, editor of *Daedalus,* I'd participated in a number of studies sponsored by the Academy on the causes of turmoil on university campuses around the world in the late 1960s and early 1970s. As a result, I was better informed than the average faculty member about the conflicts and tensions which had disturbed the balance of academic communities across the world.

I saw the Vietnam War as the trigger for turmoil in the United States, but not the underlying cause, especially since the student rebellions in Germany, France, and Japan were as politically volatile, and as capable of producing as many *enragé* student leaders, as the student movement in the United States. I thought the sources of the problem lay in the content and style of academic instruction in the modern university. Training in critical reasoning was no immediate help to the Japanese students who were battling their society over environmental issues. They needed first a curriculum which would examine the human relationship with nature, and assess the changes in that relationship in modern times. Life in the large organization for the disciplined modern professional offered few opportunities for emotional growth, and the nihilism of most modern aesthetic expression compounded the problem. This was particularly difficult for my Canadian students, who wanted affirmations of what it meant to be Canadian, not training in the critical assessment of other cultures.

At the University of Toronto, President Bissell had tried to head off battles between the University's various constituencies by establishing a commission to examine the institution's governing structure. Halfway through the process, the Faculty Association had rejected the President's recommendations for faculty participation on the commission, and voted to select faculty representatives by direct election. The commission, not surprisingly, given the electoral process, finished up with a membership comprised of student political leaders, faculty who were deans or heads of existing university colleges, and smaller delegations of support staff and trustees. It was fascinating to watch this political process play itself out, to try to figure out where the tension points were within the institution and between the University and its external constituencies—government, community leaders, media, and, Canada being a society where organized labor mattered, unions and their leadership.

As this case study in academic politics unfolded before my eyes, David Riesman, one of Harvard's distinguished social scientists, and a trenchant analyst of social trends in education, asked me to write a chapter providing a Canadian comparison for a book he planned devoted to the social and political phenomenon of campus radicalism and institutional change in the United States. My curiosity reinforced by this assignment, I read my way through the many studies and group submissions made to the University of Toronto's Commission on University Governance, and then began to attend the legislative hearings at Queen's Park, at which interested parties could submit briefs to the Committee through which the Minister for University Affairs would bring forward a revised Act for the Governance of the University of Toronto.

At the hearings, it became clear that the Minister for University Affairs intended to sponsor legislation which would leave the faculty of the University in a minority position on a proposed single-governing body, which would combine the roles and responsibilities of Academic Senate and Board of Trustees. Moreover, with apparent logic, but little understanding of academic communities, the government planned that the faculty representation in the University's governance should be identical with that of the student delegation. The proposal was aimed at winning political capital among Ontario voters, among whom there was a growing belief that the growth of Canadian universities in the 1960s had led to the permanent appointment of large numbers of American, British, and European émigré faculty, none of whom were interested in issues of Canadian culture and national identity. Equal political power for students in university government might enable students to serve as watchdogs for their native tradition, and thus correct the unplanned consequences of worldwide recruiting for Canadian higher education. But, at the same time, it would place a youthful group of student activists, present on campus for a maximum of four years, in the same position to influence events as the faculty, the majority of whom would devote a lifetime to their discipline and to the University. Believing this division of power and responsibility an ill-designed mechanism to meet a cultural problem I recognized as real, I called my friend, Dorrie Dunlop, learned that her husband, Edward, would be attending a meeting of the Provincial cabinet that night, and asked if he would deliver a letter to the Minister and vouch for the good sense of the writer. Given an affirmative answer, I sped back to my office, summoned what powers of rhetoric I possessed, and laid out the reasons why I thought the Minister's proposal unwise.

As I pulled my letter from the typewriter, I decided I'd better check my arguments with the University Provost, just to make sure I wasn't undermining some carefully worked out compromise. There had been no behind-the-scenes agreement, he assured me. The University administration feared the worst. With that assurance, I grabbed my letter and raced off to leave it at my friendly emissary's Rosedale house. Later in the evening Dorrie called to assure me it had been personally delivered. When the proposed legislation came down a few days later, the faculty representation had been enlarged to secure a modest faculty majority. I would never know what effect my letter had, but I soon learned that the Provost was deeply impressed by my presence at the hearings and detailed knowledge of the issues. Later he told me that, to his knowledge, no other faculty member had sat through the hearings just as an interested observer, although the deliberations were likely to shape the future of the University where we all worked. When I explained that my interest came from the American Academy studies, and from David Riesman's assignment, we spent a lively hour arguing about the differences and similarities between Canadian and American campus radicalism. The Provost thought the New Left was a North American phenomenon, organized, like the unions, across national boundaries. I disagreed strenuously. I thought that issues of Canadian identity gave the New Left in Canada a unique flavor of Utopian sentiment.

Not all my political adventures won such approval. Nothing excited such volatile and irrational feelings among male faculty, administrators, and trustees as the issue of providing day care on the University campus, and subsidizing it for needy students and employees. Normally calm men would grow red in the face, and, voices quivering with emotion, ask why the taxpayer should assist women to meet their maternal duties. The University was in the business of teaching the young. It had exclusively academic responsibilities, and should not get in the business of arranging creative play for two-year-olds. When asked in return whether women paid taxes at the same rate as men did, and whether the state's intention was not to make education equally available to women as well as men, they would answer affirmatively, but instantly follow their "yes" with "and those women should have enough self-control not to get pregnant while they're studying. If they do, it's exclusively their problem." If one then listed the sizable number of happy fathers among our graduate students and teaching assistants—men who had not been obliged to abstain from procreation while students—the answer would be a dismissive sniff or the assertion that those men had wives at home doing what wives were supposed to be doing: caring for their children.

The subject kept presenting itself for discussion because the rising tide of the feminist movement kept carrying it into the press, and because campus and neighborhood women kept raising it through direct action. The University of Toronto was bordered to the south and west by a series of small, charming neighborhoods whose streets were lined with decaying but attractive houses of the late Victorian and Edwardian eras. Many blocks of these houses had been acquired by the Province, through the power of eminent domain, so that the area would be available for University expansion. As a result, the University was an inner-city landlord, renting to lower-income people and providing only marginal maintenance to houses that were eventually slated for demolition. But the attitudes of Toronto's Mayor and city government, and of inner-city residents, had changed since the acquisition of the properties. Now, in the early 1970s, popular opinion favored preserving inner-city housing, preventing urban sprawl, and designing innovative new uses for the existing built environment. Inner-city ratepayers associations had become politically active, and were dedicated to active political intervention wherever some fragment of Toronto's history could be preserved.

These political interests converged with those of neighborhood women, many of them University students or employees, who were intent on pressuring the University to provide day-care facilities for employees and students. Predictably, a group of day-care activists occupied one of the empty neighborhood houses illegally, and began providing day-care services. When the University threatened police action, and arrest of those involved for trespass, campus feminist groups were mobilized for the occupation of Simcoe Hall, the University's administrative building. One fine spring morning we arrived on campus to find banners floating from the windows of the Senate Chamber reading "Social Justice for the Under Two's," "Infants of the World Unite, You Have Nothing to Lose But Your Diapers," "Support Campus Daycare," "Women and Children Need University Services Too." Conservative male faculty were particularly irritated by the sight of the vans of two diaper services drawn up outside Simcoe Hall. The occupiers had brought along their infants and toddlers, and had cheerfully set up a day-care center in the University's august Senate Chamber.

Some of the students involved were enrolled in Natalie Davis's classes, and since rumors were flying that the police would be called to evict the occupiers, Natalie went to visit the sit-in, hoping she could learn the negotiating points which might produce a peaceful conclusion to the occupation, and concerned to see what standards of hygiene were being maintained for the infants and toddlers, who were innocent pawns in the political game. She came back to report an extremely orderly occupation. The chairs and tables used for Senate meetings had been carefully covered, and there was adequate refrigeration for supplies of milk and baby food. Nearby bathrooms seemed to be working well despite the heavy demands of the occupiers. The leaders would keep the occupation going until the University made some commitments to campus day care. She passed on her assessment to the administration, and hoped her visit and concern for everyone's well-being would prove constructive.

When I came into the History Department after lunch on the day of Natalie's visit, the place was a hive of political activity. People were gathered in small knots in the corridors. The buzz of conversation was punctuated with exclamations of astonishment and outrage. Checking in on the situation I learned that a group of senior faculty would propose a motion to censure Natalie, at the next day's Department meeting, for aiding and abetting illegal trespassers on University property. The all-male group had put a very different construction on Natalie's efforts at opening communication between the occupiers and the administration, and none accepted that a woman might be concerned about the health and hygienic arrangements for so many infants. It seemed obvious to everyone that her only purpose in visiting the sit-in could be to incite the occupants to further defiance.

I got out my list of Department members and checked off the people I thought I could persuade to vote against the proposed censure. I needed just more than a third of the voting members, since such a motion required a two-thirds majority. Plans for an afternoon at the library put to one side, I set about finding my votes. It wouldn't do to seem as angry as I felt. The best approach would be through mockery. "Come on. What's illegal about talking to the people we teach? Someone has to talk to them, and our administration doesn't seem willing to. Universities are supposed to operate through debate, remember. Talking's part of our business. Would you vote to censure someone for talking to a union picket? What's the difference? I can't believe you really want to see the Metro Police evicting all those crying babies. That's a major part of this dangerous demonstration. You ought to walk over and see for yourselves."

By evening I had my votes, and called Natalie to tell her any censure effort would be defeated. On my way into the office the next morning I stopped in to visit the demonstrators so that my colleagues would have to vote against me as well if they proceeded with the censure effort. In fact, it never came forward, because so many people had told the proponents they'd changed their minds. But I was grateful for the occasion that sent me calling on the demonstrators. The adults were two-thirds female, one-third male. The room was crowded and hot, although the makeshift nursery seemed to be functioning well. At its center, a small circle had been cleared where a presiding officer, something like the Speaker of the House of Commons, was regulating a debate, conducted in well-modulated voices, about the rights of children and the evils of capitalism, and of its core institution, monogamy. There was a dog-eared copy of *Roberts' Rules of Order* in the room, and the presiding officer seemed genuinely interested in making sure that all points of view among the floating population of students dropping in between classes were expressed. I was fascinated by the faces in the room. Everyone showed a level of concentration and intellectual excitement I rarely saw in a classroom. People had brought along political texts and volumes on child psychology to cite. Whether troubled and questioning, or engaged in the committed exposition of the ideologue, they were alive to ideas and concerned with community in ways that seemed to me to be quite different from the nihilism I associated with radical leadership in the United States. Like Natalie, I called the central administration and explained the steps I thought would lead to a peaceful evacuation. It came a few days later, but not before the carpet had been cleaned, the table set back in its usual place, and the chairs reinstated in their usual order. "We came to make a point, not to trash the place," their tall Amazon leader said as they pulled down their banners and departed. The key point in the peaceful departure was the administration's agreement to "consider" making campus day care available.

My first year of sabbatical leave from the University of Toronto in 1971–72 gave me the opportunity to disengage from academic politics and think again. John was also on leave that year, so we had an opportunity to create a new structure of work and reflection together. I traded my office in the Sidney Smith Building for one in an old commercial building at College and Spadina, a good hike to the southwest of the campus. Its top floor was still occupied by a family of Russian furriers whose black overcoats, polite smiles, and burdens of opulent pelts were a striking change of company in the elevator from my jeans-clad humanities building colleagues.

John traded his office on the main York campus for one closer to home. Each week as we learned to slow down we read aloud to one another more, listened to more music, talked more about subjects that had always been deferred until there was time for them. We also worked hard on creating the right pattern of life for John's physical health. Just after we began our leave and I had more time to observe John's recurrent fevers, sore throats, and bouts of shivering, we began to insist to his physician that something more serious was wrong with him than the recurrent neurotic cold that was regularly diagnosed. Persistence paid off when it turned out that he had chronic malaria, a disease contracted on a trip to Iran a decade before, and now difficult to eradicate. Few physicians in the postwar era could recognize tropical diseases, and it was mostly my memories of malaria sufferers returning from the Pacific war in my childhood that led us to the Toronto Institute of Tropical Medicine and a correct diagnosis. It startled me that we literally needed time to observe one another daily to be able to register the serious problems of health or happiness that busyness obscures.

In my office in the furrier's building the pile of manuscript for the volume I'd contracted to write on urbanization and its impact on women in America began to grow at a comfortable pace, and, blessing beyond words, I could sit all morning reading in my spacious, sunny office in the creaky old building without being interrupted by the phone ringing. The only sounds were of the occasional heated discussion in Russian on the floor above, and the clanging of the street cars on College Street. I met friends who wanted to talk about writing and ideas at a variety of delectable ethnic restaurants a stone's throw from my new quarters. There was a Szechwan-style Chinese restaurant a few blocks south where the food was delicious, and a little to the west was a café where they spoke only Portuguese, a place where I could indulge in my favorite Iberian delicacies. Better still, I could leave for the office very early in the morning, and meet John for a long leisurely lunch, with time for each of us to discuss the morning's work, tell stories about the past, or laugh over the cherished idiosyncracies that become woven into the fabric of a long life together.

Natalie and I met regularly to plan a course on the history of women from early modern times to the present, she taking the time period to the eighteenth century, while I dealt with the nineteenth and twentieth centuries. The main themes were to be developed from the concepts historians used to explain the contours of society in any period: class, urbanization, professionalization, demography, the institution of the family, sexuality. Over happily argumentative lunches we mapped out a yearlong course, and discussed the documents and texts students should read. Every document had to show a woman speaking about her time; some of the texts could be revivals of out-of-print materials from earlier periods, when women's lives were studied seriously. It felt luxurious to have the time for such careful plans, and it was sheer pleasure to push one another to think through the concepts which should organize a course in history that drew from the historical record women had left, and which took its periodization not from the established one drawn from a male experience but from the trends that had affected women's lives. So many efforts at telling the history of women's lives made them a simple addition to the male narrative. People wrote about "women and the American Revolution," or "French women in the Age of Reason." It was much more important to think about a chronology that took into account the real changes and continuities in women's experience. So, for instance, when eighteenth-century Americans decided to let their sons and daughters marry on the basis of affection and affinity, rather than treating marital unions as economic arrangements between families, this was an indicator of a major change in American society, one part of which involved no longer seeing women as items for barter in economic exchange. Such a departure marked a new era in women's experience of their sexuality, and was in its context as profound a social revolution as the political changes of 1776.

Life reached an important marking point in the spring when John's father died in ripe old age. The two men had managed a life of love and friction, in which each craved but could not manage deep communication with the other. Sometimes we can only see our parents clearly when their lives are seen in the round, at their conclusion. So it seemed with John and his father. We spent an early spring in Vancouver sharing memories with John's sisters and their families, taking the time for me to meet many of John's childhood friends. Since my father had been an orphan, and my mother the child of a family whose members had scattered across Australia as soon as age and the capacity to support themselves allowed, the large Conway family gatherings centered around the four devoted siblings had a fairy-tale quality for me. I liked counting up the array of nieces and nephews, tracing the genetic links between them all, observing the large velvety brown Conway eyes and strong roman nose in so many male and female variations. I also liked seeing the way John and his sisters had banded together as a family generation, sharing an approach to life and a degree of verbal virtuosity that left all their partners in life looking on in amused appreciation. I often tried to imagine what it would be like to face life from within a tightly knit cohort of siblings, to share some of the feelings of a tribe.

I thought of the Conways ruefully as I paid the duty visit to my mother made possible by a year of leave. She was once again settled in one of her pretty North Shore houses in Sydney, set among the flowers only she knew how to grow so luxuriantly. She lived as completely in the past as ever, though she still showed her usual business acumen. Her rages were as sudden and violent, and her jealousy that her children had formed other bonds in life was undiminished. After a perfunctory inquiry about John's health, and an even more perfunctory one about my professional life, she acted as though I were her unmarried child, still dependent financially and emotionally on her powerful maternal resources. No amount of conversational legerdemain, or swiftly executed pirouettes around a subject that involved spouses, marriage, careers, and life in other countries, could divert her from this stubborn course. I wondered whether a team of amused children might have managed a collective confrontation resulting in a different course, but as the sole member of my generation trapped in this dyad, I felt exposed. I contented myself with what I took to be the surface activities of checking on her finances, always soundly and conservatively managed; her health, always better than she maintained; and the house, in excellent repair—and spent sunny hours in the garden pruning roses under her eagle eye, and counting the days until I could set out for home.

But we never live only on the surface of things, and a few days before I left I astonished myself by an eruption of near psychotic rage, so primal, it must have come from the deepest recesses of my psyche. My mother lay, as was her custom in the afternoons, resting on a sofa in the glass-enclosed room which looked out on the lyrically beautiful garden. An elaborate rockery, a picture of the rock gardener's art, bloomed just beside the shallow steps leading from the back door into the tranquil beds of flowers. The picture inside was in marked contrast. Food had become a near anorexic obsession with my mother, her skimpy diet, smoking, and steady consumption of alcohol rendering her face and body skeletal, like the starving animals that had haunted me from a drought-stricken country childhood.

I was just back from a flying visit to my brother and his family, and I was worried about them. They didn't seem happy, and although nothing was said to indicate the sources of tension, the set, closed-down expression on my brother's face as he said good-bye had stayed with me. It hurt to see him worried about what must be more than the usual financial pressures of a young and growing family. Here, on this Sydney afternoon, my mother was indulging in her customary monologue about her wish to see the marriage end. Her jealousy of anyone who replaced her in her children's affections made her full of malice, and her self-involvement meant that she hadn't the slightest concern for her son's happiness. I knew she talked in the same way to others about me. All she wanted was to regain her power over her children. Something in me snapped momentarily. She was evil. I had to end her power for harm now. My eye lit on the rocks outside. There was the weapon. It would be a matter of seconds to smash that skull protruding so clearly through her emaciation.

Civilization reasserted itself. I got up and left the room. It would be better not to come alone again—ever. I couldn't handle this woman's capacity to make objects of those around her. Turning living, breathing people into lifeless objects to be possessed was the ultimate sin and my rage at it in my mother was so overwhelming that I was losing control. Later, in the miraculous calm which descended when my plane took off from Sydney, I realized my rage was for myself, too. I was just as much an object to my mother—my life since leaving home nonexistent. The outrageous insensitivity to my brother and his family had simply given me permission to feel what I wasn't conscious of on my own behalf.

I arrived home in Toronto, shaky, off-balance, unable to

sleep. If I took a sleeping pill, it would lock me in dreams in which I was repetitively battering my mother's frail and emaciated body. Finally, explaining my dilemma to a sympathetic John, I gave up trying to sleep. Over the long nights before sleep came, I read my way through twelve volumes of Proust. The leisurely pace and monumental detachment of *À la Recherche du Temps Perdu* were the perfect remedy for my tornado of the psyche. When the storm was over it had passed for good.

I was soon deep in preparation for the fall semester and the delights of teaching the new course Natalie and I were offering on the history of women. We had expected a hundred undergraduates in History 348, but the actual enrollment was over two hundred, and the larger lecture hall we secured was always crowded with a sizable contingent of graduate students and faculty auditors. The word had got around that History 348 was the most intellectually exciting course on campus, and the lectures were highly charged events. Neither of us ever got through our prepared lecture, since we encouraged people to interrupt with questions. There were some protests from the female majority in the course about having to deal in a mixed-sex group with issues of sexuality or female response to domination, subjects about which women were trained not to speak. There were many different schools of feminism represented in the audience, including some extreme radicals who wanted to exclude men altogether.

We solved this problem by scheduling an extra all-female discussion section, and leaving the regular lecture hours and discussions open to all comers. As the undergraduates realized that many of the intent listeners and questioners were faculty from other schools and disciplines, their attitudes to learning changed. Seeing other people attending voluntarily, to learn, made them think about the course as more than just "credit hours." Soon there were no more complaints about the amount of reading required, and the tutors reported that the tutorial discussions were hot and heady with excitement. Students brought friends to the tutorials because they were so interested in the material they'd read and already discussed heatedly in their homes and residence halls. What fascinated everyone was that we were showing that an historical narrative could be constructed using the records created by so-called inarticulate women, and that to use these records suggested profound questions of reinterpretation for the standard chronology and periodization of the past. "What excites me," I heard a woman student say to a group of her friends walking ahead of me to class, "is that I'm seeing myself as the subject of history. That means I can change it if I like."

Early that same fall I began chairing a new standing committee of the Canadian Association of University Teachers on the status of women in the academic professions. The national body had a professional staff which was far more liberal than the local leadership of faculty associations, and far more attuned to questions of bias because of the tenure and appointment disputes in which they were regularly involved. This assignment allowed me to export to other parts of Canada the approach and methods the women's group at the University of Toronto had used to highlight problems of bias in promotion and salaries. Now I had the weight of the national professional association behind me, with a staff which could help and advise women's groups on other campuses as they began their own investigations. For most situations, it was clear that, from now on, it wouldn't be necessary to appeal to the Legislature to ventilate issues of discrimination. The lesson of the University of Toronto's experience had been a striking one. The Ontario Legislature was still waiting to hear how the University of Toronto proposed to eliminate sex bias from its salary structure before it would sign off on the year's appropriation. A few written inquiries from the staff of the Canadian Association of University Teachers to universities in other provinces usually prompted the central administration to conduct its own study, and seek advice from the Association about acceptable mechanisms for remedying the effects of sex bias.

My colleagues on the committee were senior faculty from universities across the country, and their conversation around the edges of meetings transformed my sense of the country from a regional to a national one. Their friendship gave me an academic network I'd not had before, one that was outside a group of specialized historians. So what began as a fairly parochial concern with my own institution grew into a set of national concerns. The cases of bias we heard about were far more striking than any I'd experienced, and they set me thinking about my feminist concerns in a larger context. Why was bias against women so strong in the academic world? How could it be addressed without creating an even stronger, more covert pattern of hostility? Did it exist because universities had grown out of celibate male religious communities? Or was there something more fundamental at work, I didn't as yet understand. The easy answer was to adopt the formula already becoming a catchphrase in the popular feminist movement and make bias against women inherent in patriarchal institutions. But that didn't satisfy me. There had been times in the patriarchal West when women had been free to create knowledge, and those counterinstances were too frequent to make the general explanation very satisfying. I wanted to know *why* the modern university had developed its particular form of hostility.

This combination of absorbing teaching and instructive new professional duties seemed a full and lively set of assignments, completely occupying my attention until my mind was jogged about the University of Toronto by a call from the President's office. During my absence on leave a new President, John Evans, had been installed at the University, and he wanted to see me. I noted the time of the appointment in my schedule, and thought no more about it. I'd been critical of many aspects of the University's previous leadership, and didn't expect that the search committee would have come up with a real departure from the past. The new President was an alumnus, a former Rhodes Scholar, and someone highly regarded as an innovative and socially responsible reformer in medical education. As an Australian, I'd always thought the Rhodes Scholarship the kiss of death for any promise of future creativity. Rhodes Committees in Australia picked the perfect cookie-cutter version of upright colonial manhood, and passed over the people with rebellious imaginations or critical minds. I assumed the selection process worked the same way in Canada. I didn't expect much of medical doctors either, since the medical profession in North America represented one of the most conservative social and political groups in the country.

The appointment was rescheduled for mid-October, so that by the time I went to keep my appointment with President Evans, my head was so filled with all these new tasks and interests that it took me a while to grasp what the meeting was about. John Evans was in the process of building his new administrative team and, to my astonishment, he wanted my advice about it. He was planning to structure his new administration around the five standing committees of the newly legislated Governing Council, the single body which had replaced the old Senate and the former Board of Trustees. There would be the traditional committees—on Academic Affairs (previously the preserve of the academic Senate), Finance, and External Relations and Alumni Affairs—and two new committees—with mandates for the oversight of the University's internal community, and its planning and institutional research function. He thought there should be a vice presidential appointment concerned with Internal Affairs, because the internal climate of universities was so tempestuous at the moment. Every day there were fresh reports of student riots on American campuses. And these had their counterparts in France, Germany, and Japan. The problem was that the demands of running an institution the size of the University of Toronto usually pushed issues of internal relations to one side. He wanted to appoint a strong person at the most senior rank in the University to ensure that relations with faculty, students, and employees stayed at the center of everyone's attention. I'd written about the climate at the University of Toronto, and the tensions leading up to the development of the new governing structure. What did I think of the idea? Would it work?

I felt the academic's instant panic at being presented with a practical problem—I was only trained to analyze what events meant after they happened. But it was flattering to be asked to apply what I knew to the present. I said that the plan might work if the new vice president was viewed as a serious academic, and not one of the scholars manqué who usually ended up in the student affairs side of universities. I thought there would be three major sources of disaffection within Canadian universities in the decade ahead. The feminist movement was not a fleeting phenomenon, and women students would continue to exert pressure for equal status and for an equal claim on the resources of academic institutions. The New Left critique of capitalism would make universities a logical target for demonstrations which could generate publicity, and win recruits whenever the response was heavy-handed or could be construed as repressive. Young Canadians cared passionately about sustaining and strengthening Canadian culture, and would be harshly critical of universities they thought unwilling to foster Canadian studies and recruit Canadian scholars. Whatever form the troubles took I thought the University would do better to try to manage them internally, rather than relying on police riot squads and much-publicized arrests.

Observing my interviewer as I talked, I had to admit I'd been wrong in all my earlier expectations. The Canadian Rhodes Scholarship Committee had clearly chosen well in John Evans's year. There was none of the fake British stuffiness about him that I found so trying in Australian Rhodes Scholars. Tall, energetic, and athletic, he talked wittily, with an elegant turn of phrase, and an occasional mordant self-mockery which was very disarming. Although he'd only been on the job a few months, I was surprised by his intimate knowledge of the place, the province, and the possibilities waiting to be realized in Canadian intellectual and scholarly life. He might be a medical doctor, member of a conservative profession, but he was clearly a most unusual one, with a powerful and highly original intellect.

As the meeting wound up we agreed that I'd provide him with a list of the people I thought he should consider for the new position, and a list of some of the issues I thought might be on the new appointee's agenda. I left feeling energized by the conversation. Earlier in my life I had dreamed about the political vibrancy of an Australian society which somehow managed to retain the energies of the talent lost in the brain drain to better-equipped and more competitive academic institutions elsewhere. Marriage and the move to Canada had set that dream aside. But the same problem existed in Canada. Perhaps this man was the kind of leader who could make that happen for Toronto? If so, I knew I was going to enjoy watching the dream fulfilled, in the place I now called home. I tried to imagine a situation in which it wasn't necessary to say to my brightest fourth-year students who came to consult me about graduate study, "Well, of course, you've got to get away. The big question is whether you want to go to England or the United States." A few years later, whatever the choice, the flood of letters would arrive about whether or not to come back, and in most cases, like my own, some other society captured the energy, the dreams, and the will to make them happen.

Although I thought of myself as a mature professional, with aspirations to make a difference in the scholarly profession in which I worked, it had never entered my mind that I had any talent for running things. My life had expanded suddenly because I'd moved from advancing my own career to thinking about other women like myself. And I'd grown bored with the internal politics of my little world of historians; I had started concerning myself with the affairs of the university where I worked. I came by that perspective quite naturally. I was married to a man a generation older than I, whose daily life was absorbed by similar concerns, and I lived them with him. But although I freely offered him advice about his role, my training as a woman meant that, even as I celebrated my thirty-seventh birthday, and knew I was a mature adult, I never saw myself as a potential candidate for major administrative responsibility comparable to my husband's. So when, at our next meeting, John Evans told me he thought I'd be the best person for the job, I was utterly dumbfounded. I said I'd think about it, and went back to my office to try to digest this turn of events.

"That man's out of his mind," I told John over dinner that evening. "He thinks I'd be a good candidate for the Internal Affairs job we've been talking about. I've never run anything in my life."

John was amused at my astonishment. "He's not crazy. Just very smart. You love to run things and you do it very well. You'd be good at the job."

When I listed all the reasons not to accept the invitation— the book I was working on, my scholarly career, the time commitment which would encroach on our life together— John dismissed them one by one. "You can write a book at any stage of your life. This is an opportunity which will teach you a lot you might not otherwise learn. You aren't only a scholar. You need a life of action, too. We aren't the usual married couple. I believe in this kind of service to academic institutions for you as well as for me. If you want to do it, we'll manage about the time involved."

I knew I was just hitting my stride as an historian. I thought about the growing group of graduate students I wouldn't be able to work with as closely. Beside it I placed the outside chance that, by changing my life, I could help make an institution, which served as a model for the rest of Canada and its leadership, become aware of the ways in which it shortchanged women as faculty and students. I thought about the potential energy such a change might release. And then there was the prospect that a rich province of the old British Empire might be persuaded to create an institution so strong that the most original and powerful Canadian minds could grow and flourish within it. The significant observation, the great creative insight, might not have to be pursued elsewhere. It was a difficult choice.

"Besides," John said, "it's a tough job running universities these days. That man needs help, and you ought to give it to him. You can have a private life another day."

I was convinced. A day or two later I stopped by Simcoe Hall and, after satisfying myself that the head of the new administrative team had a real, not token, commitment to equality for women, signed on for a three-year term in charge of Internal Affairs. We never even discussed the rank of the appointment, because it didn't occur to me. I just assumed that because of my age and very recent promotion I'd be a vice provost or some similar designation. It wasn't until I saw the docket for the December meeting of the Governing Council that it registered that the President was sticking to his plan of making the post a vice presidential one. When the University News Office called up to schedule an appointment to help them prepare a news release, I was frantically busy trying to get into shape the paper I was to present at the coming month's Annual Meeting of the American Historical Association, so I tried to satisfy them by offering to send a detailed curriculum vitae. "You don't understand," the genial voice on the other end of the phone explained, "you're the first woman to hold vice presidential rank at the University—and that's *news*." When the University photographer showed up at my home that evening to take the photograph to accompany the story, it began to dawn on me what I'd just done.

12.

LEARNING ON THE JOB

When I arrived at my new office on the second floor of Simcoe Hall on January 2, 1973, to officially take up the job I'd actually begun to perform back in November, after agreeing to the appointment, the newness of my place in the scheme of things was comically expressed by the furniture in the room. It looked like a furniture store. Two large desks, two commanding black desk chairs, several sofas and occasional chairs, and assorted filing cabinets were jumbled haphazardly about the room. Clearly two different sets of orders had been issued to the Physical Plant Department to equip the new office, and the bureaucratic result was a room so crammed one had to sidle in the door and squeeze past the furniture to get to the telephone sitting on the floor, already ringing insistently.

The nervous-looking temporary secretary who arrived shortly thereafter surveyed the chaotic room. "Just make a list of the phone calls," I told her. "Your job for the day is to get one set of furniture moved out." I was already on my way out the door to teach a class when she raced into the hall after me with a question: "Which set do you want taken away?" "I don't care," I said, laughing. "You decide."

The furniture-littered room was symbolic of some of the problems of the institution I was about to take part in running. The University of Toronto had grown rapidly through the previous two decades, including the opening of two new suburban campuses. The enrollment in its fifty-three faculties and schools rivaled those of some of the giant flagship campuses of American state university systems. In the process of growth it had acquired a bloated and entrenched bureaucracy, and since the level of public funding had been steadily rising, the financial side of the organization had tended to take over the management of the campus, while presidents and provosts struggled with the recruitment and staffing of burgeoning new schools and faculties. Like many Canadian universities, its nonacademic administration had provided a comfortable home for retired British army officers and former colonial administrators, men (for there were almost no women) who carried with them the attitudes of their formative years. They were philistines, believers in hierarchy and discipline, embodying the concern for bureaucratic procedure which had been the bane of the old British Empire in its waning years.

The tasks of building and expanding had been the primary ones, while the institution's relationship with the Province of Ontario, which provided just over 80 percent of its operating funds, and 85 percent of its capital needs, had been primarily taken up with the development of a system of formula funding, which favored expansion in graduate education and provided little leeway for program improvement in undergraduate education. Some faculties, such as Medicine, and some departments in the Faculty of Arts and Sciences, such as Political Economy, a uniquely Canadian blend of politics and economics, met a world standard of achievement. Many more stood at the pinnacle of Canadian excellence, but others merely filled out the expected roster of any university curriculum. The principal barrier to achievement had been access to funds for research and instrumentation, and the problems of managing growth. There were inherent tensions in Toronto's relationship with the Province, because the political process of allocating capital funds for universities set Toronto at odds

with the other provincial universities, and ministers and senior civil servants could become exasperated with Toronto's
claim to be the prime center for graduate study, with its ac-
companying richer grants.

One consequence of the poorly planned growth was a fairly
gritty urban campus with too few intervals of green tranquillity, and no space for sociability, save for the old central campus. There the Victorian bulk of University College looked
across a verdant circle of green to Simcoe Hall, a graceful
building housing the central administration, and Convocation
Hall, the University's major ceremonial auditorium and
meeting space. The buildings completing the circle around the
inner green were statements of past priorities. They were the
library, already swamped by student numbers, the Medical
School, the neo-Gothic Knox College, a Presbyterian theolog-
ical school, and the discreet modern shape of the campus
bookstore and the University of Toronto Press. Campus
bookstores might be in back alleys elsewhere, but the Press
symbolized the University of Toronto's responsibility for giving expression to Canadian culture, a nonprofit beacon
against the commercialism of American publishing.

This charming core was dwarfed by the sprawling periphery of blank city streets, parking lots, and mediocre buildings.
The place of women within the institution could be instantly
understood by the ample and stately space assigned male sociability and recreation at Hart House, an elegant and stately
neo-Gothic building overlooking the green tranquillity of the
central campus, and the utilitarian redbrick women's athletic
building, set on a side street, providing a fraction of the Hart
House space for a female student body about the same size as
the male.

The campus mood in 1973 went with the history of expansion. Many faculty were relatively recent arrivals hired to
cope with the growing student enrollment, which had reached
forty thousand on the downtown campus. A sizable number
were Americans, who simply assumed they were living in a
province of the society centered on New York and Washing-

ton. The sprawling urban campus couldn't convey to new arrivals what the old University, with its cluster of denominational colleges and its small cadre of professional schools, had been like. Then there had been a real faculty community. The older, all-male faculty world had hummed with sociability around Hart House, the college common rooms, and the comfortable houses of faculty, mostly within easy walking distance of the campus. By the time the era of expansion came, faculty couldn't afford housing close to the campus. People commuted long distances. Some didn't even respect the Oxbridge traditions so cherished by an earlier generation, which liked to see itself as embodying the same distrust of the social sciences, scorn for graduate education, and conscious elitism which they'd learned at Oxford or Cambridge. Office buildings and classrooms were crowded, libraries and laboratories inadequate for the numbers to be taught. Tempers were shorter and manners cooler than in the past.

The student body of the early 1970s had two novel components. There were some 4,500 graduate students, evidence of the University's new role as producer of the doctorates needed for Canada's expanding universities, who lived in poor housing near the campus, lacked facilities for sociability, and served more and more as the underpaid course assistants for Toronto's larger and larger undergraduate courses. Then there were the American exiles, young men escaping the draft because of their unwillingness to serve in the Vietnam War, radical, alienated, searching for ways to politicize the Canadian universities they took to be just like their own.

There were also points of tension in the University of Toronto's public relations, because, in an era of growing populism and concern with democratic versions of Canada's national identity, it was seen as the educator of the city's and the Province's old elites. Its relationship with the city government was perpetually strained by its building programs, every additional square foot of which took dollars from the city tax rolls. Each effort at new and needed facilities was progressively more and more in conflict with urban reformers interested in preserving existing housing, and retaining the integrity of old neighborhoods, to sustain a vital residential core in the inner city.

John Evans and his new team wanted to change all this—dismantle the bureaucracy, manage the campus in the interests of its students and faculty, be a better corporate citizen in the inner city, work more cooperatively with the other universities in the Province, and build the University's capacity to support research, so that the brilliant scholar would remain in Canada, to add luster and new knowledge to its embattled national culture. Some of these objectives were at odds with one another, but John Evans, a skilled and visionary executive, planned to release energy and promote a creative synthesis of objectives through a highly collegial style of decision making. While everyone on the administrative team had a specific portfolio of responsibilities, the group met weekly to discuss all key decisions, so that actions in one area didn't frustrate initiatives in another, and to ensure that there was a rough working consensus on the handling of contentious issues. For a novice, it was possible to sit at these weekly meetings and be instructed in every aspect of managing a complex academic organization, including its relationships to its external constituencies.

Everyone looked forward to these weekly meetings. The issues were endlessly fascinating, and the information absorbed invaluable, but the most enjoyable part was to listen to the President sum up, and provide the prescription for action on the issue of the moment. He did this with such incisive wit, vivid imagery, practical insight into organizational and political behavior, and genuine concern for a collaborative style of action that the group was amused, instructed, and encouraged to surrender petty jealousies. He was unselfconsciously patriotic, and looked at the issues facing Canadian universities from a national point of view. Most visionary leaders lack the skill and application to focus on the details necessary to translate the vision into reality. John Evans had both sets of skills to a remarkable degree, so that working on his team became a concentrated seminar on both the style and substance of leadership.

It took me a little while to adjust to the pace at which my life changed. An academic's life is busy, but usually on a schedule she or he can control. It allows time for quiet reflection and for periods of study, interspersed with the busyness of people, lectures, papers, publication deadlines, and hours devoted to counseling students. I had always thought myself expending my full complement of energy on these satisfying activities, endlessly diverting and delightful because of the pleasure of coming to new ideas and insights, and because of the quirky originality of generations of students. Now every waking hour in an eighteen-hour day was allocated, from my first meeting at eight in the morning till I finished dictating the day's correspondence and memos sometime after midnight. Every thirty minutes or so I had to focus on a new subject, and often make a decision about it without the usual careful and exhaustive study that is the core of an academic's life.

Used to giving texts close attention, I quailed before the volume of the day's mail. Some things had to be skimmed, others quickly handed on to subordinates. In time I came to select the three or four issues I would expend most of my energy on, leaving others to what I thought of as housekeeping, given a routine level of maintenance activity, while the attention is elsewhere. Not a gregarious person, I now lived my entire life in meetings.

The cast of characters on any given day could be mind-boggling. I might start out mediating the battle between the wrestling coach and the Director of Athletics, listen to the tragic complaints of some hapless faculty member denied tenure, meet a wide-eyed delegation of students certain that their plans for a campus center would usher in the millennium, talk to the Dean of Nursing (convinced that the only woman member of the central administration would respect her school) about where her faculty should fit in the University's priorities, move on to a meeting with architects about new athletic facilities, worry over budgets and staffing for student services, and end the day with a delegation of cleaning women complaining about sexual harassment. It was a little like having a ringside seat at a daily serial drama, except that I had to do something about each installment.

Some groups had unrealistic expectations of the first woman in the University's senior administration. Feminist groups expected me to wave a wand and provide the money for an entire new department of Women's Studies, complete with the necessary library collections and freely available day care. The more utopian among them also expected that at the same time I would bring about the dismissal of a third of the male faculty so that women scholars could be appointed in their place. Women faculty hoped I would remedy the salary inequity our ad hoc group of women faculty had revealed to the Legislature in the closing year of the previous administration. The change of leadership had been used to buy time to rectify the problem, but it was now squarely on the new administration's agenda. Many expected that, by some magic associated with my mere presence, the institution would begin to hire more women scholars. Junior male faculty denied tenure were confident a woman would have more heart than the formal University procedures allowed, and that I would instantly be swayed by the merits of their case. These aspirations I more or less expected. What I hadn't bargained for was that the people who'd been invisible to me before— women administrators, secretaries, lab technicians, researchers appointed on soft money, cleaning women, career counselors—all had the same kind of hopes. The association of lesbians and homosexual men (the word *gay* had not yet entered common speech) hoped I'd attend their social functions. So did the just-formed group of witches—spawned by the conservatism of Toronto's cluster of schools of theology. In the past, I'd been a socially conservative woman with some radical ideas about equality for the only world I knew, the world of working professionals. Each day on the job was a lesson in the functioning of political and sexual hierarchies and the attitudes which upheld them in occupations and areas of society I'd never thought about.

Preoccupied as I was with my university world, I was startled to discover that I was also a symbol for legions of other women. Before I learned to ration the time, my dinner and lunchtime calendar filled up with commitments to speak to unions of women schoolteachers, business and professional women's associations, women's athletic associations, women journalists, guidance counselors, women lawyers, trades-union women, Catholic women, conventions of every occupation remotely concerned with education. I'd never thought of myself as a resource before, but each time I talked to a wildly enthusiastic group of women, or a mixed audience in which the women members radiated excitement and enthusiasm, I came to see that the mere symbol of an office in a formerly male hierarchy assumed a meaning which went way beyond my personal identity. Without planning to I'd become a public person.

Every woman who is the first to enter a new occupation, or who is one of a tiny minority, knows she mustn't make the smallest mistake, in work or dress or deportment, not just on her own account, but out of responsibility to those who'll come after her. But now I had a larger audience than simply my professional colleagues. These audiences all wanted to know the same thing: How to make it in a man's world? What was the secret? How had I gotten to be where I was? What do you do to make the men around you listen to you? How are you going about changing things? Often, my questioners just wanted to see someone in the flesh on whom to project their own aspirations. Sometimes the bright faces would look anxious. Then the personal questions would come. Was I happily married? Did I have children? Did I ever get tired? How did I manage my time? Did my house ever get dirty? What did I do if someone in my family got sick?

Over time, the accumulated experience of answering all these questions made me look back at my family and childhood, to see what was exemplary about them. How *did* I learn to manage time? The answer was simple. I had only to recall my mother's flawless management of two or three people's jobs on Coorain, my family's remote sheep station in the Australian outback. She'd managed to be cook, laundress, baker, dressmaker, gardener, schoolteacher, housecleaner, and bookkeeper on the station, all without the slightest sign of hurry, and she'd always set aside two or three hours in the day for reading. Did I ever get tired? The answer was almost never. I could see my mother's quick, vibrant step, and my father's delighted smile at a piece of work well done, a practical problem solved, something well managed. They had been people of enormous, driving energy, visibly thriving on work, joyful about what they were doing. My energy was in my genes, nourished by my childhood, and unsapped by ambiguity about what I was doing as an adult. The problems that prompted the invariable question about energy came from the conflicts about work versus domestic responsibilities in the urban world, and the guilt about having domestic help, induced first by the uniquely North American child-study movement and then by feminists who hadn't been able to imagine well-paid and dignified work in the household. Both kinds of guilt did sap working women's energy, as did the spoken or unspoken messages of husbands who were jealous of their wives' time involved with others.

It was easy to meet some of the expectations. It didn't take too long to educate the conservatives on the Governing Council that the taxpayer was not getting a good return on the money spent on educating women if the women could only devote half their attention to study because of perpetual worries about child care. Once that proposition was accepted, it was only a matter of dealing with the prejudice which insisted that women who chose professions and careers should forgo childbearing until the conclusion of their formal education. Given the statistics about the numbers of male lawyers, doctors, engineers, and graduate students who married while their education was in process, and asked why women alone should be required not to reproduce during their student years, most gave their reluctant assent.

For many years pressure on available space had been given as the reason for not providing a University child-care center. As soon as the need moved to the top in priority, there was more than adequate space. Once space was assigned, some of my long-suffering staff had to exercise the patience of Job and the wisdom of Solomon mediating between the conflicting philosophies of child care among different University groups. Nonetheless, the building conversion went forward, a staff was hired, and after that, one of the pleasures of walking past the site off St. George Street was the sound of children playing and the kaleidoscope of brightly colored jungle gyms and toys which decorated the play area.

In a budget the size of the University of Toronto's, then about $125 million, it was also no major problem to find the money necessary to eradicate the effects of bias on the pay of women faculty. There were so very few of them, just 340 out of 2,380 full-time faculty. It was a more complex task to figure out how to make the adjustments by a process which all concerned, male and female, could accept as based on merit. The social scientist who had helped our women's ad hoc group analyze the University's salary data came up with the solution. Every woman faculty member should be asked to assign herself a male peer from within her department or a related one. The choice should be regardless of rank, and based upon an assessment of teaching, research, and professional service activities. Department chairmen should also be asked to assign a peer ranking to all women faculty in their department, again without reference to rank and reflecting the same criteria. Where the woman and her Department Chairman agreed, there could be an automatic adjustment of any existing salary differential. Where they did not agree, an activity analysis questionnaire was administered to the woman and her male colleagues of the same rank, and to whatever individual she chose as her equal in performance. The results of all this peer ranking were then coded, to preserve the confidentiality of all involved, and the coded data were then reviewed by a committee made up of male deans, an associate provost, and a group of senior faculty. The exercise was so painstaking, no one could quibble about the results. In a surprising number of cases, the woman faculty member and her chairman selected the same peer. The undervaluation of the woman's work had not been conscious. People just hadn't been asked to think about the matter seriously before. In more than half the cases where there was a difference of opinion in the peer assessment, the review group made substantial adjustments. These were the cases in which it was safe to assume that there was genuine, conscious bias at work.

I was a disappointment to the feminist proponents of Women's Studies. I thought it a basic error in strategy to allow those, almost exclusively women, who wanted to study women's experience to be driven out of the core disciplines of the humanities and social sciences, segregated in a separate underfunded department without sponsors in the expense allocation process of the university, and so swamped with students that their research output could often not be competitive with more traditional faculty. This led to what I thought of as specious ideologies about "feminist" or excessively nurturant teaching styles as a justification for less real research. Overly nurturant teaching, from which all overt criticism has been removed, seemed to me to run the same danger for the young as permissive child rearing, because both obfuscate the nature of power and thus limit the possibility of rebellion. I didn't think it was possible to get around the fact that the relationship between teacher and student had been and would remain an asymmetrical one. The asymmetry could always be reduced by showing courtesy and respect for the less powerful member of the learning team, but I didn't think courtesy and respect were sex-linked characteristics. It was true that much rudeness and harassment of students was allowed to pass under the guise of the Socratic method, but there was no biological imperative about that. I'd met a fair share of hectoring women teachers in my time.

I was also something of a curricular conservative, believing that people needed a firm grounding in a single discipline before they became involved in more eclectic, interdisciplinary work. Given the choice, I would have put money into funding research about women, fostering the careers of conventional scholars who were interested in studying the female experience, and, over time, achieve a slow cumulative effect on the mainstream of scholarship. One couldn't legislate a change of heart, or a new set of research interests among self-regulating professional scholars, but I thought the incentive of research funding, and the career enhancements it provided, would exert a steering effect.

My views didn't fit the contemporary desire for an instant alternative curriculum, and within the next decade scholarship about women became a thriving collective enterprise, although mainstream departments tended to appoint their token woman and continue with their previous agenda of business, disregarding the broader questions raised by research which took women's experience, rather than men's, as normative. No matter how strong the performance of separate women's studies programs, it was basic research that was most needed—in medical schools, on heart disease in women and about breast cancer; in engineering and architecture, so that urban design and transportation planning, which ignored how women had to spend their time, didn't compound the stress of women's two careers; in law schools, on legal philosophy and a system of law that recognized the conflict-ridden nature of the family; and on the reality of domestic violence. These changes required an alteration in the very core of academic institutions, not at the periphery, and I thought separation would slow that process. There was also a political problem about separating the study of women into special interdisciplinary programs. It could, and later did, make it possible for embittered and conservative male academics like

Allan Bloom in his *The Closing of the American Mind*, to scapegoat feminist scholars, and to blame them for every change in the academy they didn't like, or hoped to persuade others to regard as second-rate.

I did manage to meet expectations about the handling of rape on campus, something that happened to cleaning women as well as students and faculty. I told the chief of the campus police that I wanted to be called instantly, no matter what the hour or what I was doing, to be notified personally if there was an incident of rape or alleged rape on campus. That meant I'd get the report before there had been time to cover up any details of failures in security, and quick enough to insist on the right counseling. The next time there was an incident it occurred at 4:00 a.m. I wasn't called. "I didn't want to wake you up and worry you," the chief said. The notification had come at 7:00 a.m. "I'm paid to be woken up and worried about safety on the campus. Every minute you delay you are countermanding orders, and wasting the taxpayers' money." I knew he was an extremely thrifty man, and the notion of preventing waste worked.

The requirement to notify a Vice President the minute a threat to a woman's safety on campus occurred did raise the profile of security for women, and did enable us, by diligent study of the pattern of events, to raise the standard of an already very efficient campus police service. The rate of violence and crime on campus was minuscule compared with the problems that existed on urban campuses in American cities. In the late sixties and early seventies, the University of Toronto, right in the downtown area of the city, occupying 125 acres, operated with a security force of twenty-seven people. Across the border in Rochester and Buffalo, it was a different story, but the pattern of public order in Canada was maintained except in moments of extreme crisis.

I was always puzzled when women asked me how I managed to make people listen to me. When the hands shot up at question time during my public speaking appearances, "How do you make your voice heard?" was sure to come up early in the session. Real participation in academic life requires pleasure in disputation, insistence that others clarify their ideas, interrupting the stream of talk to insert one's own question or to raise a counter point. It also requires doing the work necessary to contribute to the discussion and willingness to trust one's own judgment.

When I was appointed to the Budget Committee, a group of senior administrators and faculty who reviewed the budget submissions of all the University's academic and nonacademic units, I discovered that I didn't understand accounting readily. It took me time to spot where revenues were being inflated, costs from one year to another speciously reduced. The time it took me to digest the mountains of figures left me bleary-eyed, and still uncertain of how things were being counted. So I asked one of the friendlier accountants from the Budget Office to come in an hour early for a few mornings to give me a crash course in accounting, quickly mastered the necessary concepts and language, and was soon arguing as confidently as the next person.

In my childhood in the Australian outback there were no experts to rely on. If a piece of machinery didn't work, one figured out its working parts and fixed it. If someone broke a bone, someone else made a splint and did the best possible job of setting it. That approach to life stayed with me. If I didn't understand something, I worked at it until I did, because there was no point in taking on any task unless I could contribute to it. It was sometimes embarrassing to have to stop the discussion and say, "Wait a minute. I don't understand that. What am I missing?" But most people respect an honest question, and love expanding on their particular area of expertise. The rare encounters with condescension usually offer valuable insights into character and motivation, and time usually provides ample opportunity to even the score with the condescender.

One area of the institution I had to keep on asking questions about was the personnel system. I couldn't understand why the women secretaries who did much of the administrative work of the institution couldn't be promoted to management positions. The system for assigning points in the job-rating scheme seemed to mystify rather than explain things. A person's job classification was governed not by knowledge and the importance of the tasks, but by how many people formally reported to an individual, a concept derived from military ideas of rank but not applicable to civilian activities. The span of responsibility in a secretary's work could be very great even though no one formally "reported" to her. The system of classification was hung up on "command" while most organizations functioned just as much on securing consensus, on facilitating communication, and on the ability to listen to others. An efficient secretary or administrative assistant might actually stand in for her boss half the time, yet receive no credit for it at salary review time. But what was worse was that she couldn't take the knowledge derived from a secretary's job and use it to progress to other ranks in the nonacademic side of the University. Men didn't seem to get stuck in the administrative assistant category, because people seemed to be able to see and register their contribution to the job. A woman's contribution was invisible, or, if it was visible, people actively resisted having her move to a better job because they were so dependent on her skills.

I decided that no competent woman would work for me without getting coached for a better position. I took the time to ask the opinion of the person often better informed than I was about people and information flows, and remembered to thank them when the judgment paid off. Every three months we reviewed how we were managing the work, and what we could each do to make it flow better. Although it wasn't supposed to happen, I sent them to meetings in my place, gave them assignments, reports to write, things that would build a record of self-directed competence. We worked the office schedule so that the secretaries could take the classes that would make them promotable—accounting, economics, organizational behavior. When I knew there was a good job coming up I sent them off to apply. The competent ones never stayed more than eighteen months, making my office, on occasion, a less smoothly working but always happier place. My only failures were with women just about my age, accustomed to hierarchy, and unable to forgive me for the gap that yawned between the interest of my life and theirs.

In time I came to see the modern complex organization as dysfunctional because of the formulation of its job categories around gender stereotypes. So much energy and talent was underutilized because of the dead-end jobs to which women were assigned, or which they had once sought at a time in their lives when they needed predictable hours and no unscheduled overtime. Human resources just weren't used well, and the most spirited defenders of the system were the so-called human resource professionals, their minds so boxed in by their job category systems, and their sex-biased task analysis, that they couldn't imagine a fluid organization where people's capacity to learn and grow mattered. Once I understood how it all worked I always refused to have the jobs of my secretaries and administrative assistants classified. I wanted to be able to pay them for the long hours they worked and the intelligence they contributed to the enterprise, something I could only do outside the gender-biased classification schemes that were set up to make such recognition impossible for most women.

Even more arcane than personnel systems was the business of raising money. In Canada that was mostly a matter of building good relationships with the federal or state bureaucrats who handed out grants, because private donations in support of education were modest, shaped by the belief that education was a public sector responsibility. I began to learn my way around the maze of jurisdictions in Toronto and Ottawa, searching for funding for a new athletic building at the University of Toronto. As a first step in overcoming the anonymity and lack of recreational space on the campus, we wanted to build a new athletic building—a multipurpose gym space, an indoor track, squash courts, and an Olympic-size pool for aquatic competition.

The quest proved an education for a rebel against Australia's compulsive athleticism. Blessed with abundant good health and energy, I'd never thought much about health and fitness in adults, although I had some good examples of the need to do so in my own family. Now I had to speak persuasively to the federal officials in the Department of Health about the way our new facility could be programmed for community use. That meant learning all the current research about community health. To my astonishment, I learned that women in my age group were the least fit segment of the population, and that a third of the visits by women to physicians concerned lower back pain, a condition that could be relieved by simple exercise. But instead of being encouraged to exercise, most women were prescribed muscle relaxants and tranquilizers. Here was another terrible waste of human energy, and all because women were taught to look delicate, and not to develop physical strength, a definition most male doctors then also accepted.

The assistant I hired to work with the architects on developing the program for the building was a Canadian distance runner, an Olympic athlete who taught in the school of Physical and Health Education. I'd always had the humanists' bias against PHE, but now I discovered from John Evans, my health-reforming boss, that medical schools were often bastions of ignorance about healthy life-styles, and that some of the most creative work in exercise science was being done in schools of physical and health education.

As we made the rounds of the health bureaucracy my new assistant eyed my gait and asked me if I'd ever been a runner. "A distance runner in high school," I said, "a long time ago, and an occasional jogger now." "You still move pretty well," he said. "You ought to try serious running again. You'll have even more energy. What size are your feet? I'll bring you some running shoes. My coach gets them free from the athletic shoe companies." Before long he had me getting up an hour earlier for a daily run before breakfast, and reading the first publications that heralded the new vogue for health and fitness.

By the time we secured our grants from the Province and the federal government, my sedentary ways had been permanently changed, and my attitudes transformed toward taking personal responsibility for my health. I had the enthusiasm of the convert in my encounters with officials, and this personal involvement plus the superb brief my staff turned out won us the money that allowed the project to go forward. In my mind I had a map of the bureaucracy marked with all the nodal points at the state and federal levels where one had to win approval to secure a grant. The process of finding new money was easier than I'd thought—marshal the case, find the real decision makers, move the process along by personal cultivation—it was really all quite rational.

That wasn't the case when we set about securing a permit to build our new facility. My life became a blur of heated and unhappy ratepayers' meetings at which I was the target for the accumulated wrath of the local residents about the ways of their vast, and usually anonymous, corporate neighbor. I knew not to take the barrage of complaints personally, and recognized a lot of the inflated rhetoric as political posturing, but I was startled and instructed by the intensity of the local residents' feelings. Some were owners, some renters. None wanted a huge blank-faced athletic facility dominating the local skyline. They just didn't believe me when I said it would be available for community use, and that the standard of design would be better than the University had demonstrated in recent years. I realized that there was an invisible boundary in the neighbors' minds which meant that facilities that were theoretically open were not so in practice.

Somewhere in the residents' mental imagery of space, the University was an impermeable monolith, and changing that perception was going to take time and persistence. I remembered how utterly unaware of the neighbors I'd once been, the typical commuter who felt entitled to the large inner-city

campus and simply didn't register the neighborhoods surrounding it. Eventually the effort at communication paid off,
enough local residents began to believe that the new building
could be a valuable community resource, and the permit to
build was approved. In the process, I'd been given a series of
lessons in cultural geography I never forgot.

In December when I cast up a balance sheet for the year,
and tried to decide what had been accomplished through all
the meetings, the ceaseless activity, the efforts to persuade, the
efforts to judge issues and people, the endless dealings with
the often conflicting aims and needs of constituencies, I realized that I'd write history differently in the future. The interaction of individual, institution, and environment was even
more complex than I'd understood, and the tangible results
often elusive.

In some ways the mere fact of there being a woman in the
office responsible for managing the University's services *had*
made them more responsive to the needs of women students
and faculty, though whether with ill will or genuine commitment wasn't yet clear. In some very inconspicuous ways our
relationships with the city and neighborhood were improving,
the processes by which we worked on planning were better
and more inclusive, maybe a few budget decisions had been
more responsive to community needs. Some grievances had
been settled while others simmered on. Life would be incom-
parably better for the children and families served by the day-
care center. Women faculty were paid equitably across the institution for the first time. But now my horizons on that subject were so enlarged that their tiny number was dwarfed by
the larger cohorts of lab assistants, secretaries, cleaning
women, and infirmary nurses. The list kept growing. I could
see the impersonal momentum of the large institution moving
along its path, like a planet in space, with a few individuals
trying to alter its course, deflect it from collisions, bring it a
little nearer the sun, eagerly trying to accumulate the energy
to nudge it in a more creative direction. I understood now
why the great medieval historians had studied institutions.

They had a life of their own. Liberal individualism might make modernists study individuals and political movements, but redeploying a bureacracy was the real challenge, and that was hard to achieve when the University's central management had so little discretionary income available to create incentives for change.

If I looked at myself, the balance sheet looked different. I was a changed person. I'd been pushed beyond the boundaries of my orderly but narrow professional life, made to think about a range of subjects I'd ignored, or of which I'd previously been oblivious, energized by working with people I admired and respected, reaffirmed and instructed in my feminist ideals, creatively engaged in a broader set of concerns than my life had encompassed in my earlier incarnation.

The effort had boosted me over some important areas of ambiguity about my own identity that I'd been unaware of in the past. I hadn't known I liked running things, or that I was a forceful personality. It seemed ludicrous that I could be approaching forty and unaware of something so basic about myself and my motivations, especially since I'd made myself a scholarly reputation analyzing a similar lack of awareness in women leaders of an earlier generation. I was the most private of women, but I was now operating with a public persona that seemed to matter to a lot of people. I hadn't minded the inevitable harsh criticism and the politically motivated attacks that go with any public role. I'd watched many attacks on John during our years together, and had come to understand the stereotyping and projection of hostility on the available authority figure, which is characteristic of communities of students and hypercritical faculty. So I never took the bad opinions of my critics too much to heart, or the political machinations of opponents too personally.

The area of my job which brought me the most opprobrium was the vexed one of maintaining public order on campus. This was no small matter when the sit-in and the confrontation involving studied rudeness and vituperation were the standard techniques of the student left, while, in Canada, the picket line at union contract negotiation time was a common occurrence. The previous administration had followed contradictory policies with campus dissenters. Occupiers of buildings were routinely arrested and charged with trespass, sometimes by campus police, sometimes by the Metro Toronto police. Then, when the culprits ended up before a magistrate in court, the charges were frequently withdrawn.

I thought sit-ins should simply be left to run out of steam, since they become boring for all concerned if ignored. I also thought that if there were serious breaches of the peace on campus, those arrested should be brought to trial and the charges made to stick. With this in mind I made a point of being present wherever there was violence or potential for it on the campus, so that I could form my own assessment of the situation, and, incidentally, if demonstrators had to be removed physically, could give informed testimony as to the appropriateness of the decision and the manner in which it was implemented.

Magistrates who had tended to deal leniently with student protesters were often startled by my appearance in court. The judge hearing a case in which union picketers alleged undue physical force had been used in removing them when they obstructed entrance to the University's administrative building looked at me in some curiosity. I had dressed with care that day to look the model of a British Empire lady of impeccable upbringing. When it transpired that I had been the person to issue the order to remove the demonstrators who were throwing punches, he looked even more curious. When I testified that I had observed the defendant kick the shins of one campus police officer and punch another in the stomach as they were attempting to clear entry to the building, the case was won.

After the scuffles at the administration building I realized that the incident might have gotten out of hand, and that it might have been necessary to ask for assistance from the city police. To be better prepared next time, I went to call on the Superintendent of the local police division, to explain who I was and open up the lines of communication. He had followed the reports of the recent incident in the press, and told me he thought I'd tried to have people taken into custody without enough campus police to manage the situation. Remembering the sprains and bruises that had needed medical treatment after the event, I was inclined to agree with him. Our campus security people were just that, trained to secure buildings and direct crowds, but not for physical restraint.

The trouble was, I explained to the Superintendent, anyone in my position was reluctant to call the city police on campus because they normally arrived with sirens blaring, consulted no one, and proceeded to act on their own assessment of the situation. Standards of order and propriety were different on a university campus, so that some collaboration between the police officer in charge and the appropriate University official was necessary to maintain the margin of control necessary for safety, yet still allow what often looked like raucous and unseemly dissent. "If you could only come in plainclothes on an old yellow school bus or something like that," I explained, "and then agree to consult with me, or my deputy if I'm away, we might call on you more often." After a return visit we agreed that some such arrangement might be made to work informally.

The event which tested the agreement came shortly thereafter when an angry student crowd, supplemented by groups unaffiliated with the University, battered down the locked doors of Simcoe Hall and disrupted a meeting of the University's Governing Council. Under discussion at the Council were allegations by the local branch of Students for a Democratic Society and Italian laborers from a local construction union that University doctors were prejudiced in their assessment of Italian workers in workmen's compensation cases, and a series of issues relating to University disciplinary procedures. The subject of Italians was the more heated because a public lecture given by an American sociologist whose views of southern Italians were thought racist had been disrupted by a similarly tough crowd. In that case I had mistakenly decided to work through the event using campus police, only to be outnumbered and outmaneuvered by the disrupters. My faculty critics thought I wasn't tough enough on student dissenters, and unwilling to defend unpopular ideas. In fact, I shared their concerns but was unwilling, unless other avenues were exhausted, to turn the campus into a semi-militarized environment, which was just the mood campus radicals wanted to contrive and exploit.

The situation around the disrupted Governing Council meeting built up too quickly to summon outside assistance, so when our small group of security men were pushed aside I took the precaution of observing the legal niceties by personally barring the doors to the meeting room and telling the unruly crowd of yelling intruders that they were trespassing, and asking them to leave. The disrupters had had the forethought to bring along several TV crews with them, so that for once, we had a clear record of the jumbled events of a building occupation.

The disrupted meeting was immediately adjourned, to be reconvened several days later, this time with full police protection. When I went over to the station to explain the situation and lay out the request for help, I was met with smiles and friendly laughter. They'd all watched the TV news the night before, seen me issuing my warnings, and thought I'd make good material for the police force. When I explained to them that Simcoe Hall had thirteen entrances, and many ground-floor windows, they whistled in astonishment at the chutzpah of anyone who'd try to protect this building with the tiny security force we had. In this friendly atmosphere I was able to explain how hot tempers had become on campus, and my hope that we could conduct the reconvened meeting without incident.

As the police team arrived on campus I had to laugh at my idea of bringing them unobtrusively anywhere. They did come in plainclothes in an unmarked series of buses, and my new friend, the Superintendent, present in person, stayed close by the door where I was standing beside President Evans watching the process of checking people into the building. Toronto's finest riot police were all well over six feet tall, in splendid physical shape, and, even dressed in jeans and sweaters, couldn't blend into any crowd. They'd come in such numbers, and so quietly, that not even the wildest zealot was tempted to acts of provocation. After that collaboration we worked easily together through bomb threats, wild rock concerts, threatened arson, computer crime, and all the other hazards of a large urban setting.

After the usual spring madness of student demonstrations in 1974, it became clear that the favorable tide of Provincial funding, on which the hopes for building the academic strength of the University rested, was on the ebb. The change in the external environment came from three principal causes: the rapid rise in inflation caused by the energy crisis, a shift in government priorities occasioned by the sudden downturn in the birthrate of the late 1960s, which meant that the plans for building Ontario's higher educational system must be scaled back, and the refocusing of government spending on solving the problems of the spurt of urban growth in the Province in the previous decade. This meant moving to investment in urban transportation, community colleges, hospitals and recreational facilities, while holding rates of increase in higher educational spending well below the rate of inflation.

The years of student turmoil on campuses had taken their toll in public support, while the media treatment of educational issues was negative, hostile, and often avowedly anti-intellectual. The wholesale importation of foreign scholars during the sixties had helped open a wedge between higher education and popular sentiment, because universities seemed less emblems of Canada than suspect forces of Americanization. Indeed, there was legislation under discussion which would forbid the employment of noncitizens in Ontario universities, unless no Canadian with appropriate credentials could be found for the job.

It made no difference to explain in impassioned session with the Minister for University Affairs, or the Provincial Prime Minister, that several decades of institution building were at the point of yielding a high-quality research environment in Toronto, one that could keep the best talent in Canada. The response was clear: Ontario would be different from its southern neighbors, building a vibrant urban environment even as America's cities were decaying. Harvard might be one of the world's greatest universities, but the cities of Boston and Cambridge were decaying around it. The cost of world-class research just couldn't be borne across the board and also allow for investment in other valued social priorities. The bitterest pill to swallow was the comment that designing a transportation system which could slow the rates of increase in pollution was important for all citizens, and it was cheaper to hire transportation experts from M.I.T. than to try to develop that expertise on the ground in Ontario.

These opinions made for gloomy discussions at our weekly staff meetings. No one feared managing what had been a growing institution into a steady state, but overseeing a steady decline in real resources was not an appealing prospect. Not surprisingly, much of the weight of discussion shifted to building private support, and the planning of a major fund drive for the University. The problem was that Canadians were used to contributing modestly to capital drives, but were firmly convinced that operating funds should come from tax revenues. The more careful the investigation, the more limited the prospect of sustaining operations through private support seemed. In the past, the University had not invested in a highly professional public relations, fund-raising, and alumni affairs staff, so the task of building support would be slow to yield returns—and carried out against the grain of public sentiment.

The job which had seemed such a chance to build a promising future had to be redefined with this sea change in the external environment. The daily routine of meetings was now filled with anguished discussions with heads of services about how to cut back staff, hours, facilities. The most painful were the meetings with loyal people whose departments or services were to be merged or closed down. Then there was the exasperation of watching the talented leave while the less gifted remained.

There was no one to blame for the turn of events. The government's decisions made sense for anyone not concerned with building and retaining Canada's intellectual elites. Undergraduate education would be of more than average quality, but not far above. The critical mass of research talent would build only in isolated fields. The innovative observation, or the creative vision, would be realized elsewhere. The tide would doubtless turn again in public funding, but not for a decade or so, and by then the task of building quality would have to be begun all over again.

For someone drawn to academic administration by the dream of building a better academic environment for women, recruiting more women faculty, developing new services and supports for women students, the change presented a serious moral problem. I didn't relish letting go the men whose jobs were eliminated to help us bring revenue and expenditures into line. Anything women now achieved would be possible only at the expense of the males already in the institution. It was a dismal prospect, and it sent me home every night with a heavy heart.

13.

A DIFFERENT CHOICE

EARLY IN 1972, as coeducation became the educational fashion of the moment in the United States and feminist groups in universities across North America campaigned for the establishment of programs to study women's lives, Stephen Graubard asked me to write an essay for *Daedalus* examining the reasons for both trends.

His request set me reading the history of nineteenth-century colleges, and the history of the early public universities which were the first to admit women. My exploration coincided with the preparation for the course on the history of women Natalie and I were to teach in the fall of 1972, in which one of the major themes was the extent to which modernization and the expansion of commercial capitalism in the eighteenth century had resulted in the decline of women's sociability groups, while strengthening those of men in both their working and leisure activities. The women merchants who'd been so successful in the English wool trade were put out of business by its expansion across the Channel to the Continent, because they were tied to home and family. The eighteenth-century women silversmiths, like Hester Bateman, whose dazzling work was so sought after by collectors in the twentieth century, hadn't been able to pass on their craft to their daughters as production moved out of the household and men's guilds were able to monopolize the training of apprentices. New systems of distribution eliminated the market women and fishwives whose collective life had made them important components of eighteenth-century bread riots and street crowds. With the loss of business activity and skill went the experience of collective life, so that modern bourgeois women were shaped by isolated domesticity in ways not experienced before.

My life of learning to work beside my father on our lonely sheep station in Australia was a modern anomaly, a function of our isolation and the shortage of male labor. It had meant that as a female child I sat on the edge of the male working groups who gathered together to manage some major task like drafting or branding sheep or cattle, and listened to them talk to one another about life. The stories of war, natural disaster, wild sprees in the city, horses that refused to be broken, the complicated and temperamental machinery that had to be maintained allowed for the exchange of a kind of sympathy and common understanding I knew my mother had never had. When she met other women on social occasions, there were always men present, and the conversation didn't explore any deep aspect of women's experience. It stayed politely on the surface of things.

In this context my reading about the founding of women's educational institutions in North America, and on the debates about education which preceded the decision to educate women and men together in the same classroom, at both school and university level, posed some fascinating questions. What had led Mary Lyon, the founder of Mount Holyoke, to buck this major trend in modernization when her college opened its doors in 1837? What was the difference between being educated in a classroom with boys or young men, and being with a group of female peers?

The standard view of the reasons for establishing coeducation in the United States was that it was the product of liberal egalitarian sentiment, democracy in action, leading to the wish to treat women as equals with men. But when I read the legislative debates about establishing tax-supported public education for women in the northeastern states where it first appeared, the discussions were economic and very practical. In a labor-scarce society, women needed a certain level of education so that they could take on the work of teaching elementary school. The cost of establishing two public systems was too heavy a burden for the taxpayer, so there had to be only one. I noticed that wherever communities were large enough to build more than a one-room school, the building had two entrances—one marked Boys and the other Girls. I wondered what the message of the two entrances was, since those entering were bound for the same classroom. Perhaps it was a statement that sex boundaries were still to be maintained there, so that the same boys and girls would have a different experience in the classroom, even though they sat side by side.

It was instructive to read the discussions about the founding of Mount Holyoke alongside those which led to the foundation of Oberlin, both institutions of the reforming 1830s. Mary Lyon's driving passion to educate women was about them and their intellectual and moral life. Her discussions of the curriculum—whether it should include science, how much time should be spent on physical exercise, how much for moral philosophy—were all aimed at the women's capacity for future action, for a purpose in life that went beyond marriage and domesticity.

My imagination was gripped by an early Mount Holyoke student's letter home to a friend. Miss Lyon wanted to produce "hard marble" women, the student reported, not "soft marble," which was easy to shape but quickly crumbled before the forces of the elements. Hard marble was more difficult to shape, but it could take a brilliant polish which would last, and which was impervious to wind and weather. The gripping image came from the cemeteries of New England, places everyone visited. The young women who hung on her words would have known how one had to brush the moss and lichens away from soft marble to read the fading inscription, and how the polished headstones retained their luster, and their message, undimmed. The luster and the imperviousness to external circumstances were dynamizing images for women's self-directing will. Women in Mary Lyon's institution were prepared for the disciplines of the mind and expected to put them to the test of action.

Oberlin, founded within a few years of Mount Holyoke, was the creative American solution to a problem never experienced in the Old World. In the settled East there were many institutions for the preparation of Protestant clergy, but in the new settlements of the Ohio Valley, occupied after the War of 1812, the cost of traveling east and of paying tuition was prohibitive for the sons of newly established western farms, where food was plentiful but cash almost nonexistent. In response to the problem, many young men seeking training for the clergy found work on the farms of Eastern-educated men, clearing the woods and mucking out the barn in return for their training in Latin and Greek. No one counted the labor of the farmer's wife and daughters in the cost of the young men's education, although it was a woman's job to labor on the laundry, mending, and cooking for the enlarged households.

So when a group of Ohio men planned the establishment of Oberlin College, they thought first of acquiring a farm, building college buildings on the farmland, and enabling talented young men to earn their education there by substituting farm labor for tuition fees. Late in the day the planners remembered about the laundry, cooking, cleaning, and mending, the tasks of the farmer's wife and daughters, and quickly developed plans for the admission of women to Oberlin. Women students in the first classes at Oberlin were assigned a male student for whose laundry, mending, and cleaning they were responsible—service activities they performed on Mondays, when no classes were scheduled, and for which they were not paid. Men's unpaid manual labor on the farm was fitted in around the academic schedule, as was women's valetlike work for the men. But women took care of their own laundry, mending, and ironing on their own time. Moreover, classes which involved public speaking or disputation, such as rhetoric and debate, were closed to women. They might learn but never speak about their knowledge in public. Their minds were for the private delectation of their male partners.

The Oberlin Trustees' records make clear that the presence of women was also seen as a sure guarantee against what they called "monkish vices." Women's presence was to ensure the heterosexual conformity of the men. The training of women's minds was advocated as an effective means of ensuring that they would be cultural resources for their husbands when these young men took up the challenge of ministry in the cultural desert of frontier society in the Mississippi Valley. Women's education here had a derivative purpose. It was not for the women's capacity to act, but to enlarge their capacity to support the action of others. No one talked to Oberlin women about becoming as lustrous and resistant to external forces as hard marble, though many steely female wills were forged by the experience of study there.

It mattered that women lived in a relationship of service to their fellow male students because that changed the terms on which they entered the classroom. A great many of them became ministers' wives, as the founders had planned, but the rebellious minority took the learning on their own terms—the prohibition against public speaking, and the experience of hearing their scholarly productions read by a male voice at commencement, were simply goads to action on their own behalf.

In coeducational academies, where the secondary role of women students was not so vividly symbolized as at Oberlin, trouble quickly developed between the sexes. Something happened that no one had planned. Women did better academically than men. After the first few years of coeducation at the University of Chicago, a troubled President William Rainey Harper urged his trustees to authorize the establishment of a separate college for women, because it was embarrassing to have them carrying off the lion's share of the year's academic honors. At Cornell, the tension between the men and women was symbolized by the decision of male fraternities to ban any fraternity brother seen fraternizing with the Cornell women at Sage College. At Berkeley, the initial warm welcome given women students by the men quickly changed to hostility when they took most of the academic laurels at year's end.

So the message was clear. The initial experience of coeducation was ambiguous. No one wanted women to excel on their own terms. Their presence in the classroom was either explicitly (as at Oberlin) or implicitly secondary to men. That seemed, to me, to be an equally strong theme in the discussions of coeducation at male elite universities in the 1970s. The discussions about merging Yale and Vassar, or Harvard and Radcliffe, focused on the social adjustment of men and women. They should study together because as adults they would live together, and the presence of women stopped some of the less attractive aspects of adolescent male sociability. Everyone seemed to believe that it was psychologically healthy for the young to live side by side during the transition from adolescence to young adulthood. There was no latter-day Mary Lyon to talk about the fact that women and men follow different developmental paths during that critical transition. In contemporary America that transition for men involved separating from family and forming the identity of the working self—developing the capacity to relate ideas to action. Generativity was a secondary responsibility to work, and a secondary responsibility which came later in life.

For young women the tasks were different. They had to form two quite different images of the self: the self as generative, and the self in relation to work. In the coeducational setting it was often the helping role in work that was learned, and the identity as a woman was often the self as seen by male friends and lovers—the fragmented female self-image which comes with the internalized gaze of the male assessing female desirability. No one talked about women's intellectual life as the driving purpose of the proposed new coeducational institutions, because women were simply to be added to an ongoing enterprise designed to maximize male talent.

There were always discussions of the changes in plumbing necessitated by coeducation and shared residences. Some mention was made of the need for women's athletic facilities. But there was no discussion of what was needed to relate mind and action during this complex stage of female life. American educational discussions always focused on social adjustment, and the bourgeois comforts of emotional satisfaction. I thought there was much about the contemporary role of women to which young girls or their male counterparts should never be comfortably adjusted. American society needed a stronger focus on civic virtue, and a greater concern for social service on the part of the young, instead of encouraging early marriage where social service was limited by the boundary between family and society. The pattern of women's voluntarism wasn't a sufficient remedy, for it defined civic concern in gendered terms I thought should be rejected.

It seemed to me that the cozily domestic, introduced too early in youthful development, had the effect of obliterating or muting civic and social responsibility. My nineteenth-century feminist theorists about social evolution had all worried about where and how commercial societies could instill social values that went beyond personal satisfaction and self-interest. I agreed with them that the development of the civic virtues tended to be slighted in exclusively commercial societies, and that leadership and the talent for action came from an education which did not take the paired couple as its social norm. William James, America's greatest psychologist, had worried in the 1890s about how Americans could find the moral equivalent of war, and I thought his worries still entirely justified.

It was touching to read the history of the foundation of Mount Holyoke. Mary Lyon's battle to raise the money for her institution showed a hard marble woman at work, harvesting the pennies New England farm women could scrimp together from within their already frugal housekeeping bud-

gets, coaxing bigger gifts from churches and from large do-
nors. It had taken so long for the pennies to add up to the
necessary sum to start the building in South Hadley, where
the aim to educate women on their own terms first found architectural expression.

Sophia Smith's benefaction for the college which bore her
name had been generous, but there had been the same painstaking scrimping by early classes of Smith alumnae to contribute the extra pennies needed to add up to the cost of
building the first gymnasium for women. The endowments
that supported women's colleges had grown slowly, and never
rivaled their Ivy League counterparts. It troubled me to think
of them being casually turned over to male direction, because
I knew no male-directed institution would suddenly allow
the needs of women to drive financial priorities. And I knew
from my daily work at the University of Toronto what efforts
of will and political finesse were required to redirect any allocation of resources in times of surplus, let alone in times of
scarcity.

In the summer of 1973, Natalie, whose accounts of her life
as a student at Smith made the great women scholars who'd
given her her love of learning seem like household presences,
told me that the presidency of Smith would soon be vacant,
and that she had written a long letter to the Search Committee setting out why she thought I'd be the right person for the
job. She had, by then, become a member of the History Department at Berkeley, after much pondering what would be
the most creative choice for the future. Although her departure broke up one of the most creative partnerships of my
life, I'd urged her to make the move. It was an indicator of
the intellectual environment we lived in at the University of
Toronto that neither of us could find a collaborator within
our own fields. I knew Natalie was a dazzling scholar, and
that she should be teaching in an institution where there was
a large cadre of graduate students up to her level of work. Beyond feeling pleasure that my most admired colleague wanted
me to be custodian of the institution she cherished, I gave the

matter no more thought. I was busy learning to swim in the choppy seas of my new administrative life, rooted in Canada, and far too preoccupied to think of change.

When the letter from the Smith Search Committee turned up on my desk in December, I knew I had to schedule a meeting with them, if only as a courtesy to my friend and collaborator. The few documents which accompanied the invitation tickled my curiosity. Smith's educational budget for its 2,800 undergraduate students was larger by far than the entire Faculty of Arts and Sciences at the University of Toronto, four times Smith's size in enrollments. I wondered what it would be like to think about educating students drawing on such resources.

I liked the delegation from the Search Committee I met at the Century Club in New York. They were a mixture of trustees, alumnae, students, and faculty—all full of intellectual energy and enthusiasm. They seemed worried about the trend to coeducation among similar male colleges like Williams and Amherst, but energetically convinced that Smith's mission was to educate women. I thought their worries misplaced. I was working with women students in an institution of some sixty thousand students. I taught, by preference, at night, when the part-time women came in droves to the downtown campus. I knew what their battles were, how hard it was for them to feel entitled to take the time for expansive nonutilitarian learning.

One of my favorites was a tiny blond woman in her forties, mother of four, alone in life because of divorce. She worked in a suburban computer center and was often late for class. I tried to convince her that her time was worth money, and that a cab to and from the commuter station to the University campus would give her that extra hour in the library she needed. But she had no past experience of spending money as an investment in herself and her talents and couldn't change her ways. She continued to arrive at my class white-faced and tired from her long commute by public transport. She needed to change worlds to see herself differently, a vision that could only come from the moral support of her peers, and a counseling service expert in unraveling the conflicts and self-denigration of older women. My few minutes' pep talk after class wasn't enough.

I thought there were thousands of women like her in every major city in North America who would jump at the chance to have four years to devote to self-development. The discussion was lively, but I went away unconvinced that this was the job for me. I thought I could help the cause by what I was writing on the history of education, but I liked what I was doing in Toronto too much to think about the subject more.

Beyond a polite thank-you for making the time to meet with them, I didn't hear from the Search Committee again until April 1974, by which time they had slipped from my consciousness. It was John who insisted that I accept the invitation to visit the Smith campus and learn more about the college. "I know more about this kind of New England institution than you do," he said. "You should take it very seriously. I've had my ten years in Canada. I'll go with you wherever you want to move now. It's your turn."

John and I had wandered about the Smith campus on an August visit to the Connecticut Valley in the late 1960s. We had admired its leafy central core landscaped by Frederick Law Olmsted, its focal point the tranquil water of Paradise Pond, its residential center of gravity the neo-Georgian quadrangle to the north of the old campus. But we had seen it in the depths of summer somnolence, while en route to visit the MacLeish family in Conway—never in full session with the students who were its raison d'être.

Spring comes to the Connecticut Valley a good two weeks before the first crocuses in Toronto, so on my April visit I left a grey city to see a campus ablaze with crocus, daffodils, scilla, and rich strawberry and cream magnolias. Brighter than the spring flowers were the faces of the young women I saw everywhere. I could spend months at a time at the University of Toronto without ever hearing a female voice raised.

Here the women were rowdy, physically freewheeling, joshing one another loudly, their laughter deep-belly laughter, not propitiatory giggles. The muddy afternoon games on the playing fields produced full-throated barracking. I was entranced.

The student who took me for a tour of the campus thought I was a parent of a potential freshman, so I had to quickly invent a suitable female relative from whose point of view I could ask questions. My guide was a sophomore from the Midwest. She planned to major in economics, but she had interests in religion and philosophy, and might elect a double major. She was planning to live and work in Washington D.C., perhaps for the government, perhaps for a research organization. Her house in the Quad evoked a strong response in me, impressive though the science labs, library, art studios, music building, and athletic facilities had been. The space was ample and well furnished, the notice board awash with political notices, the rooms sizable, each door alive with signs, posters, ironic comments, cartoons. There was a notice for a house meeting that evening, and, in response to my inquiry, I learned that each house was self-governing in all but a few respects. Office was elective, and hotly contested. I realized that this was a real alternative society, a place of true female sociability, where women ran things for themselves.

The faculty I met displayed the justifiably wary curiosity of people presented with a total stranger as a potential President. The women clearly fit Natalie's description of the scholarly figures who had transmitted their love of learning to her. The men were more recognizable as academic types, so that I thought I could guess where they'd done their graduate study. I'd recently been spending a good amount of my time at the University of Toronto cutting budgets, scaling down or closing services, thinking about how to make do. This didn't seem to be part of Smith's experience. In fact, the Trustees and the Search Committee spent most of the time I was with them asking what I'd plan to raise money for, what I thought could be improved. They assumed everything was possible, even as they worried about bucking the trend to coeducation.

Educational quality was what everyone cared about, and there seemed to be no limits to the efforts everyone was prepared to expend to achieve that.

What worried them was whether Smith could raise money effectively if it insisted on adhering to its mission to educate women. Could it continue pricing its tuition competitively while not admitting men? What would happen to the quality of its academic life if women from elite prep schools were all counseled to enroll at Harvard or Yale? Would there be enough women of talent to go around in the coming decade of the eighties, when the cohort of young people was dramatically reduced in size?

I thought the case for women's education in an all-female student body was easy to make. One had only to explain the historical trends which had confined middle-class women to domesticity, unravel the ambiguous motivations which inspired coeducation, push people to think whether the classroom experience for young women and young men was really the same, and point to the outcomes in the careers of graduates from women's colleges. In any event, one could also point out that women's colleges were the only truly coeducational ones so far as faculty were concerned. It was the Harvards and Yales which were single-sex institutions in that dimension. As for the worry about numbers of applicants, that seemed part of the preoccupations of a small segment of American society. A college for women should be concerned with the whole age spectrum of potential students, not just entering eighteen-year-olds. And even among the eighteen-year-old population I thought it foolish to be so preoccupied with entering test scores. That preoccupation was part of the American quest for security in a formless society which eased its anxieties through developing statistical measures for everything. I was from a tradition where one sought to educate not only the very gifted but to expand the potential of those who were not precociously high achievers. There was a very large cohort of women who could benefit from a Smith education, and whose motivation, character, and capacity for growth were as important as the way they tested at age sixteen or seventeen. Smith had always been a leader in women's education, and there was no reason why it shouldn't continue to be so in the changed mores of the 1970s. I was glad that Trustees, students, faculty, and alumnae had all been polled and had voted overwhelmingly that Smith should remain an institution for women. I thought Smith could take the lead in reaffirming that purpose for other women's institutions.

On the plane on the way home to Toronto, reflecting on my two-day visit, I realized that there was a distinct likelihood that I might be invited to become Smith's next President. I had to think seriously about how to weigh that possibility against the other possibilities in my life. If I remained at the University of Toronto there was surely the possibility of heading a Canadian university in the future. I'd be forty on my next birthday, so the question was what to do with my life for the next decade. I knew I wanted to quit administration by the time I was fifty, because my life would never be fulfilled if I didn't do the writing I knew was in me, and if I left it later than fifty, the urge and the energy might begin to fade. I'd already begun to miss the pleasure of sitting alone at my desk, focusing the mind, and finding out what I knew through what appeared on the page. I'd been in love with words since childhood, and I craved the sensation of clarity that comes from working to shape a text. With each day spent poring over budgets and memoranda I missed the excitement of having imagery begin to flow from some nonverbal part of the brain, the sense of discovery as one made the connections between parts of one's experience which one wasn't even conscious were linked until they appeared on the page. But there was no telling whether this private passion might, or might not, be successful in shaping events, so its call on my time and energy must be deferred. The next ten years must be for action, doing what I could to seize and shape the energies being mobilized in the feminist movement, for the ends I thought would endure beyond the fashions of the moment.

Where would I be most effective? What could one person do to shape events? I'd already begun to be haunted by the time consumed in the bureaucratic processes of administrative life. One had to process so many feelings for others, wait while the people with minds for minutiae fussed over petty detail, listen endlessly to complaints about the human condition. Some days I would count how many hours closer I was to my death, hours in which nothing had happened but the same repetitive human complaints, or ritual committee maneuvers that were substitutes for thought.

I could write the script for most academic committee meetings. My most hated ones were devoted to nit-picking about the hours of credit assigned a course. How many minutes of a chemistry experiment were the equivalent of learning to conjugate six French or Russian verbs? I couldn't care less about such silliness. It was the total conspectus of a student's experience that mattered. Then there were the budget discussions. How to equate books and journals to microscopes to ensure exact similarity of treatment between departments. I always wanted to shred the pettifogging papers on the subject and focus the discussion on how students learned. But for many of my academic colleagues these were subjects worthy of countless hours of discussion. Sometimes I imagined a gifted anthropologist from Mars arriving to interpret the documents surviving from this long-dead academic culture. I decided she or he would conclude that the participants were incapacitated by shyness and could only manage sociability through the ritual of the academic committee. If I was going to let my mind be numbed by such things, where would I have most leverage, the most direct personal effect?

In worldly terms, most people would assign a higher value to running a university, but I wasn't interested in the empty forms of status. I wanted to know that whatever form of service I took up would matter, not just as a notch on a list of achievements, but because there was some contribution I could make that would warrant setting aside the private pleasures for a life of ceaseless activity. I didn't have to worry that

John would mind the demands of whatever I chose to do. He had said that it was my turn to decide what work should dictate the circumstances of our lives, and I knew he meant it.

The most important consideration was where my work would have the greatest impact on women's education. It might touch greater numbers of women indirectly if I ran a Canadian university, but the influence would be fleeting, and the institution would revert to type the minute I left, like some hybrid iris or daisy lacking cross-fertilization. If I went to Smith I might be able to prove to a doubting public that a women's institution could thrive in the modern world, that in itself it embodied important aspects of modernity. If I were successful, it might be possible to make it an intellectual center for research on women's lives and women's issues, research that could have influence far beyond Smith's lyrical New England campus.

On different days I felt differently about the choice. The wrench of leaving Canada would be far more powerful than my earlier uprooting from Australia. I'd come to love the country, the region, the political society, deeply, in an adult fashion. I was now in a life-stage where growth and adaptation were slower than in the twenties. I'd leave an important part of myself behind in Canada, because I'd found my adult professional self there. Some mornings I knew I couldn't do it. On other mornings, as I read the paper and read about another women's institution abandoning its past for the wrong reasons, I couldn't wait to get started.

In June, John and I were invited to dine with the Smith Trustees in New York, an occasion I took to be another stage in vetting the various candidates' backgrounds. In fact, it was the Trustees' point of decision. The next morning, while we were at breakfast, the phone rang, and I heard myself saying yes to the job.

My appointment was to begin a year hence, on July 1, 1975. That meant that there was time to bring most of the projects I was working on at the University of Toronto to a conclusion, and to depart with a sense of closure. It was startling to realize how much I'd learned about managing a complex institution under John Evans's tutelage, and that of my friendly and helpful colleagues on his administrative team.

Even though not yet formally in office, I found that I spent many weeks divided between the two institutions. I'd spend Sunday evening through Tuesday in Northampton, catch an early flight to Toronto on Wednesday, head for the office, and spend the rest of the week on Toronto affairs. The demands of managing two jobs at once kept me moving so fast that I was barely conscious of the passage of time until the farewell parties began, a new spate of press interviews and photographer's sessions occurred, and I was faced in the same week with the interesting tasks of approving next year's budget for the institution I was about to run and deciding on the fabrics for the redecoration of the President's house at Smith. Carpet samples and curtain materials made the change seem real. So did my last farewell gift. It was a Metropolitan Toronto Police Officer's badge, presented with considerable style by my old friend and working partner from our local police division.

We took a long holiday in the British Columbia Gulf Islands in June and early July, slowing down to watch the seals play, hike in the hills in search of colonies of bald eagles, and swim in the sparkling summer ocean. We'd rented a cottage on a remote island, with no telephone service, so I had to drive quite a way to make whatever phone calls business required from a rickety public phone by the ferry landing. Under these conditions the rest of the world began to slip away, so that it was quite a shock when John turned to me one morning over breakfast and asked, "How does it feel to be President of Smith College? It's the first of July today."

The question caused me a moment's panic. I wasn't quite ready to assume the new persona. "Let's burn our passports, assume a new identity, and find work taking tickets on the B.C. Ferries," I said. "No one would ever find us, and we'll keep on living this simple life together."

A week later I left John behind in Vancouver, returned to Toronto to pack up our belongings, and give delivery of the house to its new owners. Then I slowly packed the silver, a mountain of official mail, the few treasures too precious to hand over to the movers, and myself into the family car. Leaving this much-loved city was proving even harder than I'd anticipated. I'd been pushed out of Australia by family circumstance, the experience of discrimination, frustration with the culture I was born in. Nothing was pushing me out of this wonderful setting except a cause, and the hope to serve it. All the farewells had been said, yet I still didn't want to leave. I drove slowly along my familiar route downtown, stopped to get gas at the service station on Bloor and St. George Street, where the Jamaican mechanic had always been so skillful at raiding wreckers' yards to find spare parts for my aging car. Then I drove past the University that had been my world for the last eleven years, past the Royal York Hotel where we'd stayed on our first night in Canada, and on to the freeway going west and then south around Lake Ontario, headed for Buffalo and the United States.